Vic Davis c̄ Frida
San Angelo, TX
27 Jan 2018

Scalpels and Sabers

missing Frida + our pups

Nineteenth Century Medicine in Texas

Sylvia Van Voast Ferris ★ Eleanor Sellers Hoppe

EAKIN PRESS
Austin, Texas

FIRST EDITION

Published in the United States of America
By Eakin Press, P.O. Box 23066, Austin, Texas 78735

ISBN 0-89015-514-3

for my daughter, Charlotte,
with my profound admiration
for achieving independence over poliomyelitis,
and
for my daughters Beverly, Nancy, and Melissa,
all, always in my heart,
and
for my physician—husband, Curzon,
who eased my grief long ago
and daily secures the sun for me
Sylvia Ferris

In gratitude and love
to all my family,
especially
my father, the late Erle Dees Sellers
and
my brother, Dilworth Parramore Sellers,
twentieth century physicians
Eleanor Hoppe

The practitioner of the medical art has the privilege of feeling assured that he is useful; and the art itself, in every stage of its imperfection even to its final advancement, will continue to be of most singular service to mankind — relieving the sick, to use the expressions of Hippocrates, from the greatest of evils, from diseases, from pains, from sadness of mind, and from death.

— Dr. George Cupples
Address to TMA, November 1853
Meeting in front of Austin Methodist Church

Contents

Surrender of Santa Anna, a painting by William H. Huddle. Dr. Alexander Wray Ewing treats General Sam Houston after the Battle of San Jacinto, 21 April 1836.

Foreword

The history of medicine has a glorious past. During recent years, however, it has been stated and taught that any knowledge pertaining to medicine that was over five years of age was of no value. It has also been written that of all the scientists that have ever lived, eighty percent are still alive. What horrible misstatements.

It has been the fallacy of every generation since the Renaissance to think that they have solved the mysteries of life and God. I am afraid that some of the present generation is falling into this same error.

Knowledge is somewhat like a river flowing down to its outlet. It picks up tributaries of knowledge along its descent, but we are far from the outlet. We are still very ignorant about the fundamental causes of life and disease.

We must remember that today medical treatment is still an art of human relations as well as scientific exactness.

In picking the period of 1800 to 1900, Sylvia Ferris and Eleanor Hoppe are to be congratulated for writing about a period of Texas medical history during which many fundamental discoveries were being made. The knowledge for the eradication of smallpox, which had been a scourge killing millions of people since antiquity, was made by Edward Jenner in 1798; the first abdominal surgery was performed by Ephriam McDowell in 1809; the discovery of ether anesthesia was made by Crawford Long in 1842; the introduction of antiseptic surgery was done by Lord Joseph Lister in 1865, and causes of infectious diseases were discovered by Robert Koch and others about 1878.

During this period communications were slow and the ingenious Texas physicians devised many of their treatments by trial and error. For example, moldy bread which undoubtedly contained penicillin, was given for sore throats. These pioneer physicians were brave, bold, brilliant, and self-sufficient.

Medicine is the oldest learned profession in the world and it is rooted in the past. Each successive generation of physicians stands upon the shoulders of its predecessors, and the future before us is largely the creation of those who have gone before.

I heartily recommend that you read this excellent book by Mrs. Ferris and Mrs. Hoppe and that it will give you the pleasure that it gave me.

WILLIAM M. CRAWFORD, M.D.

Fort Worth, Texas
January 1985

Preface

The practice of Medicine is an Art, not a trade; a calling, not a business; a calling in which your heart will exercise equally with your brain.

— Sir William Osler

Bringing together some obscure and not-so-obscure facts about doctors and medicine as it was practiced in Texas in the last century, we hope to further the understanding of Texas medical history. Spotlighting certain individuals who were perhaps typical of many others, a picture emerges of the diversity of doctors who lived then and of their hardships, their courage, their strengths as well as their weaknesses.

Roughly sketched historical events provide background, but the facts are far from complete. Undoubtedly, we have not incorporated all noteworthy medical events in Texas history. On the other hand, some material which has little significance for the whole story is included for human interest, humor, or for its uniqueness.

We hope that the material we have gathered enlarges appreciation for the varied contributions made by Texas doctors of the last century. In politics, science, industry, and countless other endeavors, the achievements of many doctors enriched the development of our state, and imprinted the century with their mark.

But along with the more shining examples of doctors, we have included rascals, scalawags, and mediocre men in our story, readily admitting that many doctors of the last century failed to meet the ideal. Even so, considering the hardships and medical deficiencies of the moment, a significant number of nineteenth century Texas doctors measured up quite well.

We strived to focus attention on their practice of medicine

which, unlike other realms of science, is often referred to as the "art of medicine." That largely indefinable term was particularly applicable in the nineteenth century when doctors, despite the lack of scientific facts, endeavored to ease pain and heal. They often improvised in makeshift situations, relying on intuition and remedies concocted by trial and error.

Those who practiced on a frontier such as Texas were additionally handicapped by the far distances from centers of learning, by living conditions in remote areas, and by economic hardships. All things considered, most doctors of the last century used everything within their means to prevent illness, heal the sick, and alleviate suffering; indeed, they practiced the art of medicine.

Part of that art of medicine was caring and giving of self. The family doctor was counselor, confidant and comforter. He expressed concern, provided hope, and maintained a compassionate attitude. He was sometimes called a "messenger of mercy." In turn, the doctor received the trust and respect of his patients. At best, his story was one of service, self-sacrifice, dedication to his profession, and devotion to his patients — all qualities which bear emulating in the centuries to come.

Now, even as science and technology gather momentum and race through the twentieth century, unimaginable medical miracles await the not too distant twenty-first century. The intangible heart of medicine must not be lost in the press of progress. Without heart, healing might become mechanical. Instead, the advances of medical knowledge and technology can supplement, rather than supplant, the ancient practice of the art of medicine.

In our research, we found conflicting dates and discrepancies on numerous facts, as well as the usual varied spelling of a great many names. Our purpose was not to resolve these dilemmas but to be as consistent and accurate as possible. We have purposely omitted footnotes or endnotes, desiring to avoid the pretense of extensive scholarship; we hope our bibliography, however, will help other researchers.

One medical historian has compared the task of compiling medical history to that of assembling a mosaic. Bits and pieces are found here and there — some are related, some are not.

Our bits and pieces of medical history are assembled like a

patchwork quilt, with fabrics of many threads — some silk, some hemp, some pure gold — and more than a few knots. Scraps of stories about medical personalities add colorful variety. Medical progress forms the pattern by the end of the century.

Here then we present the batting, the inner part of that quilt, which makes up our nineteenth century medical story of Texas.

Acknowledgments

We wish to thank the people who assisted us, and gave us advice and encouragement:

Dr. James G. Burrow of Abilene Christian University read our outline and made helpful suggestions. We are honored that Dr. Burrow, medical historian and writer, consented to write an introduction for us; he is an author of medical books: *AMA: Voice of American Medicine,* and *Organized Medicine in the Progressive Era: The Move Toward Monopoly.*

Dr. William M. Crawford, past president of the Tarrant County Medical Society and member of the American Association for the History of Medicine offered suggestions on our material. Dr. Crawford is a noted medical historian and author of many articles on medical history. We appreciate the foreword he wrote.

Dr. Fane Downs, of McMurry College, gave information on the Texas Revolution chapter.

The personnel in the various Texas medical school libraries helped us, particularly: Dr. Jonathon Erlen and Ann Goertemiller at UTHSC in Dallas; Dr. Larry Wygant and Dr. Inci Bowman at UTHSC, Galveston; Joyce Ray at UTHSC, San Antonio; and Elizabeth White at Houston Academy of Medicine, Jesse H. Jones Library, Houston.

The personnel in the following museums and libraries also helped us, particularly: Kristine Fredriksson and Rebecca Herring at the Museum, Texas Tech University, Lubbock; Tom F. Shelton at The University of Texas Institute of Texan Cultures, San Antonio; Uli Haller, assistant archivist, at the Rosenberg Library, Galveston; Wayne Daniel of the Fort Concho Museum Library, San Angelo; Lila Jefferson, Mary Harper, Shay Bennett, and Laurie Dudley, at the Abilene Public Library; Connee Leetsch, Edith Roebuck, and Lisa

Dunn at the Dyess Air Force Base Library, Abilene; Gifford White, historian and writer, Austin; and Michael R. Green, State Archives, Austin.

Librarians at other libraries who aided our research include: Richardson Library, Barker Collection, UT Austin; Abilene Christian University Library, McMurry College Library and Hardin-Simmons University Library, Abilene; and Daughters of the Republic of Texas Library, at the Alamo, San Antonio.

Thanks to Betty Afflerback and Nancy Bierschenk at the Texas Medical Association in Austin, who opened their files to us. Thanks also, to John Heslip for his drawing of the Button Seal.

We are appreciative for the many friends who shared their books and historical material with us.

Especially, we would like to thank our families and friends for their patience and understanding while we worked on this project.

Introduction

A generation that has heard much about the "magic bullets" of chemotherapy, the wonders of antibiotics, and the virtues of the thiazides likely knows little about the themes narrated in this book. When modern medicine sometimes makes more progress in a week than the healing arts once made in a century, the humble past of medicine is easily forgotten. This volume portrays medical life in a modest era when the Texas frontier brought out not only the crudities of medical practice but the valor and heroism that so often attended it.

Sylvia Ferris and Eleanor Hoppe of Abilene describe vividly medical practice in these exciting years. The authors show the struggle of frontier physicians, who with meager skills and resources, combated diseases of unknown origins and uncertain cures. They show the depressing life of government doctors in frontier forts and how the physicians in frequent wars and frontier forays put down the scalpel only to take up the sword. They describe the role of some eminent physicians in Texas history and their rise to political prominence in the state.

Many native Texans with outstanding physicians in their lineage who served the people of the state in the nineteenth century, will be pleased with this book, and any layman can read it with enjoyment and profit.

JAMES G. BURROW, Ph.D.
Professor of History
Abilene Christian University

1

Setting the Scene: *North of the Rio Grande*

Here they brought a man to me and said that a long time ago he had been wounded with an arrow through the right shoulder, and the arrowhead was lodged over the heart. He said that it gave him much pain and for that reason he was always sick. I touched him, felt the arrowhead, and saw that it traversed the cartilage. With a knife I had I opened his chest to that spot and saw that the point was crosswise and was very difficult to remove. I continued to cut, inserted the point of the knife, and with great difficulty I finally extracted it. It was very long. With a deer bone, using my knowledge of surgery, I took two stitches, following which he bled profusely all over me. With hair from a skin I staunched the flow of blood. When I had removed the arrowhead they asked me for it and I gave it to them. The entire village came to see it and they sent it into the back country so that those who were there might view it. Because of this operation they had many dances and festivities, as was their custom. On another day I cut the Indian's two stitches and he was well. The wound I had made was no more apparent than a crease in the palm of the hand. He said he felt neither pain nor any discomfort. And this cure gave us among them and throughout the land control of all that they considered valuable or cherished.

— Cabeza de Vaca (1490–1564)

The first recorded surgical procedure — performed in Texas in 1535. De Vaca was the first Europeon physician and surgeon in the United States.

For three hundred years after the explorations of Cortes, Cabeza de Vaca, and Coronado in the early 1500s, Texas was a remote northern outpost of the vast Spanish Empire in the western hemisphere. Medical treatment and facilities were available in the Spanish provinces below the Rio Grande. In 1524, Cortes had established the first North American hospital in Mexico City. By the close of the sixteenth century, there were at least ten hospitals in Mexico. No such medical amenities existed north of the Rio Grande.

From time to time, expeditions of conquistadores traveled that vast territory hunting treasure for their Spanish King. On these long journeys, priests often accompanied them and tended to the spiritual needs of the soldiers.

In cases of illness, the priests administered what help they could, but few medical supplies encumbered the arduous trips. They sometimes administered the more common treatments of bleeding and purging. They were also accustomed to prescribing medicinal herbs of Spanish, Mexican, and Indian origin, but they were medically untrained. The priests were sometimes more effective saving heathen or sinful souls than diseased or wounded bodies.

Some of the priests remained north of the Rio Grande in the missions the Spaniards established from Nacogdoches to San Antonio. Their main purpose was to convert the Indians to Christianity.

The priests were helpless, however, in dealing with the epidemics and fevers that plagued Spanish Texas. Repeatedly, the Governor of the Province of Texas beseeched the King of Spain to send medicine and doctors for the wounded soldiers, as well as for the citizens stricken with illness. Indian depredations, epidemics, and intermittent fevers took their toll, but medical supplies and trained medical help remained inadequate.

The weather, *whatever* its nature, was considered a cause of illness. After a violent drop in temperature one January, Governor Cordero wrote:

> This variation, so sudden and extreme, has produced the following effects: all living here have suffered much, and among the rational, it has brought on a catarric fever, epidemic and inflamatory, which demoralizes the faculties.

In another instance, the Spanish governor wrote in 1819, of one unspecific epidemic which, he stated, was,

> . . . doubtless caused by the terrible drought that has been prev-

> alent for a long time. Although only one person has died of the prevailing disease . . . if it does not rain and lessen the heat a little, it will spread with even greater malignity.

Even though such theories lacked foundation in medical science, Spanish authorities initiated several health measures in their territory in the new world. They sent a ship carrying vaccination material to prevent the spread of smallpox; they established hospitals at remote outposts and attempted to staff them with qualified medical personnel; and in the interest of public health, they passed various ordinances and made sporadic attempts to enforce them. These measures, although inadequate, were the groundwork for medical developments later in the century.

Spanish King Charles IV hoped to protect his subjects in the New World from the devastating effects of smallpox, a disease which was probably introduced into Mexico in the sixteenth century by Cortes and his followers. Upon hearing of Jenner's discovery of vaccination with cowpox in 1798, the King realized the importance of sending the discovery to the new world for prevention of the dreaded disease characterized by skin eruptions that left its victims disfigured with small pock marks. In 1803, he sent his personal physician, Dr. Francisco Xavier de Balmis, and two assistants on a strangely equipped mercy mission to the Spanish dominion across the sea.

Twenty-two children sailed with the medical team in a small Spanish ship. On the long voyage to the New World, cowpox virus, which had been dried on threads, was transmitted to the children. The doctor kept the virus alive by vaccinating two children each week to ten days with the virus taken from the festering sores of two children vaccinated the previous week. After the living chain of smallpox virus reached Mexico, de Balmis offered vaccination to the population, after first vaccinating the young son of the viceroy. But it was not until April 1806, that the provisional governor of San Antonio de Bexar received an active vial of the vaccine fluid and a paperful of smallpox scabs. Several months earlier, the first shipment of vaccine from Mexico City had evaporated on the long journey.

Using the new shipment in the Alamo infirmary, Dr. Federico Zervan proceeded to innoculate twelve children, six belonging to the troops and six belonging to the settlers. This experiment was unsettling to the townspeople who feared the disease and did not understand immunization. Eventually, upon seeing the children free of disease, the townspeople ceased their resistance and accepted vaccination material from the authorities. The innoculation experiment continued for several years, and in time, the threat of smallpox lessened. Thus began the eradication of the smallpox scourge in Spanish Texas.

The success of these earlier experiments led the way to the Mexican government's program in San Antonio in 1830 for compulsory vaccination of all children, the first such attempt in the state.

The Spaniards, who established hospitals at intervals along their frontiers, realized a hospital was needed north of the Rio Grande. There they opened a military infirmary in a partly damaged area of the Mission San Antonio de Valero, often known as the Alamo. The word alamo is the Spanish word for cottonwood, and according to some historians, the eighteenth century Spanish mission became so-named because of the many surrounding cottonwood trees. During Mexico's War with Spain, a company of Spanish soldiers from Alamo del Parras, Coahuila, Mexico, used the mission as barracks. From this association probably originated the name. Although makeshift infirmaries had existed there previously, the facility established at the Alamo in 1805, is considered to be the first hospital in Texas.

As in most frontier garrisons and Spanish outposts, the medical personnel of this hospital treated the civilian population as well as military patients. Among the diseases treated at the Alamo were malaria, smallpox, pneumonia, influenza, gonorrhea, and syphilis, as well as arrow and bullet wounds received fighting Indians.

Dr. Federico Zervan, a "professor of surgery and medicine," was in charge of the Alamo military infirmary. A dignified but colorful character, he entered sleepy San Antonio in 1805, with an impressive retinue accompanied by beasts loaded with trunks and boxes. Among his valuables were an organ, two chandeliers, six large portraits, and one hundred and thirty-eight books.

Dr. Zervan was probably willing to accept this frontier post in hopes of leaving his personal troubles behind. Even before leaving New Orleans in 1803 after his wife died, there was a clouded issue of some forty thousand dollars owed to his brothers-in-law. They legally, but unsuccessfully, sought to prevent Dr. Zervan from taking possession of his wife's property, which included sixteen slaves. Further disputes were to follow Dr. Zervan.

In his new post, Dr. Zervan treated the sick and wounded for the small sum of sixty *pesos* a month. In addition, he was responsible for preparing medicines and carrying out administrative duties, which at first, he discharged in a satisfactory manner. Unfortunately, he had to contend with many insurmountable problems.

The equipment at the Alamo infirmary was not adequate. Beds were made of bamboo or reeds "in order to avoid the dampness of the ground."

Sometimes there were more patients than beds. During one influenza epidemic, in addition to patients in the beds, an additional seventy-two patients were scattered about the building receiving treatment.

Medical supplies, usually arriving by packmules, were not plentiful nor regularly received. Dr. Zervan received seven boxes of supplies in the spring of 1807, which he had ordered nine months earlier. The list, representative of medicines widely used at the time, included the following:

> Senna, sugar candy, cochineal, rhubarb, epsom salts, Jesuit's bark (cinchona officinalis), incense, cream of tartar, cantharis (Spanish fly [pulverized green blister beetle]), American ipecac, opium, borax, catholic extract, three dozen rubber bougies, one rubber catheter, tarter emetic, wine, spirits of scurvy-grass, olive oil, frog cordial with mercury, simple cordial, divine cordial, one box of surgical instruments for operations for trepan, 12 pointed Spanish lances, thin catgut, two large syringes, Hispanic pharmacopoeia, active mercury, corrosive sublimate, sweet mercury, white arsenic, black bromide, four American cupping glasses.

Though Dr. Zervan remained in good personal standing with the governor of the province, he was not popular with the townspeople. They thought him indifferent and ineffectual. They doubted Dr. Zervan's abilities, since much of his treatment and medicine did not produce miraculous cures or healing. In fact, the townsfolk were so disillusioned with the effectiveness of Dr. Zervan's methods, they petitioned the town council to remove him. However, the doctor's friend, Governor Cordero, staunchly defended the doctor with the wise observation that the people freely chose Dr. Zervan's ministrations; they were not forced to accept his treatment.

The governor probably became weary of interceding for Dr. Zervan, who had the dubious distinction of being the first doctor in Texas involved in a civil suit for irregularity of practice. This notable controversy involved Dr. Zervan and his good friend, Father Juan Manuel Zambrano, with whom he lodged. The two were accustomed to spending leisure hours together gambling. Unfortunately, the doctor lost five hundred *pesos* to his friend and host. The friendship rapidly deteriorated when the doctor could not pay his debt. Petty hostility ensued, as the priest sought payment for "unpaid board," and the doctor countered by seeking payment for "professional services." As arbitrator, the governor required both men to cease the quarrel, but thereafter, Dr. Zervan's friendship with the governor flagged. In 1807, Dr. Zervan returned to Mexico after resigning from military service. Undoubtedly, Dr. Zervan's exit from the city lacked the pomp of his grand entrance.

Dr. Jayme Gurza was Dr. Zervan's replacement at the Alamo hospital for the next four years. One of his chief problems was the deterioration of the building itself, which was fast falling into a state of neglect; the roof leaked whenever it rained, and some even expressed concern that the crumbling walls would fall down. Dr. Gurza submitted a report, which resulted in some repairs, but more were needed.

Dr. Gurza also had to contend with the same problems of his predecessor: the scarcity of equipment and supplies. Governor Cordero authorized thirty new beds made of bamboo or cane, but there were only enough sheets for fourteen beds. Dr. Gurza requisitioned sheets for each bed, but the order was not filled for three years. Mattresses, too, were a source of complaint. Those in use were stuffed with moss rather than more comfortable wool. Dr. Gurza predicted "evil results that the patients may experience for lack of this essential article."

In addition, the cost of requisitions and maintenance was a constant source of dispute with the Spanish authorities. In 1808, Governor Cordero reprimanded him for excessive hospital expenses, such as 688 *pesos* for "moss, wool, and other effects for beds." Authorities also considered the expense of medicinal brandy outrageous: "one hundred twelve *pesos* being charged for two barrels of brandy used in the pharmacy," an amount allotted for thirty patients over a six-month period.

A change in Spanish government in 1811 brought about Dr. Gurza's imprisonment, probably because he was a foreigner. An oath of loyalty soon thereafter achieved his release from prison. Several months later, he requested a discharge from government service due to illness. When his request was honored, mention was made of "the rigorous zeal with which this meritorious doctor has fulfilled his duty."

The next year, the governor of the province of Texas reported a scarcity of funds in meeting the expenses of the hospital. The situation did not improve. In 1814, the surgeon then in charge of the hospital, Dr. Francisco Farina, again reported a scarcity of supplies, particularly of drugs, to the Spanish governor at Monterrey. The governor instructed the surgeon to make a list of needed drugs, which he did. Later, the governor replied that he had received the list, that the drugs had been ordered from Vera Cruz, and that in due time the drugs would be sent to San Antonio. This exchange was the last dated reference to the Alamo as a hospital.

The hospital closed soon thereafter. The building, then badly neglected, was sold at auction. The troubles endured at the Alamo hospital only foreshadowed greater troubles to come almost a quarter of a century later.

A man ahead of his time, the Spanish Governor, Don Antonio Cordero, wisely instituted sanitary measures in the township of Bexar. He posted an order for each and every settler:

> I hereby order each and every settler of this city and its suburbs. . .
>
> . . .in addition to taking away all dead animals from town streets or lots — leaving them considerable distance from the city — not to kill animals within their own lots, being careful to cover up the blood with dirt afterwards; lastly, I order them not to harbor any filthiness in front of their homes or around their lots; those who disobey this order will be prosecuted by law.

Further, he ordered the military to: "comb . . . hair daily, and change clothes at least every week, in order to prevent infection with sores and other diseases which are prevalent."

In spite of the earlier attempts to promote public health, the Spanish empire's political problems thwarted well-intentioned efforts. As Spanish rule came to an end, a sad state of affairs existed. What little money the Spaniards had was needed more below the Rio Grande to end the Mexican rebellion, than to finance health measures on a remote frontier. Governor Martinez, the last Spanish governor, reported the following:

> . . . this province, separated so far from all communication with the other provinces, has not within its bounds even a mediocre physician who could prevent the infinite number of deaths that occur for lack of medicine and medical attention. The nearest physician is 150 leagues away and, even though at one time there

was a large drug store here, there are now to be found only cans with only a remnant of their contents, and this is spoiled.

After repeated requests to the Spanish viceroy for a physician, officials promised that Don Jose Maria Aleman would come to Texas. Three boxes of his medicines did arrive, but the doctor reportedly fell off a mule in San Luis Potosi preventing him from making the journey. The doctor wrote: "If your Lordship would like to have a book with illustrations for those who attend the sick," he volunteered, "I shall be glad to forward one."

When San Antonio suffered an epidemic in 1819, the boxes of medicines were opened, even though at that time, the city still had no physician. This situation was remedied in 1820, when Don Jose Joaquin Villaverde came to San Antonio as "this city's physician."

Dr. Villaverde reported on the medical needs to the Spanish authorities, saying:

> I have decided that, with the greatest economy, the sum of one thousand pesos annually must be spent for medicines. Wishing to be one of those who contribute to the welfare of humanity, for my salary I shall be satisfied to receive merely four hundred twenty-five pesos annually.

This arrangement did not succeed. The poor settlers were unable to pay for their medicines, resulting in the cancellation of the doctor's contract. In his book, *The Medical Story of Early Texas*, Dr. Nixon has called this the "first recorded attempt at socialization of medicine in Texas."

An interesting historical note on the Spanish era is truly a vision awry. The last Spanish Governor of Texas, Antonio Maria de Martinez, had high hopes and dreams for the future of Spanish Texas. He wanted trained soldiers, a network of highways, and a chain of *presidios*. He anticipated thriving commerce, safe travel, and an end to both banditry and hostile Indians. He visualized Spanish families colonizing the expanse of Texas land north of the Rio Grande.

For forty months, the governor worked to carry out his plans, but no help came. Spanish authorities did not share the extent of his dream, or if they did, they were too busy fighting the Mexican revolt. No Spanish colonists arrived, and there were no funds, few soldiers, and scant medical and building supplies.

In that propitious moment, the governor was approached by Moses Austin, a former naturalized Spanish subject, who wanted to bring families of Americans from the Louisiana Territory to colonize Spanish Texas. Here then was the answer to the Spanish Governor's dream: the colonists could not only fight the Indians and protect borders, but they could settle and develop the land. While becoming the Spanish King's loyal subjects, they would also provide revenue for Spanish coffers.

Little did the governor expect that Spain would lose its hold in the New World. Neither could he foresee that these settlers, a new breed of people, would become instead fervent free-thinking Texans, their spirit of independence as large in scope as the vast territory north of the Rio Grande.

Dr. Villaverde, known as the first Mexican doctor in Texas, remained in Texas only six months after the Mexicans gained control of Spanish interests in the New World in 1821. At that time, he was allowed to resign and return to Saltillo. Apparently, the medical department of the army, not satisfied with his required diploma, gave the following explanation: "his appointment is nullified because he did not exhibit a copy of his title."

Other frontier outposts in Texas had trouble keeping medical personnel as well. The records indicate only a handful of Mexican doctors were in and out of that area during the fifteen-year period of Mexican rule. Some of these served short periods with the Mexican garrisons. Dr. Augustin LeFarza was assigned to the post at Nacogdoches in 1829 from Matamoros. When he arrived in San Antonio on his way to Nacogdoches, he requested a discharge due to poor health. It was not granted. It seems the doctor's health was stronger than his desire for frontier life, and several months later he completed his assigned journey. He was given another command at Matamoros the next year, but the protest of his commander may have prevented his leaving the post. The record is silent on Dr. LeFarza's subsequent service.

In addition to such personnel problems, medical conditions were no better under the Mexican regime. A hospital was badly needed, but none took the place of the abandoned Alamo hospital. The sick and wounded were carried to hospitals further south.

Medical supplies were even more difficult to procure than in the days of Spanish rule. Severe medical shortages still existed below the Rio Grande. There were additional problems in raising sufficient cash to send supplies northward. In 1830, a shipment of seven boxes of medicines to the Twelfth Battalion at Nacogdoches was delayed several months in Goliad, because the treasury did not have the funds necessary to complete the journey. The authorities demanded cash in advance from Nacogdoches, a request which those in charge could not meet. Only after repeated letters and threats did the medicines finally arrive at that destination, but the quarrel over payment did not end for some time. Even a matter of ten *pesos* due the freighters in Matamoros was not easy to settle.

The medical picture in Texas north of the Rio Grande was soon to change. Improvements were gradually brought about with the coming of the American and European settlers.

2

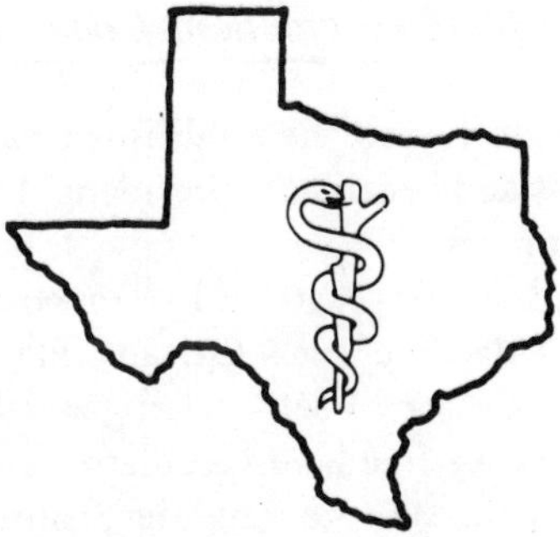

Seeking the Frontier:
Texas Fever

. . . for the impulse to {go} to Texas both as to soldiers and moving families exceeds anything I have ever known.
— December 1835 letter of Micajah Autry, Alamo hero

Throughout the nineteenth century, doctors came to Texas from the east, north, south, and even from Europe. These physicians played a strong part in settling and developing that part of the western frontier that is now the Lone Star State. A mixed lot, some were of the highest calibre, indeed builders and shapers of the state, while others — charlatans, medical adverturers and opportunists — took advantage of the pitiful ignorance of others. For good or ill, their influence was felt in many aspects of frontier life, their contributions not limited to the traditional area of healing.

The reasons they rode, walked, or traveled hundreds of miles from their homes and families were as varied as the men themselves. In addition to many of their immediate personal reasons for coming, however, they shared in common basic desires for land, a new way of life, and better health.

Dr. James Long, a plantation owner from Natchez, Mississippi, was a man with the premature vision to free Texas from Spain early in the nineteenth century. Married to Jane Long, who came to be called "the mother of Texas," he established for a short time an *early* Republic of Texas and became its president. History, however, gives him scant recognition.

This self-educated doctor practiced little medicine after serving as surgeon in the 1815 Battle of New Orleans. He preferred the life of a soldier to that of a doctor. A self-styled general, in 1819 he assembled an army of seventy-five land speculators and adventurers to march overland across Louisiana, to force the Spanish out of Texas.

His ragtag army consisted of forty armed horsemen and foot soldiers bearing sabers and short knives. Packmules hauled food supplies and ammunition. As they marched, General Long recruited additional troops with the promise of 64,000 acres of rich Texas land to be given away when a new government was established. His army soon numbered three hundred.

They met with little resistance from the Spanish garrison at Nacogdoches, and on June 23, 1820, all Spanish troops surrendered. Proclaiming Texas a free and independent republic, General Long immediately established a civil government under a supreme council of which he was the president.

This group then proceeded to enact laws for the new Republic of Texas and to provide revenues by the sale of public lands. A newspaper printing shop and various other agencies were established at the capital city of Nacogdoches. Trading posts were opened throughout the nearby territory to carry on official and commercial business in the name of the Republic of Texas.

One of General Long's enterprises in Nacogdoches was to publish *The Texas Republican.* This newspaper — which survived only about two months — advertised Texas for the taking.

General Long made plans to conquer all of Texas. Maintaining a solid stronghold in east Texas, he surmised that the Spanish could be easily pushed back across the Rio Grande. His plan included enlisting the aid of the pirate Jean Lafitte, who held Galveston Island and kept Spanish ships out of the Gulf of Mexico. General Long wanted the pirate fleet allied with his Republic of Texas navy.

Lafitte appeared agreeable, but the wily pirate told General Long a much stronger land force was required to conquer all of Texas and hold it. Until Lafitte had such assurance, he would not aid General Long.

General Long soon returned to Nacogdoches where he learned that a strong Spanish army had surprised his forces there, killing or capturing most of his Republic of Texas officials and soldiers. Long crossed over into the United States join his family.

The reality of a free republic was shattered, but the dream remained. For some time, James Long plotted and planned for another expedition to free Texas. His zeal to establish a Republic of Texas never diminished, but his army did. When at last, with only fifty-two men, General Long stormed into La Bahia in October 1821, he found a fruitless victory: Captain Don Francisco Garcia, who surrendered the garrison, claimed to share Republic of Texas sentiments with General Long. Four days after the attack, however, seven hundred Spanish troops arrived from San Antonio surprising Long's men. Upon seeing the reinforcements, Captain Garcia again changed his mind, unsuccessfully attempting to shoot General Long. It was said that the only damage was "the rape of a lock [of hair] which the whizzing lead cut from the general's head."

All the while, the Spanish shelled the fort without success. Trying another tactic, they pretended to be enemies of the Spanish Royalists, initiating a cease-fire. Once more, General Long was deceived, and he was soon taken prisoner. He was then marched to Mexico where he was killed a few months later after striking a guard.

Thus ended James Long's attempt to free Texas from Spain and establish a Republic of Texas. Even though this multifaceted entrepreneur had a limited medical career, a brief military career, and a short political career, his words and his actions ignited a long-lasting flame for freedom.

Ironically, Dr. Long is little known or remembered as perhaps the first Anglo-American doctor to perform a surgical act of healing in nineteenth century Texas.

While searching Galveston Island in 1821, Dr. Purnell [Parnell] and a small detachment of General Long's army encountered a large number of Karankawa Indians. In the resulting skirmish, the Indians were supposedly driven off the island. Although the Indians suffered several casualties, the only damage to the Americans was a slight wound to Dr. Purnell. An arrow had pierced the skin of his head and skewered his hat to his scalp. After the battle, Dr. Long extricated the arrow with his broken sword, accomplishing a successful surgical procedure.

For some doctors, land itself, not therapeutics, was the chief motivation in coming to Texas. While some only wanted to become property owners, others hoped and planned to engage in land speculation.

The United States, recuperating after the War of 1812, suffered some difficult times. Many banks closed during the panic of 1819. Poverty replaced wealth, as other businesses failed. The United States Congress, reacting to the poor economic conditions, required cash for land in 1820. Since few had cash, few were able to buy land. Many were eager for new answers to escape this difficult plight. All at once, rumor spread like wildfire that Spanish Texas's rich lands were free, or pennies an acre at most.

Land promoters, called *empresarios*, fanned the flame. They negotiated with the Spanish government to introduce settlers into Texas. Mexico separated from Spain just as approval was granted for the Austin colony. The fire that was the desire for free land reached fever pitch. It was called "Texas Fever."

Reports differ as to the amount of land parcelled to each *empresario,* but generally an *empresario* received one to three *haciendas* of five *sitios* for a minimum of one hundred families. A *sitio* or league of land was 4,428 acres. Married men, single men, wives, children, slaves, farmers, and ranchers all received varying amounts of acreage. Originally, colonists were required to "become Mexican citizens, be Catholic, and of good character." Later they only had to promise to occupy and develop the land within two years.

Requirements for acceptance to colonize, however, became more stringent. Later the rules read that "no frontiersmen who has no other occupation than that of a hunter will be received. No drunkard, nor gambler, nor profane idler, nor any man against whom there is even probable grounds of suspicion that he is a bad man." Infringements upon these rules were harshly dealt with: public whipping, property confiscation, and exile to the United States.

A total of twenty-six grants were made under the Mexican *empresario* grant system from April 1823, to May 1832. Over twenty-six million acres of Texas land were finally distributed.

On the first of August 1821, Stephen F. Austin arrived with nine men to explore the area that was to become the First Austin colony. Among them was a Dr. James Hewitson, a native of Ireland, who in January 1822, took the place of Dr. Villaverde as surgeon of the San Antonio army hospital at twenty *pesos* a month.

Dr. Hewitson also treated the townspeople, but his services were not satisfactory, "because he applied the same kind of medicine to all kinds of diseases." The governor of Texas wrote to the military authority in Saltillo in January 1823, that Dr. Hewitson was not qualified for his position and that he had taken his instrument case from him. Sending him to Saltillo, the governor did note, however, that "Dr. Hewitson's conduct is not bad, and he professes our holy religion."

Apparently, Dr. Hewitson engaged in the mercantile business while practicing medicine in Saltillo. According to John J. Linn, Dr. Hewitson "was well posted in Mexican affairs." He had an extensive medical library for that time with books on pathology, anatomy, practical physics, the nervous system, arteries, autopsy, botany, surgical operations, and general medicine.

Land looked more lucrative than the medical field, so in 1828, Dr. Hewitson became an *empresario*. He joined with Colonel James Power to obtain a grant from the Mexican government to establish a colony between the Guadalupe and Neuces Rivers, the Colony of Power and Hewitson. Together they were authorized to bring in four hundred families, half Mexican and half Irish-Catholics. A cholera epidemic in 1833 was a major setback. Other hardships were brought about by General Santa Anna and his Mexican army on the move which ended the progress of the colony.

In November 1821, Dr. Robert Andrews enthusiastically wrote to Stephen F. Austin that he and a group of fifty others anticipated moving from Arkansas to Texas. He planned to bring his own medicine and asked Austin while in New Orleans to "buy Thomas's [*sic*] practice if convenient," an instructive book on the Thompsonian [so-called later: Thomsonian] treatment being popular at that time.

Dr. Andrews, one of the first physicians to help Austin establish his colony, became Austin's friend. When Austin went to Mexico City in 1822 to confirm the permission to colonize which had been granted his father, he was accompanied part of the way by Dr. Andrews. While waiting to hear that Austin had returned from Mexico City, Dr. Andrews remained in Saltillo.

Dr. Andrews's sojourn there was not easy, pleasant, or profitable. Practicing medicine, he made only about seventy to eighty dollars a month, barely enough to meet his expenses. At one point he was robbed of what little he had except for the clothes he wore. He described his predicament in a letter: "I live at present on hope altogether, there being no call for a Physician . . ."

Discouraged with his predicament, Dr. Andrews also suffered failing health. He desperately desired to change his circumstances and become a working part of the Austin Colony's bright future.

Apparently, his hopes were not realized. He claimed that if he could only return to Texas for a short time he would willingly diet on "catfish and wild onions without salt or greas[e]."

While several colonies were established in Texas, none were quite as successful as the First Austin Colony. The first families to settle in the broad valleys between the Brazos and Colorado Rivers under the terms of Stephen F. Austin's original colony, numbered two hundred and ninety-seven and came to be known as "The Old Three Hundred." Of those, the name of only one physician appears in the records of the General Land Office at Austin, Texas. James A. E. Phelps is listed as receiving title to a *sitio* of land in Brazoria County on the 16th of August 1824. It is unlikely that any American or European physician settled in that area to practice medicine before that date.

During the decade following establishment of the colony, many more doctors came to Texas. The Register of families introduced by *Empresario* Stephen F. Austin includes the following doctors who took the oath prescribed by Article Number 3 of the Colonization Law of the State of Coahuila and Texas dated March 1825, and the dates of their arrival:

> Thomas J. Gazley, a married doctor from Ohio, who arrived 16th of November 1828. "Wants his land at upper end of McGinty's Prairie and at upper end of a little prairie on the Colorado between this and that of a tiny plain above."
>
> William D. Finley, a married doctor from Ohio, who arrived 18th of January 1829. "Has a six months delay to bring his family . . ."
>
> James B. Miller, a single doctor from Kentucky who arrived May 10, 1829.
>
> Robert Peebles and his wife. He was a doctor from Louisiana who arrived 10 September 1829 with one child and five dependents.
>
> Asa Holdridge, age twenty-seven, single doctor from Louisiana who arrived 1830.
>
> Christopher G. Cox, age twenty-seven, married doctor from Tennessee, arrived February 1830 with wife, child, and one dependent.
>
> S. J. Moseley, age twenty-seven, a single doctor from Tennessee arrived March 1830.
>
> Lyman Conkrite, age twenty-six, married doctor from New York, arrived January 1831 with wife Sarah and one child.

Samuel B. Watts, age twenty-three, a single doctor from Alabama, arrived February 1831.

J. S. Counsel, age thirty-three, single doctor from Louisiana, arrived March 1831.

Richard Marsh, age twenty-four, single doctor from New York, arrived May 1831.

Erasmus D. Downer, age thirty-two, a single doctor from New York, arrived May 1831.

A. C. Taylor, age thirty-two, a single doctor from Illinois, arrived May 1831.

Branch T. Archer, age forty-three, widower from Virginia, arrived June 1831 with three children and two dependents.

T. F. L. Parrott, age twenty-eight, doctor from South Carolina, arrived in this Country in November 1831.

J. D. G. Varrelmann, married doctor from Germany, arrived in 1832 with wife and six children.

Joseph E. Field, age thirty-three, single doctor from Massachusetts, arrived probably in 1833.

Alexander Ewing, single doctor from Pennsylvania, arrived March 1833.

Amos Pollard, married doctor, arrived from New York in December 1833.

John Y. Wallace, age thirty-four, married doctor from Pennsylvania, arrived 26 February 1835 with wife Eliza and two dependents.

Upon presentation of a diploma, the town council of San Felipe de Austin granted Dr. Robert Peebles, originally from South Carolina, a provisional license to practice medicine which he did for two years. In fact, in 1830, he became a member of a Board of Physicians with the authority to examine the credentials of other doctors desiring to practice in the municipality. He was one of three physicians on the first board of health of San Felipe which convened in 1831.

An interesting account of this examining board indicates that they took their duties seriously. In 1831, Dr. C. G. Cox and Dr. J. B. Walls were summoned before the Town Council and fined twenty-five dollars each for breaching municipal ordinances by practicing medicine without obtaining a license. Dr. Walls paid his fine without protest; Dr. Cox objected, paid his fine, and petitioned for remittance. The Council demurred.

In addition to his medical responsibilities, Dr. Peebles engaged in land speculation. In 1835, Dr. Peebles and two friends received a grant of 400 leagues (1,771,200 acres) from the Mexican Governor, an allotment termed "one of the clumsiest land steals in all history." This bestowal required Dr. Peebles's on site residence. He lived in Monclova until the Mexican troops advanced on Texas. Four days before Santa Anna and his army reached San Felipe, Peebles loaded the Texas land records in a wagon and sought safety back in Texas in Nacogdoches. In October 1836, he delivered the records, including evidence of his own illegal transactions, to Stephen Austin.

Regardless of his problems with this transaction, Dr. Peebles became land commissioner for Austin's Colony at a time when less than honest land deals and dealers certainly existed. To Dr. Peebles's credit, he kept the goodwill and friendship of Stephen F. Austin.

Another of the first physicians who came to settle with the Austin Colony had little time to practice medicine there before he was tarred and feathered, his *quid pro quo* for taking what some reports call an "adverse political stand" against Stephen F. Austin.

Actually, Dr. Lewis B. Dayton (Deaton) disagreed with, and loudly objected to, Austin's Land Office fees and Surveyor's fees of twelve and a half cents an acre imposed on the colonists. Dr. Dayton stirred up the populace, arguing that the original contract with the Spanish government called for Austin to settle three hundred colonists at his own expense with only land as remuneration.

Dr. Dayton was arrested and charged with making slanderous accusations against Stephen F. Austin in 1826. After a trial and conviction of disturbing the peace as an agitator, law enforcers stripped Dr. Dayton to his underdrawers, shaved his head, tarred his body, and clothed it with the contents of a feather pillow. As an object lesson, he was then marched down the street and ordered to leave town, a command that he apparently accepted with no further resistance. Stephen F. Austin, who was away when this incident occurred, later said that it would not have taken place had he been there.

Dr. James Grant owned a large estate near Parras in Coahuila. At one time he sold certificates for one hundred leagues of land, and following his death, his estate included unlocated and unsold certificates for three hundred leagues of land.

Grant's business deals were offset by the part he played in the Texas Revolution. Dr. Grant had been with the Texian army when they captured San Antonio late in 1835. Believing that many in Mexico would help them overthrow Santa Anna, Dr. Grant and other leaders recommended an invasion of Mexico through the lower Rio Grande. The General Council commissioned James Fannin, Grant, and Francis Johnson to act according to plans for such an invasion, a fatal move for Dr. Grant. One week after the Mexican General Urrea's army decimated Johnson's detachment not far from San Patricio, they killed Dr. Grant and most of his men at Aqua Dulce Creek.

After the war for independence, other groups lured settlers to Texas with prospects of land ownership. Dr. John Cameron, an *empresario*, obtained a grant to colonize along the Red River, but apparently the venture was not successful. Later, he was given a grant of land in the Panhandle. Imprisoned in Mexico with Ben Milam when General Cos dispersed the Legislature, Dr. Cameron and Milam escaped and made their way to Texas. Fighting for Texas Independence, Dr. Cameron helped capture San Antonio when General Cos surrendered. Dr. Cameron, who spoke fluent Spanish, was invaluable as an interpreter. Dr. Cameron and John L. Woodbury were also given an exclusive privilege to work iron and coal mines in Texas for twenty-three years.

Dr. Ferdinand Charles Herff came to America because his group was offered land in Texas in 1847, by the German Nobleman's Immigration Company. He was one of a courageous group of free-thinking, liberty-loving Germans who immigrated to Texas between 1845 and 1850. These people were dissatisfied with political conditions in Germany at the time.

Dr. Herff became a leader in the practice of medicine in San Antonio, but he first settled a colony in the wilderness. There he tended the sick without the advantage of European medical centers where he had been trained.

Some settlers came to Texas to improve their finances. With a scarcity of money in the United States, many people incurred extensive debts from which there was little hope of escape. Given the opportunity, these people were eager to make a fresh start. Anson Jones was one doctor who chose to come to Texas when his gambling debts in New Orleans became excessive. Unlike many others, Dr. Jones later paid back the money he owned his debtors.

Escaping other unpleasant situations also brought a number of doctors to Texas. For centuries, dueling had been an accepted manner of settling disputes. The practice, however, was now looked upon with disfavor by authorities in the United States. Leaving the

Dr. Herff's Journey to Texas

The arrival of Dr. Herff's group in Galveston in April 1847 was not uneventful. The immigrants' steamer was commandeered for military use by the United States. On a second-class substitute schooner, the group sailed for Indianola, the only port with a direct road connecting southwest Texas.

The schooner's slightly inebriated skipper steered the vessel into a sandbar, whereupon the vessel began to sink. Quickly lowering a lifeboat, the now more sober captain hastened to debark, ostensibly to seek aid. But to Baron Herff, it was clear the rascal was escaping to save his own neck. At gunpoint, he ordered the captain back aboard with: "If this ship sinks, you, my Captain, will sink with it!"

The carpenter on board repaired the leak. Five days later, landing at Indianola, the group travelled to Llano, a hard trip by oxcart through harsh terrain filled with bandits, wild animals, pesky insects, and hostile Indians. The colonists, who named their settlement Bettina, immediately began building a long one-story bunkhouse to be furnished with a row of cots. Among the group were a brewer, a miller, a blacksmith, and two physicians.

scene of a scandal was easier than answering to those who might take some appropriate action.

Many doctors arrived on the Texas scene after duelling confrontations. Hot-tempered Dr. Branch Archer had been involved in a duel in Virginia before coming west, and even the distinguished surgeon, Dr. Herff, had fought as many as twenty-one duels in Europe before coming to America. The young Baron von Herff had fought nineteen of these contests with a flat-bladed cavalry "Schlager," one with a cavalry saber, and one with a pistol.

There was a dual feeling on duels. Dueling was not considered a crime in some places. Men, particularly from the south, felt impelled to defend their honor upon occasion. Dr. J. M. Steiner was involved in a fatal duel at Fort Graham early in 1853, a fact which may explain his move to Austin in 1854. The doctor had been acquitted in a Justice of the Peace Court. There were some, however, who complained that justice had not been served. When the Army ordered a court-martial to be held in Austin, Dr. Steiner did not appear. Troops were then sent to Waco where Dr. Steiner had practiced from 1851 to 1853. Instead of arresting Dr. Steiner, the troops were arrested themselves by the civil authorities, assuring Dr. Steiner his freedom.

Many who came west had suffered unhappy love affairs or marriages. Such was the case with Dr. John R. Sibley, who fled to Louisiana and Texas after an unhappy second marriage.

Dr. Sibley's occupations were many. He was at one time "contract surgeon in the United States Army, Indian agent of the United States, land speculator, farmer, ranchman, owner of a salt mine, instigator of Indian uprisings in Texas, informant and confidential representative of Stephen F. Austin in the United States."

Born in Massachusetts in 1757, Dr. Sibley later became a surgeon's mate in the American Revolution. After the war, he practiced medicine in Great Barrington, Massachusetts, the birthplace seventeen years later of Dr. Anson Jones. Dr. Sibley married and moved to North Carolina, where his wife died. Other misfortunes prevailed. He married again, but this marriage was not a happy one. He also lost considerable property. To escape from his situation, in 1802 he moved to Natchitoches, Louisiana, the furthest outpost of the United States, and next to the Spanish domain of Texas.

For twelve years, Dr. Sibley was a United States Indian agent with a salary of $1000 a year plus a liberal allowance to make friends with the Texas Indians. This action incurred the enmity of the Spanish governor of Texas, who reported that Dr. Sibley was trying to cause the friendly Tonkawa Indians and other tribes to rebel.

While records indicate that Dr. Sibley lived for a time in Texas, he was primarily engaged in political and diplomatic activities in Louisiana. He kept Stephen F. Austin informed on European affairs as well as political conditions in the United States.

On one occasion, he prescribed medicine by letter for one of Austin's ailments:

> . . . It appears to me there is no doubt but the symptoms yours describes are produced from an affection of the kidneys which I think it probable has been brought on by your Long Sedentary habit, and I should hope that a change in that Respect with a moderate use of some cooling diureticks will Relieve you — Amongst the Vegetable Diureticks those which are Emolient are best (*viz*) Slipiry Elm Bark, Water Melon Seeds. Mauve or Mallows, the Inner Bark of Pine, Casteal Soap. . . . these are all used in form of tea Sometimes a small Pill of Opium may be Proper . . . your diet should be more Simple than Ordinary and Wine and Ardent Spirits used more sparingly.

Dr. Sibley, who later was "captain of the militia, justice of the peace, parish judge, and a state senator of Louisiana," died only one year after Texas became a Republic. It was said that he was "a man of large properties and many achievements." Like many others, Dr. Sibley may have escaped a lifetime of misery by making the journey west. All who came were not so fortunate.

Some doctors came to Texas because they or someone in their family had health problems. Believing that climate was related to disease, they sought what they felt was a healthy area. Many had asthma, hay fever, or other respiratory ailments, which often improved in dry climates, particularly in the drier areas of the frontier. Doctors as well as others were enticed by reports such as those by Mary Austin Holly, cousin of Stephen F. Austin. She declared in 1836:

> While we claim nothing unreal, no poetic exaggeration, or fictitious excellence for this region, we could confidently assert that no state on the continent is more eminently favored by nature in fertility of soil and salubrity of climate than Texas or presents a like combination of natural advantages . . .

In 1848, Viktor Bracht wrote:

> Here the expectations of many, who came to find a healthful climate, were either surpassed or at least justified. The experiences of many German physicians have confirmed the truth of earlier reports about the climate. In truth, the healthfulness and pleasantness of the climate of the entire region far surpasses that of the northern, western, and even southern parts of the United States.

One traveler in the 1870s claimed: "Let a man travel six weeks in western Texas; and if he is not cured . . . of whatever ailment he has, it will be because there is no blood left in him."

The Texas Almanac and *Emigrant's Guide to Texas* [1873] said:

> . . . there is no State of greater healthfulness than Texas, while many portions of the State, as Austin and San Antonio and the hilly regions farther north and west, are the resort of consumptives who almost invariably recover and live many years. It is a fact not to be gainsaid or denied, that for pulmonary complaints there is no climate in the world more favorable than that of the section we have indicated.

Speaking of the Davis Mountain country in the 1880s, Walter B. Stevens bragged: "It tones up weak lungs and enables the asthmatic to whoop and enjoy life." He also claimed: "there are springs all about which possess a whole apothecaryship of medical qualities."

F. V. Hayden said Central Texas had "a climate which brings visitors for profit, pleasure, and health from all parts of the world."

A myth circulated that it was nearly impossible to die in Texas — a claim that no one wanted to dispute. Another rumor circulated that it was a "rare thing to hear any one cough," and the "Statistical Report on Texas, 1835," translated by Carlos Castaneda, claimed, "Nowhere in Texas is yellow fever or bubonic plague known." It was further reported the same year that ". . . no sickness is known there; and truly, doctors in this section will not prosper."

In spite of the rumors which indicated a poor business outlook for doctors, many came west. With the exception of fighting for freedom, the basic reasons which induced the earliest American and European doctors to come to Texas, continued to attract physicians from other parts. By mid-century, over six hundred physicians had flocked to the new state, and thirty years later, over 3000 doctors made Texas their home. Although some of those by that time were native sons, out-of-state doctors increasingly continued to settle in Texas, that promised land of "catfish and wild onions."

While going to Tulane University in the 1850s, Dr. Green P. Reagan from Mississippi, decided to make his home in Texas. He accepted the offer of a Dr. Calaway in Flatonia, Texas, who was looking for a partner. He and his older brother Adam made the journey with a light wagon and a good span of mules, along with several other families. The caravan trip was described in this way by Rocky Reagan in *G. P. Reagan: Country Doctor:*

> Along the route Dr. G. P. had several occasions to use his medicines and seldom a day passed but some grandmother sought him out for advice. 'Sassafras Tea' for fever — Richweed root boiled to purify the blood — rusty nails soaked in vinegar, a teaspoonful three times daily for added iron in the blood, these and many other remedies were always in use. One of the ladies had a severe headache — with a sharp lance several incisions were made in her temple, a small glass or suction cup was placed over the incisions until a certain amount of blood had been drawn. The headache relieved, the patient was required to remain quiet for a time. A baby was delivered in one of the wagons — a roaring fire, plenty of hot water and cloths scorched over the fire to purify them — and all was well. The caravan rolled on.

Pioneer doctors continued to come into Texas by horseback, wagon train, rail, and ship.

3

Learning to Heal:
Medical Background

To expose all the errours and prejudices of mankind, would be to write the complete history of the whole world. Religion, Philosophy, Morality, Education, Law, Politics, the Sciences in general and amongst these last, Medicine in particular, have been, and still are, so encumbered with errours and prejudices, that even the man endowed with the superior mind, with a correct judgment, with profound and extensive information, can never entirely free himself from their tyranny.

— Dr. Theodore Leger in 1838

Remote from centers of learning, Texas was considerably behind in the theories and practices of medicine developed elsewhere. Frontier medicine, however, was similar to medicine practiced in the United States during the colonial period. Much of this medical knowledge was based on misconception, but the fact was not altogether a handicap until later when scientific medicine emerged.

Nineteenth century medical theory concerning the cause of disease was based on several conflicting ancient concepts. One of these was the theory of contagion: "the spread of illness by either invisible animals or chemical poisons through contact with animals, inanimate objects, or other patients." Germ contagion was theorized in the sixteenth century by the Veronese physician, Hieronymus Fracastorius. For many centuries, however, science did not pursue the development of this theory, and little was accomplished to further the progress of medicine.

The other more accepted concept was the miasmatic theory: "the body was assaulted by poisons called miasma or effluvia that were released into the air by filth and decaying matter, especially vegetable matter." Among recommended treatments were general cleanliness, fumigation, and removal from the poisonous site.

As early as 1799, the prominent early American physician Dr. Benjamin Rush wrote: "disease is the offspring of putrid vegetable and animal exhalation . . . [and] filth acted upon by a hot sun in a moist state." Such testimony indicates that much orthodox medical treatment at that time, even by well-trained physicians, was based on this stultifying theory.

Dr. Jabez Heustis, Surgeon General of the United States Army in 1817, affirmed that diseases were occasioned, among other things, by bad air and miasmatic exhalations arising from swampy situations. Even fifty years later, Dr. Austin Flint, author of a popular textbook on the practice of medicine, upheld the putrid-vapor thesis. He wrote that endemic diseases, those known to prevail to a lesser degree in certain areas, "must be caused by poisonous miasmas (which) emanate from the soil." He went on to assert that widespread epidemics "must be diffused through the atmosphere."

Civil War notes also referred to this theory. One writer says, "In the case of typhoid, removal from the miasmatic locality is needful if the outbreak seems due to purely miasmatic influences."

Belief in the theory of miasmatic contagion was strong in Texas, supported by the fact that epidemics seemed to thrive in areas where putrid-vapor existed. The connection between decaying vegetable matter and illness is shown in this comment by a person in Stephen F. Austin's colony: "The colonists were . . . not a little molested with disease arising from the rapid disafforesting of the wilderness and the consequent decay of vegetable matter."

As late as the epidemic of 1867, people fled low areas or moved out of town to escape illness. Dr. J. D. Giddings of Brenham built a large Greek revival house on a high location, believing that it would be safer than a house on a lower level in the town of Brenham. Travelers were warned to get away from the coastal areas where epidemics thrived. For this reason, many from the coast moved to San Antonio, which was considered a more healthful spot.

One group believed that "effluvia rose from the mud rather than from the water." Other theories linked the climate to illnesses as well, illustrated by this comment: "This climate seems unfavorable to rheumatism, probably owing to the prevalence of open windows and drafts, and hence exposure to changes." In the absence of proven theories, such speculations abounded.

Most physicians at this time thought of disease symptoms as an imbalance of bodily humors: blood, phlegm, yellow bile, and black bile. The Greek physician Galen developed this humoral doctrine which explained body susceptibility and internal causes of disease.

Much treatment was intended to restore balance to the system, including bloodletting, purging, vomiting, and sweating. Poisons were expelled by these means, but some treatments were given for the purpose of counteracting certain bodily conditions, such as excessive dryness or coldness.

Still other treatments were based on the concept that the body's blood vessels and nerves were composed of fibers and that illness resulted from excessive fiber tension or weakness. Appropriate medicines or tonics were then recommended to relax, stimulate, or strengthen the fibers.

Medical practice was based on these concepts for centuries, and scientific medicine made little progress.

TYPES OF DOCTORS: DIFFERENT SECTS

There were many different types of doctors: allopaths, Thomsonians, homeopaths, eclectics, hydropaths, and neo-Thomsonians to name a few. Each had a different system of practice, but all were based primarily on the same erroneous theory of contagion. Consequently, a patient's well-being was little affected by which medical sect his physician represented.

The majority of physicians were allopaths, or "regular" physicians. They utilized all measures proved valuable in treatment, including medicines which produced bodily reactions opposite to the disease. Some treatments or medicines were so harsh that they were termed "heroic" measures.

As an example, some allopaths dared to perform surgery, considered an extreme measure by other sects. But the most popular "heroic" treatments were based on the drastic steps of "bleed, puke, and purge," either one or all three. "Diseases desperate grown," they believed, as Shakespeare did, "by desperate appliance are relieved, or not at all."

Believing that the proper way to restore health to a patient was "to let the blood out of him," a majority of regular doctors bled their patients copiously for almost every known disease. It was not uncommon for the physician to extract as much as fifty ounces at a time, bringing the patient close to fainting.

In this procedure, a blood vessel was severed with a lancet, or by scarification. A scarifier was a spring-loaded instrument containing many knives which punctured the skin. Cupping involved drawing blood through several small skin perforations made by the scarifier using a cupping glass or "wet cup." In some cases bloodsucking leeches were effectively applied directly to the patient's body, a bizarre method not favored by either patients or doctors.

Such "heroic" treatments left the patients weakened and susceptible to infections. In addition, these treatments actually killed some patients who could not stand the shock of the accompanying violent convulsions. Understandably, the fear of bloodletting was terrifying for the sick.

Allopaths treated dysentery patients with repeated doses of an emetic, such as tartar, ipecac, or opium to induce vomiting and sweating. Purging was accomplished by giving such drugs as calomel, castor oil, or mercury.

With orthodox treatments such as these, a disenchanted public looked to other types of doctors. The various medical sects grew larger in number and were well represented on the Texas frontier.

Thomsonianism, which spread through the nation in the first half of the nineteenth century, developed out of the thinking of Samuel Thompson, a poor New Hampshire farmer. He blamed his mother's death on poisons administered by the orthodox physicians of the day. When his wife became ill, after losing confidence in the medical treatment available, he called in several root and herb doctors. His wife's recovery convinced him of the benefits of botanical remedies. Soon after this in 1805, he gave up his farm to become a traveling herb doctor, making use of his longtime interest in roots and herbs.

By 1811, he began to teach his method of practice, and a society of followers was formed in Maine. The next year he began describing his practice in a "medical circular." Fearing others would profit from his ideas, he patented his system in 1813. Later, he claimed to have sold over 100,000 patent rights. By 1822, he had expanded his pamphlet into a book entitled: *New Guide to Health:* or *Botanic Family Physician, containing a Complete System of Practice, on a Plan Entirely New; with a Description of the Vegetables made use of, and Directions for Preparing and Administering Them to Cure Disease, to which is Prefixed, a Narrative of the Life and Medical Discoveries of the Author.* Despite the length of the title, the book became very popular and went through many printings.

In the book, Thompson described his method of treatment which was based on restoring heat to the body. Since he mistakenly believed that disease was the result of cold, he recommended the use of steam baths, as well as the use of "hot" substances, such as cayenne pepper. He relied also on the therapeutic value of *Lobelia inflata*, used as an emetic drug, sometimes called Indian tobacco. Such emetics were used to clean out the system and were followed by a series of tonics prescribed to restore health. Thompson also prescribed capsicum and bayberry.

Each purchaser of Thompson's book — which sold for twenty dollars — received membership in Thompson's Friendly Botanical Society and the right to practice Thompson's method on members of the purchaser's family. Chapters of the society were organized in many communities, and the members met to give advice and assistance to those in need. In some parts of the nation, local "infirmaries" were opened to provide steam baths and other treatments in keeping with Thomsonian practices. [The "p" in Thompson's name is usually dropped when the word *Thomsonian* is used.]

National conventions of the Friendly Botanical Society were held. In 1835, at such a convention, a move was made to establish a medical school teaching Thompson's system of treatment. Thompson, however, saw this move as alarming, since he believed medical education, usually based on a formal study of the sciences, only confused and prevented use of his methods. Those who wished to institutionalize his system did not fully understand that the appeal of Thomsonianism was based on the ability of each family to treat itself after proper instruction. After Thompson's death, disagreements among his followers caused fragmentation of the movement about 1845, and numerous botanical medical schools were founded with varying programs.

For all its drawbacks, the Thomsonian movement made several contributions. One was the use of the herb lobelia. Thompson claimed no credit for this, however, as other practitioners had used it previously. Some believed Thompson's chief contribution was his recommendation of drug therapy with prescribed dosages. Prescriptions were simplified since each drug was given a number.

Thompson performed a service by pointing out shortcomings and leading a revolt against "heroic" practices of the day. His herbal treatment probably did less harm than blistering, bloodletting, and other standard medical practices. He should also be credited for speaking against the use of poisons at a time when small doses of calomel, arsenic, antimony, nitre, and opium were standard treatment. In addition, he attacked what he felt were unjustly high medical fees charged by orthodox doctors.

Thomsonianism was not to last, but Thompson's methods helped make way for needed change.

In Texas, some doctors used botanical remedies along with conventional treatments. One Clarksville doctor, Dr. W. F. T. Hart, claimed in advertisements that he "embraced the theory and practice of the Botanic system blended with regular practice." Dr. James H. Starr, Treasurer of the Republic, had been educated in a Thomsonian medical school. His records show, however, that he adopted conventional practices.

At the same time Thomsonianism developed outside the ranks of the medical profession, another threat to orthodox medicine developed within its own ranks. The system of homeopathy, fashionable among the nobility in Europe, became popular with some physicians, particularly in the cities and among the wealthier classes.

The developer of this system, who experimented around 1790, was Samuel Christian Friedrich Hahnemann, a well-educated German doctor. He became critical of many medical practices of the day, such as blistering, bleeding, and the use of cathartics. He criticized the haphazard way drugs were often prescribed and compounded.

Hahnemann conducted experiments of his own on the effectiveness of cinchona bark. Noticing that the drug produced symptoms of malaria in himself, he then concluded that any drug causing such symptoms in a healthy person would remove the symptoms or cure a sick person. An example was the effectiveness of the cowpox vaccine. The law of similars was called "similia similibus curantur," meaning "like is cured by like." His whole system, based on this

Gems of Wisdom from Samuel Thompson's
New Guide to Health

Thompson's Motto: "The study of patients, not books; experience, not reading."

"Cold, or the lessening of heat, is the cause of all disease, hence a balanced temperature of the 4 elements will result in perfect health."

"The most effectual way to destroy quackery in any art or science, is to diffuse the knowledge of it among mankind."

"It is true that much of what is at this day called medicine, is deadly poison; and were people to know what is offered to them of this kind, they would absolutely refuse ever to receive it as a medicine."

"Possessing a body like other men, I was led to enquire into the nature of the component parts of which man is made. I found him composed of the four elements — Earth, Water, Air and Fire. The earth and water I found were the solids; the air and fire the fluids. The two first I found to be the component parts; the two last kept him in motion. Heat, I found, was life; and cold, death."

"A man may have a scientific knowledge of the human frame, he may know the names in every language, of every medicine, mineral and vegetable, as well as every disease, and yet be a miserable physician . . . There is a power beyond the reach of art, and there are gifts that study and learning can never rival."

Thompson quoted Dr. Blane with this gem:

". . . The history of the start of medicine in all ages, so teems with the fanciful influence of superstitious observances, the imaginary virtues of medicines, with nugatory, delusive, inefficient, and capricious practices, falacious and sophistical reasonings, as to render it little more than a chaos of error, a tissue of deceit, unworthy of admission among the useful arts and liberal pursuits of man."

law, was described in Hahnemann's work, *Organon of Rational Healing.* These theories, he believed, had been known to the ancient world; he had only rediscovered them.

As Hahnemann's theory was tested using many drugs, the recorded results were called "provings." From these, Hahnemann concluded that after a drug was taken, all symptoms were caused by that particular drug. Thus he favored long case histories be taken which noted all symptoms. He also believed that small doses were more effective than larger doses. One dose of a drug was supposedly effective up to three months. He warned in the *Organon,* "if too strong a dose of a remedy, that is even entirely homeopathic, be given, it will infallibly injure the patient." He believed all drugs were poisonous if taken to excess, which led to studies on "infinitesimals" or small doses. Drug purity was another factor to be taken into careful consideration in drug preparation.

Hahnemann also believed in the principle called "dynamization," the theory being that a drug shaken the proper number of times gained in curative powers. He stated that if a drug is shaken properly, "the medicine becomes exalted in energy."

Although most homeopaths agreed on Hahnemann's principles, there were many who did not agree on the application of his methods. There were high-dilutionists and low-dilutionists, all arguing over the proper dilution a substance needed for maximum results. The low-dilutionists gained a greater following.

Homeopaths using Hahnemann's methods met with some success, particularly in the treatment of yellow fever. There was little that could be done to help the sufferer, and the patient fared better when treated with homeopathic measures than those who were bled or blistered. Naturally, homeopaths became more numerous and successful in areas where yellow fever was a recurring problem. Homeopathic methods also met with similar successes in treatment of Asiatic cholera.

Many homeopaths were well educated in the same manner as regular physicians. They retained their earlier training as valid, but added homeopathic practices.

There was disagreement among the homeopaths themselves, but the group as a whole came under attack by the orthodox profession.

The homeopathic sect, which organized societies that excluded many quacks, appealed to the wealthy, and became influential — an irritating threat to the medical establishment.

Regular doctors felt that the dosage given by homeopaths was too small to do any good whatever. Believing that homeopathic cures were due to natural recovery rather than homeopathic treatments, regular doctors tried to remove homeopaths from their medical societies by calling them "irregular practitioners."

"Regulars" also took homeopaths to court whenever possible. They did everything within their power to separate homeopathy from regular medicine, a fact which strengthened the organization of the American Medical Association. In the Code of Ethics adopted by the AMA in 1847, consultation with homeopaths was ruled out, and in 1859, the AMA voted to exclude all "irregulars" from membership.

Homeopathy can be credited with criticism of some of the medical practices of the time. One of Hahnemann's most important contributions was popularizing the theory that treatment with small doses or no treatment at all was preferable to more "heroic" measures. Hahnemann also should be credited with recognizing the importance of diet, rest, exercise, fresh air, and other common sense measures that many physicians of the time ignored. By 1900, many of these recommendations were incorporated into standard medical procedure, but many other homeopathic recommendations have not withstood the test of time.

By the end of the century all homeopaths were using homeopathic drugs along with regular drugs. As medical science advanced, many homeopaths abandoned their adherence to homeopathic methods. Gradually, as this occurred, the homeopathic doctors were accepted by the regulars.

Although New York had become the main center for homeopathy following Hans Gram's introduction of the practice to America in 1825, homeopathy was brought to Texas by Gail Borden, who had probably become acquainted with the practice in Europe. Borden, an early settler in San Felipe de Austin, arrived on the Texas scene in 1828. Later known as the developer of condensed milk and dried meat concentrates, Borden traveled to Europe to promote these products. On one such trip, he "became a convert to homeopathy."

Although not a physician, upon his return he assumed the title, "Dr. Borden." In explanation, he said, "It's no use to be a doctor unless you put on the airs of one." Later, for his pioneering nutritional studies, a laboratory building was named in his honor, the Gail Borden Building, at the Medical Branch of The University of Texas at Galveston. Borden County was also named in his honor.

Hoping to treat patients through the mails upon receipt of a fee, Dr. James Angell advertised in the *Galveston News,* of May 2, 1857. He claimed to be a "Homeopathist" with twenty years of experience with "Southern diseases," and he promised to send medicine upon receipt of a sum and a description of the patient's symptoms.

Alarmed about the practice of homeopathy in Texas, regular

physicians spoke out. In 1876, Dr. Ashbel Smith said in "Discussion on Amending Medical Practice Act," *Transactions Texas State Medical Association*:

> Liberty had been defined by old Prof. Gregory to be the right to go to hell in any way the traveler in that direction might elect, and so all the people of Texas, in the exercise of their sovereign rights, might patronize, and would patronize, medicine or homeopathy, just as they might choose to select, and this Convention is powerless to remedy the evil.

In some parts of Texas bitter controversies arose between homeopathic practitioners and regular physicians. One such instance occurred in Travis County when the District Judge announced his intention to appoint the homeopathic physician, Dr. G. E. Routh, to the District Board of Medical Examiners, as well as Dr. E. G. Doerr, a member of the Indianapolis Surgical Institute. The chairman of the Board, Dr. J. M. Ross of Brenham, was later accused of unethical conduct due to serving on the board with these men; he was subsequently cleared of the charges.

Sometimes the various factions worked together successfully, such as in 1881, when Dr. Routh and Dr. R. H. L. Bibb together treated four cases of diphtheria at the Governor's Mansion.

The Eclectic Sect, which grew in popularity after the Civil War, was the successor of Thomsonianism. Wooster Beach, the founder, evolved his system from many sources. The center for the movement and its main medical school was the Eclectic Medical Institute in Cincinnati, which was granted a charter in 1845. Although there were fewer eclectic physicians than members of other sects, they were numerous in the midwest and not so popular in the south. They were more often found in small towns; sometimes the eclectic physician was the only doctor in town. In larger communities, eclectics were excluded from organizations of other doctors. Eclectic physicians were often poorly educated, and they rarely specialized.

Although eclecticism was a botanical movement, it did not advocate solely botanical remedies but recommended remedies from many sources. The eclectics believed in adopting the best from other sects; eventually this led to their adopting the scientific findings of regular medicine. The eclectics copied the practices of "heroic" medicine, but they substituted regular drugs with ones they devised producing the same physiological effects.

The practice of advocating large dosages as did the "regulars," identified eclectics with that group. When the public rebelled against "heroic" practices, eclectics became just as unpopular as "regulars." Some eclectic doctors came to Texas during that time.

Only after the Civil War, under the leadership of John M. Scudder who became dean of the Eclectic Medical Institute of Cincinnati, did a new eclectic system develop. Scudder advocated "specific medication," a theory which held that for each symptom there was a specified remedy. This theory had much in common with homeopathy; both methods were chiefly concerned with symptoms. Scudder developed botanical remedies which were later sold commercially. Around the 1850s, eclectic physicians began using podophyllin as a cathartic, a substance which became known as the "eclectic calomel."

Dr. J. Cam Massie's *Treatise on the Eclectic Southern Practice of Medicine,* published in 1854, was a popular work in Texas. The work shows the rise of states' rights medicine. Those living in the south believed that there were certain differences in the diseases of those living in that region.

Dr. Massie used as an introduction a letter from some doctors in Texas which stated that diseases had "various modifications" in Texas in need of description. Written in simple language, the book appealed to the ordinary reader.

One student of the eclectic system was Dr. W. W. Payne, whose practice was advertised thus:

> His knowledge is sought from all systems of medical practice freely. Truth is received where found. Medicine used is of a safe salutory [salutary] character rather than dangerous and debilitating. Cases will be treated without the use of antimony and mercury in any form.

When Vincent Priessnitz, a Silesian peasant, was run over by a wagon, he devised a series of water treatments as therapy. After his recovery, he continued to devise water cures for any who sought his advice. His success was talked about in the United States in the 1840s, and many copied his water cures prior to the Civil War. Those who practiced this therapy stressed its safety and its economic advantage: water, which was readily available, was cheap. Also the method appealed to those who believed in self-reliance in the prevention and treatment of disease. The leaders claimed that the practice of hydropathy could eliminate the need for physicians altogether. Water-cure physicians were in demand to explain the principles to new groups of people since those who understood the methods were no longer in need of professional care.

An interesting sidelight is that watercurists took a lead in protesting the customs regarding women's dress, which they believed were unnatural and constricting. Perhaps this stand may be explained by the fact that one-fifth of those who practiced hydropathy were women.

Since there was a limited number of water-cure institutions, the principles were explained to the public in the *Water-Cure Journal*, which first appeared in 1845. Readers were encouraged to correspond with the editor to relate their experiences.

John Harvey Kellogg, whose name was associated with cornflakes, became one writer of domestic hydrotherapy in the latter part of the century. Some of his works were *The Household Manual of Domestic Hygiene, Ladies' Guide in Health and Disease, The Household Monitor of Health,* and *The Home Hand-Book of Domestic Hygiene and Rational Medicine.*

In Texas, Water Cure or Hydrotherapy was practiced by Dr. Ernst Kapp, who established a facility in the community of Sisterdale in the 1850s.

All sects were represented on the Texas frontier during the nineteenth century. All made various claims that later proved scientifically unsound or medically inaccurate. At that time, the ability to heal depended more on the individual, his skill and training, than on the particular sect that he represented.

EDUCATION: PRECEPTOR OR UNIVERSITY TRAINING

It was common practice in the nineteenth century for students to study or "read" medicine with a preceptor. Many of the doctors who came to Texas trained under this system. Older physicians often acted as preceptors for younger men who wished to study with them. Since the guidelines were not regulated, the training was only as good as the individual preceptor. In general, textbook theories were taught rather than clinical training.

The apprenticeship was usually divided into two segments of two to three years: the apprentice first "read" medicine for a period and then he served a time as an assistant — riding with the doctor on house calls or assisting him in surgery. For this privilege, the apprentice contracted with the doctor to pay a fee or perhaps run er-

Dr. Ernst Kapp's Water-Cure Facilities at Sisterdale. Drawing by Hermann Lungkwitz; lithograph by G. Kraetzer, New York, New York, ca. 1855.

Courtesy Estate of Paula Ingenhuett.
Copy from U.T. Institute of Texan Cultures at San Antonio.

rands, take care of the doctor's horse, and perform other menial tasks. Many apprentices did not finish the recommended term of service; those who did were sometimes given a certificate stating that their apprenticeship was complete.

Occasionally, a doctor studied with a preceptor prior to attending medical school. Such was the case of Dr. Felix R. Collard, Sr., a native Texan. Soon after the Civil War, he studied with a preceptor for three years while at the same time teaching school.

Upon deciding to further his medical education, Dr. Collard rode horseback from his home in Wheelock, to New Orleans, to attend classes at Tulane Medical School. After he completed two years of study there, he received a certificate to practice medicine. Many Texans, such as Dr. Collard, sought medical education elsewhere because there were no medical schools in Texas until the latter part of the nineteenth century.

There was wide discrepancy in the quality of education of Texas doctors. Some who came to Texas were educated in Europe or in highly-regarded United States institutions, while others had not finished high school.

Unfortunately, some of the so-called "doctors" who came to Texas had no training whatsoever. Due to the laxity of licensing, a person could claim to be a doctor rather easily. Some hastily hung out shingles, knowing that distances were far, diplomas hard to check, and regulations almost non-existent, particularly in rural areas.

Some Texas doctors were trained in the large number of proprietary schools which sprang up in parts of the United States in the 1830s, or in privately owned schools designed as profit-making or commercial institutions, self-supporting through student tuition. Students sometimes paid fees only if they passed final exams, but no fee was required if a degree was not granted. This practice did not foster quality training. In addition, much of the training was given by persons of questionable credentials.

Since medical schools competed with each other to attract more students, the result was a surplus of physicians, particularly in the urban areas "back east." This in turn prompted many to seek the new frontier. In fact, graduates of medical schools at the time were urged to go west to serve the frontier communities rather than compete with established physicians in the urban areas.

Whether trained by university or preceptor, the real education of many early Texas doctors began when they established practice and treated their first patient under the difficult conditions of the frontier.

Typical of many nineteenth century doctors who struggled for a university education was Robert Caldwell Neblett, an apprentice carpenter, who walked all the way from Virginia to Pennsylvania to attend medical school at the University of Pennsylvania. After receiving a degree in the 1820s, he practiced for a time in Tennessee, Mississippi, and then Louisiana, before coming to Texas in the period of the Republic. He later served in the Texas Legislature. His long walk exemplifies the determination exhibited by many early doctors to follow to the end a difficult path in the study of medicine.

4

Practicing Frontier Medicine: *Conditions and Hazards*

At 2:30 o'clock each morning, I would ride to the spring, being always careful to throw my medical saddlebags across the saddle, and would get my two-gallon jug full of water. I strung the jug to the horn of my saddle and rode home, afterwards finishing up the night's sleep. It was not always possible for me to be at the spring at this particular hour, because oftentimes I was out on medical calls . . . There was never a moment at any time day or night, that there was not a string of wagons, carriages, buggies and horses lined up waiting for their turn to secure water.

— Dr. J. B. Cranfill

In the days before railroads, the only transportation a doctor had was horseback, horse and buggy, or on foot. One doctor, however, claimed that he always rode a mule; another made calls in a sailboat. Sometimes a horse, a boat, or even a mule was beyond the economic means of a struggling physician. Dr. James McMahon of Texarkana did not own a horse and made his rounds on foot, although at times he rented a horse when his legs could not take him the required distance.

If a doctor could afford a horse, he owned not one but several, since a fresh mount was needed after a hard ride. Dr. James Addison Abney told of the clientele he treated in a widespread east Texas ter-

Dr. Samuel Leigh Southard Smith and his horse. A graduate of the University of Michigan, Dr. Smith served nine years as an army surgeon before beginning practice in San Angelo. He later became the first city and county health officer and first president of the Tom Green County Medical Society.

Courtesy Fort Concho Museum

ritory "requiring me to keep two or three of the best horses I could find and a hostler that I might be prepared to answer calls."

Dr. William L. Crosthwait had some thoughts about the reliable type of horse needed, saying:

> I've read a lot about doctors on horseback and about horse-and-buggy doctors, but I don't recall that anyone has ever given the horse due credit. Some colts are just born to be doctors' horses. A good horse has about as much sense as a doctor. A well-trained doctor's horse senses an emergency. He pricks up his ears and is alert. And he knows when the emergency is over. Going home he just droops his head and jogs along.

It was not unusual for a pioneer doctor to travel long distances in his daily practice. Often he was called in the middle of the night to ride twenty or thirty miles to attend a patient, and once he arrived, he usually remained until the crisis was over. One account of these long rides was described as follows:

Dr. Elijah James Hayes (1820–1895), born in Georgia, was a resident of Garrison, Nacogdoches County, Texas.

Courtesy Mrs. Dorothy Stimson
Copy from U.T. Institute of Texan Cultures at San Antonio

> Often Dr. Lockhart would be called . . . into the black night — perhaps fifteen miles, often twenty. One night when he could scarce see his hand before his face, he followed for fifteen miles through river bottoms the elusive lead of a white horse.

Dr. Bowers told interesting stories of his early horseback trips through Indian country from Galveston to Brownsville. He often swam the Colorado River on his pony six or seven times a day. Sometimes he camped in tall grass, and he was always fearful of lighting his pipe because the smoke might alert Indians to his presence.

Roads were poor and sometimes nonexistent. Bad weather caused further problems. Early in his career before becoming a noted surgeon in Fort Worth, Dr. Bacon Saunders lost his saddlebags one rainy night crossing a creek bottom on horseback near Bonham. When his horse slipped, his bags and equipment were buried in the mud and never recovered.

Undaunted by severe weather, Dr. Henry North Graves of Colorado City often made buggy calls described in this manner:

> Sometimes a call would come from a town of [a] hundred and fifty miles away with no railroad connection between. Dr. Graves would wrap himself in a buffalo robe and start out in his buggy. His wife would heat bricks and put them on the floor of the buggy in an attempt to protect him from the cold of the Western plains.

Once when Dr. Thomas William Shearer of Wallisville sailed to Double Bayou to see a patient, he was caught in a severe blizzard which froze the bay. Fearing the impossibility of a return voyage, Dr. Shearer spent the night with some people in a meagerly-furnished home. One account related that "they had but two cups, one china and one tin. They served turnips and black coffee for breakfast. They honored him with the china cup, which, by the way, had lost its handle."

Dr. J. H. Sears, founder and first president of the Waco Medical Association, was called on his wedding night to see a very sick man in Limestone County. Grabbing his saddlebags, he answered the call of duty, not returning for a whole week. Dr. Sears saved the life of his patient, and the honeymoon postponed was only an incident in a life of sacrifice and service.

Dr. Sears was also a charter member of the Texas State Medical Association in 1869. He served as president in 1893.

Relying on horseback for transportation, a doctor needed a good set of leather saddlebags. In the pockets were various bottles of medicines and other necessities. Most leather saddlebags, which often reeked with the odor of valerian, were stamped by the manufacturer with a version of the following: "Elliott's patent, granted 1-18-1870, AA Melier, St. Louis, Mo. sole proprietor."

The importance of a doctor's saddlebags may be seen from the following ad, which appeared in Dr. Ford's *Tri-Weekly State Times,* on 13 December 1853, after a Dr. Lott's medical saddlebags were stolen from the door of his office:

> The individual performing this jocund trick will please return the portable apothecary shop to the owner. The doctor says his drugs are powerful and might do harm in the hands of an injudicious administrator. Carry them home and let such things alone hereafter.

Other useful items were large gourds which held fresh water and were fastened to saddles. These insured that good drinking water was available on long rounds about the countryside.

Properly equipped with saddlebags, gourds, and medicines, the doctors on horseback deserved the title they were sometimes given, the "Horsemen of Hippocrates."

An eerie encounter befell Dr. Gaines Moses Boynton, one of the earliest doctors in Buffalo Gap, who was on his way home from making a call late one night. The horse he was riding suddenly stalled. To the doctor's surprise, when reaching for his hat he touched a large object in the dark, which turned out to be a body swinging from the limb of a tree. The circumstances of the hanging and the identity of the body remained a mystery.

Most doctors carried with them a small book sold by all booksellers and druggists called *The Physician's Visiting List,* published by P. Blakiston, Son and Company of Philadelphia. New editions were published annually. The 1884 edition, which was the thirty-third year of publication, included a dosage table. These books contained space for lists of appointments and fees charged.

The coming of the railroads brought new life to the frontier, particularly along the railroad stops. The railroads made available supplies of medicine and the latest equipment. In addition to making consultation possible in difficult cases, railroads also gave doctors access to centers of learning. Typical stories described how the railroads aided medical practice:

> One West Texas doctor, who served as a railroad physician, recalled riding in a switch engine to reach a patient in an emergency and, in another instance, having to pump a handcar back to town. Often he would catch a ride on a freight train, not knowing whether there would be a horse and buggy at the end of the trip to bring him back.

On the other hand, Dr. W. L. Coleman felt that the whistles and loud noises from railroad engines were detrimental to his patients' health, particularly during an epidemic of yellow fever. He explained:

> . . . it is well known that many a poor sufferer, with life trembling in the balance, has had the scales turned against him by their unearthly and at all times needless screeches. In this city of railroads, Houston, Texas, where some fifteen or twenty either center or pass through, with its several oil mills, ice, beer, and other factories in active operation, discordant and disagreeable steam whistles are to be heard almost constantly day and night, often preventing conversation for the time being. This should not

> be permitted at any time; for there are nervous sick people all the time, and the shocks from these piercing, earsplitting sounds is very injurious to them.

Apparently, Dr. Coleman did not have much success in outlawing the noise of railroads.

In the nineteenth century, changes developed not only in transportation but also in communication. Before telephone service, calls came by word of mouth, but doctors devised ingenious methods of receiving messages from their patients.

Dr. William Wallace Walker who practiced in Fayette County in the 1870s devised a system where messages could be left under certain stones, which were marked near large stumps on a main road. By checking these points, he could save himself traveling time as he made his daily rounds. Even so, there was much room for error and delay.

Some drugstores aided doctors in developing better communication by establishing a "slate service," which provided a central location for messages. While this was a convenience for Dr. W. D. Kelley of Galveston, he often wiped names off the slate saying that certain listed patients did not really need a doctor.

Telephone service brought about much change in medical practice. In the country, telephone lines were run on barbed wire fences to connect remote houses on farms and ranches with their neighbors, and more readily available medical help.

Although primitive, the telephone exchange which came into use about 1881, further added to the convenience of medical practice. The first telephone exchange, the oldest in Texas, began in Galveston in 1879. Several months later, Houston developed an exchange. About this time, the more progressive doctors began hiring someone to answer their telephone calls.

The nineteenth century doctor usually had an office in his home, his barn, or a partitioned area or room at the back of the local drugstore. Some enterprising druggists gave office space to the physician, and some physicians even started their own drugstores.

This was a convenient arrangement since it was customary for doctors to mix their own medicines. To mask the unpleasant odor of compounding medicines, doctors sometimes heated large pans of water sprinkled with cloves, citrus, or other sweet-swelling spices.

In the period of the Republic, the doctor's office usually contained a few medical books on the blood by Hunter, and on purgatives by Hamilton. Books by Eberle and Cooper were also prized in some doctors' libraries, which were usually quite small. Few medical journals found their way to doctors in Texas during this early period.

In some areas, the doctor's office was considered no place for women, who were usually examined in their homes. If the doctor could not make a house call, sometimes the husband would rent a hotel room where the doctor could call on the female patient under the watchful eye of the husband or suitable attendants.

A doctor is an angel when you need him; a devil when you have to pay him, was an old German saying. With some justification, many people living in frontier Texas feared and avoided doctors. They had heard advice, such as that given by D. E. E. Braman, who declared:

> I would further caution newcomers who desire peace, prosperity, and health, to avoid lawyers, doctors, and quack medicines, and all other unseemly monsters.

When they did seek medical help, many patients were unable to pay anything, even though doctors' fees were small. Due to the scarcity of money, even those who supposedly were capable of higher earnings were reluctant to part with cash in hand. This difficulty in collecting fees often posed financial hardship for the frontier doctor.

Most doctors had to rely on some form of barter. Peltries, produce, and animals were the medium of exchange. It was not unusual for a doctor to be paid with a cow and a calf worth ten dollars. *Dr. Cranfill's Chronicle* records rather typical practice in the last half of the century:

> While the season had been a hard one, I was enabled to collect the first year of my practice $1500 either in money or convertible trade. I was not a stickler for details in the matter of collections. I would take anything on a medical bill from watermelons to cord wood, and from cabbages to calves. I soon had an assortment of property. . .

Dr. Cranfill goes on to describe how he began his practice:

> On February 1, 1879, my wife and I moved to Turnersville to make that village our future home. In the meantime, I had gone before the medical examining board . . . and had secured a license to practice medicine. I, however, had no funds, and so my precious mother loaned me out of her small savings sixteen dollars. With this sum I bought my medical saddlebags, and with

> the help of my father I supplied my saddlebags with the necessary medicines.

An initial investment in drugs as well as in other equipment was necessary. Dr. James McMahon said he bought $250 worth of drugs in Little Rock, before beginning his practice at Texarkana in 1873.

Opening a medical practice was more profitable in some places than in others. In early Texas, one doctor desired to move from La Bahia to another location "where there was more sickness and where he could sell his drugs with more profit."

Dr. Labadie wrote to his nephew, Anthony, March 19, 1831, from Anahuac (Perry's Point):

> I have opened my drugs which have been welcomed by the people as they have been much wanted. The Colo. had employed me to attend on his soldiers. Two or three days after my arrival I got in business & since have had not less than six cases daily. I have charged on my medical book to yesterday $115.00 the worl [*work*] of only 16 days.

Not all doctors were so fortunate. Dr. Imla Keep, an early Austin colonist, found making a living difficult. His extensive practice probably yielded less than $500.00 a year, forcing him to declare bankruptcy two years later and return to his former home in Louisiana. He listed losses of $25,600, with liabilities of $5,536.00, and assets of $1,910. Dr. Keep's popularity decreased, apparently because of less than favorable results with his patients.

The situation did not improve during the days of the Republic. One doctor wrote that he and his partner were having difficulties in Austin: "I find that should we get all the practice in this Section, that it would but poorley pay a hungry son of Aesculapius!" Going into partnership with someone engaged in a more lucrative business provided security for some doctors. In Houston, a barber and a doctor teamed together for mutual benefit. Their services included "tooth-drawing, bleeding, cupping, and other surgical operations," as well as shaving and haircutting.

Contract medicine, in which the physician agreed to provide medical care for an annual fee, was popular in the South and in some parts of Texas. In fact, a form of this system had been in use in Texas, even before the Alamo became an infirmary. The Spanish barber-surgeon, Yldefonso Reyes, filling the many needs of his patients and customers with his dual career, received two *reales* from

Room, Board, and Corn

Many doctors began their practice by contracting to be an assistant for an older, established physician. Such was the case with Dr. G. P. Reagan, who became an assistant to Dr. Calaway in Flatonia, Texas, in the 1850s. Dr. Reagan was given room and board for eight dollars per month. His horse was also taken care of with only the minimal charge of twenty cents per bushel of corn. With obligations to meet and with nothing but a promising future, the young Dr. Reagan was more than willing to lighten Dr. Calaway's load.

each person monthly, for which he bled them, shaved them, cut their hair, and treated any illness.

Under any contract system, the physician was assured of an income, regardless of the economic conditions at the time. In some places there was competition between doctors for the minimum annual fee. Later, as doctors formed societies, they denounced this practice.

The doctor, however, was placed in a vulnerable position when his patients failed to meet their yearly obligations. To avoid this occurrence, Dr. John S. (Rip) Ford agreed to treat one man's family, including slaves, for $100 a year — if this sum were paid in advance.

In 1845, Dr. A. P. Manley of La Grange expressed his expectations that patients would promptly pay up at the end of the year, "for the support of his family [so] that his purse, and hands, and mind may be kept wholly untrammeled." He justified his request after stating that his charges were reasonable. These were:

> $.50 per mi day or nite; $1.00 for each visit; $1.00 for advice where consulted; $.25 per dose for medicine in all cases; $5.00 simple natural labor cases; ($10.00 to $20.00 in complicated, difficult, or instrumental cases, and mileage extra in all cases); $1.00 for each bleeding; $1.00 for extracting each tooth; $1.00 for using syringe; $.25 to $.50 for drawing each blister; $1.00 for opening simple abscess; $5.00 to 25.00 for surgical operations.

Practicing Patience

Dr. Alexander Wray Ewing, who had treated Santa Anna's wounds after the Battle of San Jacinto, was not paid for fifteen years for his services as Surgeon-General of the Republic of Texas. It took a special act of the legislature in 1852 to pay him $1000.

The average annual income for physicians in early Texas was $500.00, little enough for the long hours and hardships involved in practice. This figure varied considerably as can be seen from the following table from the Civil War period:

> Average yearly income for San Antonio physicians (including all medicines):

In 1861:	$400.00
In 1862:	$300.00
In 1863:	$1,200.00
In 1865:	$500.00
In 1866:	$600.00
In 1867:	$1,800.00 (in scrip)

Toward the end of the century, generally speaking, physicians made an annual income of around $1000. Two thousand dollars was considered quite a large income; only doctors in the larger cities could claim such figures. Doctors Anson Jones and Ashbel Smith were exceptions: Dr. Jones claimed that his practice was worth $5000 a year in 1834, and Dr. Smith surpassed that sum during the days of the Republic. In a survey of 3317 physicians in seventy-five counties, physicians' incomes at the turn of the century ranged between $40,000, the highest figure, to $1873, an average figure.

Dr. F. B. Webb of Leesburg saw seventy-two patients in 1846; for consultation and medicine, he received a total of $1059.92 and three-fourths of a cent. The odd fractional part of a cent says much for Dr. Webb's precise figuring and record keeping.

In the days before written prescriptions, doctors customarily supplied their patients with medicines. The doctor mixed, measured, and administered his medicines as needed. He counted and packaged pills, compounded powders and salves, and bottled elixirs. The medicines were mixed on the spot to suit the individual patient.

Dr. James Addison Abney described his charges for making calls and prescribing medicine in his east Texas practice:

> . . . You must bear in mind all these long rides and strenuous day and night work was done at fifty cents per mile at night. We carried an assortment of standard drugs in a huge pair of pill bags swung across a saddle and dispensed the medicine at the bedside at two dollars and fifty cents for prescription and medicine. We also carried a pocket case of instruments and three or four pairs of forceps and pulled the aching teeth and lanced the abscesses and [did] minor surgery, gratis. Out of this enormous amount of

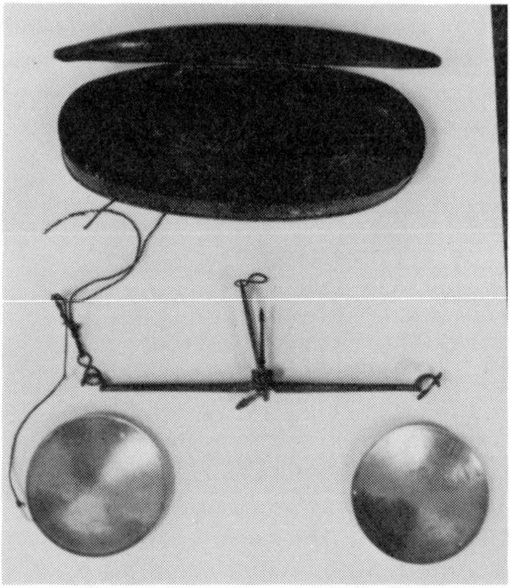

Pocket scales used by Virginians William and John D. Maclin in American Revolutionary War. J. D.'s son Junius (Jack) D., took them hopefully to 1849 California Gold Rush to weigh gold dust. No gold forthcoming, he pioneered to Texas in the 1850s, and used these scales to weigh medicine in Brazoria, Galveston, and Fort Worth. Maclin had studied medicine, but never opened full practice.
Courtesy Maclin and Ratisseau Descendants

> hard, cheap work, by tact and good management, I collected about fifty to seventy-five percent of the amounts charged on the books. I did a large charity practice that was not put on the books.

One of the first attempts at establishing standard fees was passed in 1831 by the town council of San Felipe. A "tariff or fee bill" was set up.

During the days of the Republic, the doctors themselves decided to establish a uniform rate of charges to prevent unpleasant feelings on the part of patients towards their physicians. In 1838, the Medical and Surgical Society of Houston adopted this fee schedule:

> 1st visit to patient $5.00; (each succeeding visit $3.00)
> After 8:00 pm, charges double.

Visits outside city limits, extra charge of $1.00 per miles during the day, and $2.00 per mi during the night.

Consultation visit: $20.00

Advice and prescription in the office $5.00 (extra time, $3.00 hr.)

Venesection, $2.00 extra

Extraction of tooth, $2.00 extra

Cupping, $5.00 extra

Surgical operations charged according to danger and difficulty.
Natural labor: $40.00 (difficult labor, extra charge)

Visit to several individuals of same family, charge one visit; but an extra charge of $1.00 for prescribing for each patient in the family; if persons not member of family, but only in the employ, deductions will not be made.

Medicine furnished by physician $.50 per dose.

Physicians were to present their accounts to the patient immediately on discharge of the patient, for payment then and there; if unable to pay, to sign a note for the amount.

Physicians in Matagorda, in 1840, published the following schedule of fees: day visits, $5; night visits, $10; consultations, $15; bleeding, $2; cupping, $5; labor cases, $30. They optimistically requested an immediate settlement on termination of the case.

There was great discrepancy in the matter of fees, as can be seen from a schedule of charges published by a group of Tyler doctors in 1857: daytime mileage, $1.00 per mile; mileage at night, $1.50 per mile; town visits, $2.50; prescriptions and medicine, $2.00 and upward; obstetrics, $15.00; detention, $12.00 for twenty-four hours; consultation, $6.00.

In 1845, in Gonzales, doctors charged a day visit of $1.00 per visit, night visit $2.00. Labor cases were $10 during the day and $15 at night.

One doctor in La Grange charged,

> . . . $.50 per mile day or night; each visit, $1.00; $1.00 for advice when consulted; $0.25 per dose of medicine; consultation fee, $10; simple case of labor, $2.00; difficult labor cases, $10.00 to $20.00; bleeding, $1.00; tooth extraction, $1.00; use of syringe, $1.00; drawing each blister, $0.25 to $0.50; opening simple abscess, $1.00; surgical operation, $5.00 to $25.00.

Dr. Richard S. Morgan's casebook for 1851, shows the following list of standard charges:

> . . . scarifying and cupping, $4.00; oil Riclui (castor oil), $2.50; febrifuge and blister, $2.50; quinine 30gr. prescription, $1.00; quinine 15gr. prescription, $0.50; febrifuge and cathartic, $3.00; emetic and cathartic, $2.50; pain extractor, $0.50; camomille flowers, $1.00; night visit with quinine and nitre pills, $9.00; night visit with expectorant mixture, camphor, capsicum, opium and services, $9.00; office visit without prescription, $1.00.

In the 1890s medical fees were scaled upward. *The Texas Sanitarian* of November 1892, reported the following survey of medical fees in Austin:

Day visit in the old city limits	$2.50
Visit to Hyde Park	$4.00
Visit to the dam	$5.00
Prescription in the office	$2.50 to $5
Advice without examination	$1.00 to $2
Delivery charge if not more than 4 hrs.	$20/$30
Ovariotomy	Up to 1000
Setting of fractures	$10/$100

If a patient had a contagious disease, he or she could expect to pay fifty to two hundred percent more than the standard fee. Laboratory tests, new and costly, ranged around five dollars. Cesarean sections required $250 to $500, and treatment for venereal disease required fifty percent in advance. The customary fee for treatment of nosebleeds was anywhere from seventy-five cents to more than a dollar. Dr. Boyd Cormick of San Angelo, listed a dollar and twenty-five cents for this treatment.

Obstetrical fees in eighty-nine Texas counties at the turn of the century were calculated thus in one survey:

> . . . 57.3% of doctors charged obstetrical fee of $10.00; 21.3% charged $15.00; and 15.7% charged more than $15.00.

Fixed fees for public services were unbelievably small. Dr. Ferdinand Herff served as the City Physician of San Antonio in 1855, for ten dollars a month. Dr. W. E. Saunders of Austin had to resign as Superintendent of the State Lunatic Asylum "because of insufficient salary."

Neither the fixed salaries of public service nor the negotiable fees of private practice provided sufficient monetary remuneration. Even the most dedicated doctors were often forced to engage in other businesses to make a living. "Doctoring," for the most part, did not put enough bread on the table.

Confronting danger and disaster was not uncommon in frontier practice, and nothing held more terror in the early days than the pervasive smell of smoke.

Since much early-day construction was of wood, fire was a common threat to both life and property. Water was sometimes scarce and not readily available to control fire. Often proper precautions were not taken for fire prevention. Building materials were not easily obtained to replace the damage.

The office of Dr. S. A. Owens, a founder of the Waco Medical Association, burned in 1871, a casualty of wooden construction. In the mid-1870s, fire destroyed a section of Waco, including shanties on so-called Rat Row. Several doctors' offices were burned in the area. In this instance, the fire was called a blessing because the run-down area was rebuilt with many brick buildings.

Even a building such as the quarantine station at Corpus Christi, Shell Banks Hospital, was destroyed by fire in the early 1880s. In a more personal tragedy of this period, Dr. G. M. Boynton of Buffalo Gap, lost his small son when his home burned. Dr. W. D. Kelley lost his home and all personal papers in the Galveston fire of 1885, and in Austin, Dr. Frazer's smokehouse burned.

Among other disasters confronted by doctors of the nineteenth century was the havoc caused by nature. Galveston was hit by savage storms both in 1875 and 1885, but the hurricane of 8 September 1900, "The Great Storm," caused the loss of approximately 7000 to 8000 people — or more. The storm of 1875 did less damage, but was a violent hurricane.

The brave action of Dr. George W. Peete during the storm in 1875, was praised at the subsequent meeting of the Texas Medical Association. In the midst of a tidal surge, this doctor relinquished the boat sent for his rescue to another man and his wife. They escaped, but Dr. Peete and his fourteen-year-old grandson did not. This sacrifice occurred on September 16, 1875, in Galveston.

The 1900 storm did great damage to the medical institutions: The University of Texas School of Medicine, Sealy Hospital, and St. Mary's Infirmary. The roof of the medical school was damaged, and although Sealy Hospital incurred some loss, the hospital continued in use during the disaster and afterwards. The worst damage was done to St. Mary's Infirmary, although part of the main building continued to be used. The repairs were extensive and costly.

Dr. R. H. Harrison was among many doctors from outside the city who offered their services to the stricken Galveston. He grievously described the disaster:

> . . . No pen, nor tongue, nor painter's brush, could convey anything like an adequate conception of it. Death, desolation, and dire disaster everywhere. The mangled remains of sea-beaten victims, the floating bodies of women with half-born babes protruding from their bodies, the shrieks and cries of the thousands of victims imprisoned beneath the great mass of wreckage which the waves had piled up in a semicircle around the more populous and substantially built portion of the city, which was only partially ruined — all made a scene of indescribable horror.

Dr. Harrison replaced a local doctor, Dr. Arthur F. Sampson, who had been appointed chairman of the Fifth Ward Relief Station at Fire Station Number 3. After Harrison took charge, he found "a small stock of drugs and dressing material in a little wooden shanty beside the stable for the fire station horses. He soon extemporized an operation table and some shelving for the disposition of the material, and went to work, patients coming in by the score."

Harrison also described the effect of the resulting flood upon the city and warned of possible dangers:

> The clearing of the streets of wreckage and filth in the business portion of the city, together with the liberal use of powerful disinfectants, had doubtless been of immense value; but it should be remembered that this portion of the city, which contains the majority of the best residences, is surrounded on three of its sides with an immense wall of wreckage, burying beneath it a great mass of organic matter of every conceivable character, in every degree of decomposition, and that the effluvia set free from this putrid mass must necessarily poison the atmosphere, generate disease, and enhance the mortality beyond any recent precedent.

Not only doctors but many others came to the aid of the storm victims. Upon hearing of the storm in Chicago, William Randolph Hearst commissioned a Texas doctor, William L. Crosthwait, to organize a relief train. Dr. Crosthwait was in Chicago doing postgraduate study at the time, and he was able to select five doctors, eleven nurses, and other volunteers who answered the ad in Hearst's newspaper. Hearst gave $50,000 for the expenses of the relief train, one of a number which came to the aid of the stricken city.

Dr. Crosthwait described many acts of heroism as well as other acts of barbarism and looting. He reported that a young man saved the lives of many patients in St. Mary's hospital by transferring them from wooden barracks which were later demolished, to the sturdier main building.

Holiday turned to horror for the young man, a medical student, as the hurricane approached Galveston. Planning to visit his family at their Waco ranch, Zachary Scott (later father of actor, Zachary Scott) left Saint Mary's Infirmary and walked through brisk wind just before noon to the downtown train station.

Arriving thirty minutes or so later, the tide was high. Water covered the train tracks, and no tickets were sold. Returning to the Infirmary, Scott walked more briskly as the storm unleashed its fury.

By three or four o'clock, water was knee-deep in the area, and an untold number of terrified people fled to the Infirmary. By five-thirty, water was five feet deep. The force of the storm shattering windows and demolishing walls made it imperative to move county patients in the frame building to the Infirmary, a quarter of a block away.

Hour after hour Scott helped carry nearly two hundred patients through the rising water which became shoulder-deep. By ten P. M., the storm was past Galveston. As the water receded, unidentified bodies and destruction littered the area.

Scott long remembered the sight of what had been Saint Mary's Orphanage, about five miles from the Infirmary: scattered bricks and bodies of many nuns and orphans.

Dr. Zachary Scott lived to practice medicine and retire in Austin.

The relief team organized burial squads and aided the injured. They opened a relief station from a high school. Dr. Crosthwait later wrote:

> . . . the injuries were mostly broken limbs and lacerations, some cases of exposure, but there were others who were beyond human help . . . We made generous use of whatever disinfectants were at hand, quicklime, chloride of lime, carbolic acid. The pestilence which we had feared in the wake of the storm did not materialize.

Possibly one reason was because the water supply was not contaminated; it came from artesian wells on the mainland.

After the initial aid to the people of Galveston, the relief train moved patients and equipment to the city auditorium in Houston. These measures, made possible by the generous donation of Hearst and others, did much to relieve the suffering victims of the storm.

Since the frontier sometimes attracted outlaws, physicians of nineteenth century Texas often encountered those fleeing from justice and were required to give medical assistance.

One Dr. Coe rode his horse forty miles through a blizzard in answer to a middle-of-the-night summons. Upon arrival, he discovered his patient was a wounded horse thief. This made little difference since frontier doctors were not known to reject calls for help, even from rustlers, bandits, or other thieves.

After giving his patient a hypodermic of hyoscine, morphine, and cactine, the doctor probed for the soft-nosed rifle bullet which had entered the left arm halfway between the elbow and shoulder, splintering the arm bone. A second bullet had struck the right leg above the knee, penetrating upward, and lodging in the groin. The doctor's probing, stitching, dressing, and splinting were rewarded with vicious cursing. Even so, Dr. Coe remained with his patient a few days until he was confident of his patient's recovery.

There were times doctors became victims. In 1856, a Dr. Thompson, a settler southwest of Camp Verde, went to San Antonio with a load of shingles accompanied by two companions. On the way back about six miles out of town, the party stopped to eat and rest. While sleeping, they were attacked by robbers. Dr. Thompson was killed and his companions badly injured.

Dr. Carruthers of Austin, not only lost his money to highwaymen, but lost his clothes as well. In another encounter, one highwayman who robbed Dr. Swearingen within the city limits of Austin, declared Dr. Swearingen the only courageous man he had ever robbed and said he was glad the doctor was not armed.

One frontier doctor, Dr. William Routh of Peoria, Texas, was escorted thirty miles out of town by two horse thieves to tend one of their wounded comrades. After the doctor extracted the bullet, the grateful leader of the gang offered him a double fee. The doctor, refusing the offer, accepted only his usual charges.

As he mounted to ride out of camp, one of the horse thieves admired the horse, saying, "That's a fine horse you've got there, Doc." Possibly the thief's gratitude to the doctor was not as great as his desire for a good horse, or it may have been coincidence that someone broke into the doctor's stable and stole his horse that very night.

Encounters with Indians were also a harrowing part of frontier life.

When Dr. Robert Andrews and Stephen F. Austin were surrounded by fifty Comanche Indians two days out of San Antonio on their way to Mexico, the Indians acquired some of Austin's belongings. Later when some of these items were found with a roving band of Indians, Austin's relatives heard about the discovery. For a time, they assumed that he and Dr. Andrews had been murdered.

One account of the attack says the Indians released the men upon learning that they were Americans, but they kept some of their property, including blankets, bridle, and *one Spanish grammar book.*

In February 1843, Dr. Calder, who had settled near Cedar Springs, in Dallas County, traveled on horseback to a place known today as Buckner, where some men were building a settlement. He arrived just as the sun came up, and he led a horse behind his own. After completing his business and departing, he was seen on foot pursued by two Indians. A rescue party formed and encountered a group of sixty hostile Indians, which they scattered. After searching the woods nearby, rescuers found the body of Dr. Calder, slain and scalped. Evidently, he had killed one Indian, emptying one barrel of his shotgun. The Indians, however, left the gun with him. They probably had never seen a percussion lock and did not understand its worth. Unfortunately, Dr. Calder did not have a second chance to perfect his skills with the new invention.

In 1838, a group of Lipan Indians visited Victoria. In the group was a Dr. Hanam, who had once practiced at Matagorda. At that time, he had deserted his wife and was living with a woman of the Lipan Indian tribe. They came to barter some pelts and buffalo robes for necessities. Dr. Hanam bought some preserves which he sat down to eat on the steps with his female companion. John J. Linn questioned the doctor about how he could leave civilization, and he recorded Dr. Hanam's reply in his book, *Fifty Years in Texas*:

> . . . He wished me to believe that he was doing so in a quest for scientific knowledge in regard to medicinal roots and herbs, and stated that he was acquiring a vast repertory of such know-

Dr. Spohn Treats a Rabies Victim

Arthur E. Spohn, a Canadian who came to Texas in 1868, practiced for the most part in Corpus Christi. The Spohn Sanitarium {later Spohn Hospital}, built in his honor in 1900, was named for his many achievements.

Dr. Spohn, who had trained in Michigan and New York, continued to keep abreast of medical discoveries. In spite of the scarcity of medical publications, he was able to use such knowledge he had to the benefit of the remote South Texas frontier. Because he had heard of Pasteur's discovery of rabies vaccine, he was able to advise Willie Chamberlain, bitten by a rabid wolf on the King Ranch in 1888, that he go to Paris for Pasteur's treatment, a course which probably saved his life. The victim was the half-brother of Mrs. Henrietta King of the King ranch.

Dr. Spohn also served as an administrator, for a time being in charge of the military quarantine in Galveston. Also he was director of the Marine Hospital in Corpus Christi for fifteen years. He died in 1913.

> ledge. I made no reply to all this, but was satisfied that in the balances of his desires, the squaw would vastly outweigh his thirst for knowledge.

Later the Lipan group engaged in battle with a group of Comanches. In the course of the battle, one Comanche was killed. Linn goes on to tell the outcome:

> . . . The squaw of [Dr.] Hanam cut off one of the hands of the defunct brave, and brought it to her Aesculapian Adonis with the suggestion that they should prepare it for their evening repast, stating that it was a delicious morsel. Cannibalism the doctor could not subscribe to, and he left the Indians at Gonzales, and ultimately returned to Alabama.

Dr. James Crispin Nowlin lived in Gonzales, but later settled at Center Point near Kerrville, around 1856. In that region, he discovered springs which he named Indian Springs, for the Indians who had recently left the area.

The next year Indians attacked the cabins built by Dr. Nowlin. After they fled, he joined other settlers and the cavalry from Camp Verde in pursuit. Dr. Nowlin later moved to the Guadalupe Mountains, probably encountering still more Indians in that area.

Hazards of the frontier included poisonous snakes and vicious

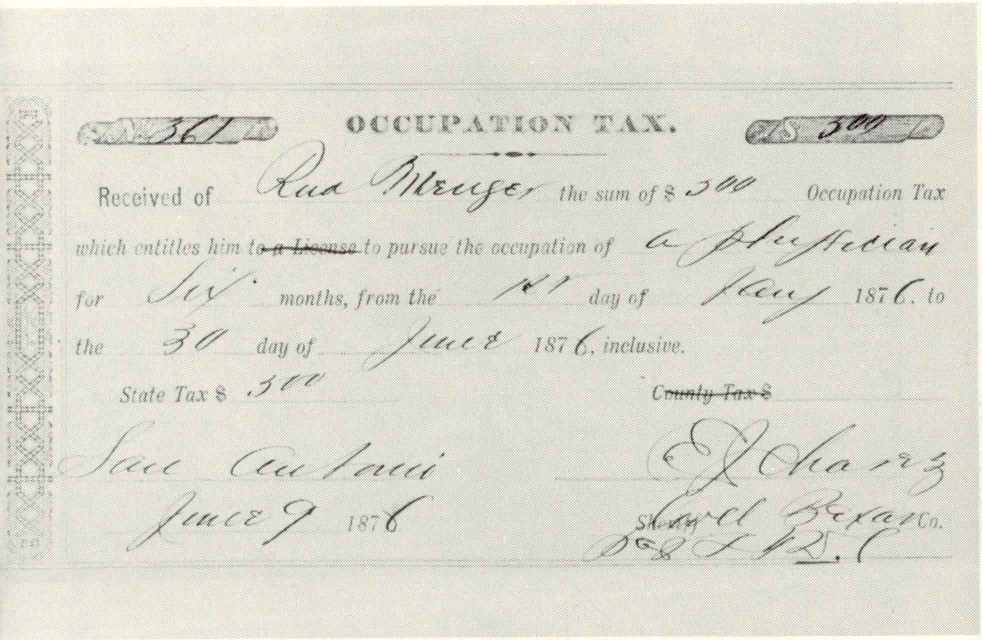

No. 361 OCCUPATION TAX. $ 500

Received of Rud Menger the sum of $ 500 Occupation Tax which entitles him ~~to a License~~ to pursue the occupation of a Physician for Six months, from the 1st day of Jany 1876, to the 30 day of June 1876, inclusive.

State Tax $ 500 ~~County Tax $~~

San Antonio June 9 1876

Sheriff Bexar Co.

Occupation Tax receipt of Dr. Rudolph Menger of San Antonio in 1876.

Courtesy University of Texas Health Science Center, San Antonio

animals, sometimes even dangerous dogs. A Dr. Bibb of Austin was painfully bitten.

On the other hand, the creatures were not always vicious. Dr. Van Zandt of Fort Worth, told the story that he was returning one night after visiting a patient when he was alerted by the sounds of what he believed were running feet. Since he had just learned that Indians had killed a man camped in that direction, he was alarmed — until he realized that instead of Indians, he had heard the "hoof steps" of a bunch of calves crossing the road.

Responding to disaster was a way of life in nineteenth century Texas, and physicians, for the most part, faced the challenges with courage and resourcefulness.

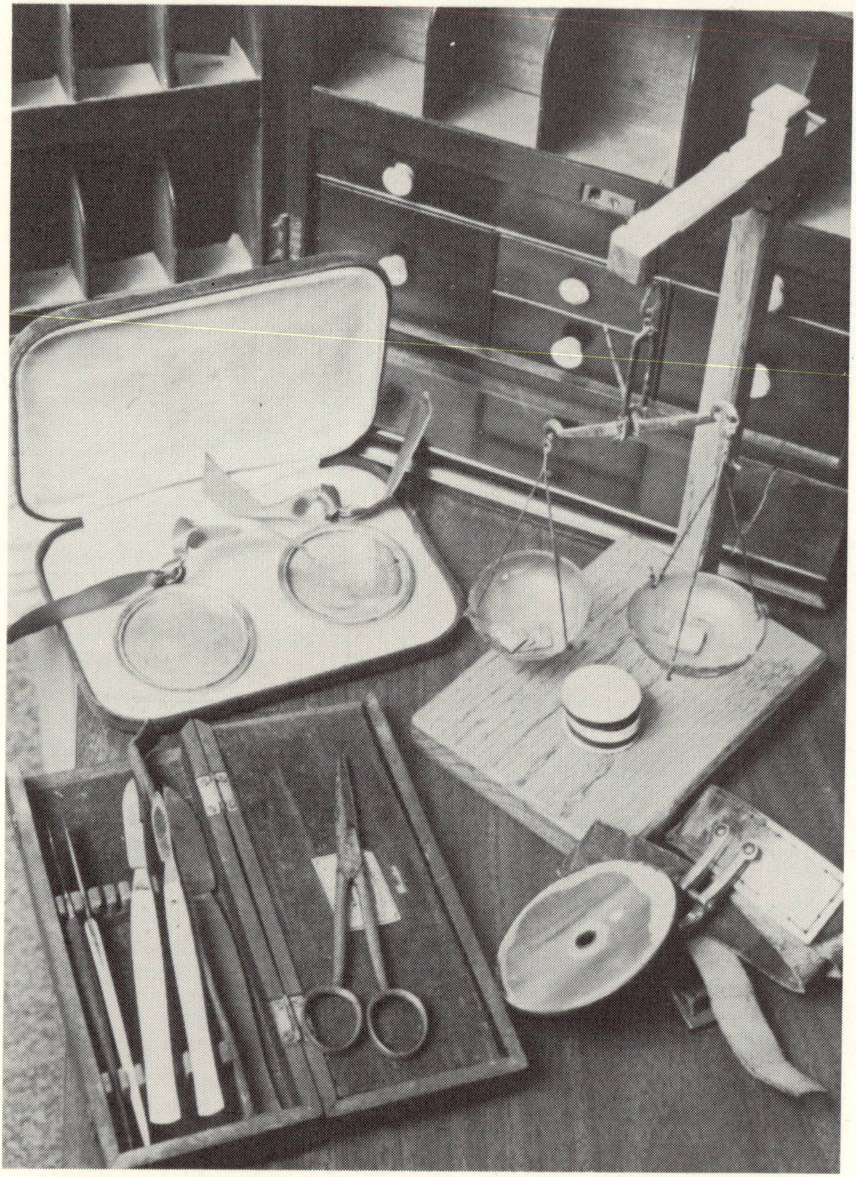

Nineteenth century medical artifacts on permanent loan from The University of Texas Health Science Center at San Antonio Library to the Institute of Texan Cultures, 1981.

Courtesy of the Archives of UTHSCSA

5

Treating Disease:
Problems and Practices

For all the ills under the sun
There is a remedy or there is none.
If there is one try to find it,
If there is none never mind it.

Some say that nineteenth century medicine developed reliable means of dealing with only two diseases: the prevention of smallpox by vaccination and the treatment of malaria with the drug quinine. Other treatments were less successful and thus more subject to change.

Calomel, or chloride of mercury, was a popular cathartic or laxative which accomplished little other than purging. Harmful effects occurred when the drug was given in large doses which caused the patient to salivate. Large doses also caused soreness, sponginess, or inflammation of the gums, as well as soreness of the tongue and the salivary glands. Sometimes, there was even a loss of teeth due to the recession of the gums.

In spite of these drastic side effects, calomel was a valuable purgative, even though the dangers of the cumulative effects from the drug were not known. Soon after the turn of the century, however, castor oil became a substitute for calomel.

Many physicians of the 1850s began more cautious treatments in their practice of medicine, opposite to the teachings of Dr. Benjamin Rush in the first part of the century. After the old "heroic" methods were discarded, physicians sought new active therapies. Although there was a decline in the use of calomel, a "through of calomel" was still a recommended treatment in frontier Texas even after the turn of the century.

After the Civil War, physicians relied on several types of treatments: antipyretics, analgesics, emetics, and tonics. Even if bloodletting was not used as much, the main intention had not changed. Physicians were still concerned with reducing temperature of the patient if at all possible. Many antipyretics were tried, usually with severe side effects.

Quinine, an alkaloid isolated from Peruvian cinchona bark in 1820, gradually became more widely used than calomel. Quinine's biggest drawback was its expense, but costs were lowered by the 1850s making quinine the most popular drug of its type. Because of quinine's wide use in the decade after the Civil War, the American Medical Association tried to convince the federal government to undertake cultivation of the cinchona tree, but the group was not successful.

Quinine effectively reduced fever by depressing heart action. Other cardiac sedatives such as the poisons aconite and veratrum viride were used for the same purpose. Not without side effects, small doses of quinine produced nervousness and giddiness; larger amounts produced ringing in the ears and sometimes caused deafness and blindness. Quinine was difficult to swallow, and its bitter taste was sometimes masked by drinking coffee.

In the treatment of malaria, quinine was an improvement over the raw cinchona bark. Gradually, it was also used for typhoid, yellow fever, and even pneumonia — diseases sometimes classified as malarial. Symptoms of malaria were easily confused with other common fevers, such as typhoid. Many other ills were diagnosed as malaria in latent form, and thus quinine was prescribed for almost everything in the 1870s and 1880s.

After the 1880s, research led to the development of synthetic antipyretics which rapidly replaced quinine. Eventually, a most popular synthetic, acetylsalicylic acid (aspirin) was developed.

Dr. William O. Wilkes of Waco said his father's preceptor gave the following advice in 1853: "When you don't know what to do with your patient, give him an emetic; he always feels so good when he gets over the sick-stomach."

Small doses of emetics promoted violent vomiting. Tartar emetic was popular, or "tartarate of antimony." When given in large doses, it lowered the frequency of the heartbeat and became an antiphlogistic. Other emetics were saltpeter (nitre), jalap, and ipecachuana. Harmful effects resulted; when jalap was mixed with calomel.

Quinine was also considered a tonic for general health, appetite, and digestion. Shine Philips in *Big Spring*, said that "Everybody took quinine in the winter to prevent somethin' — God only knew what. Some people just put it in their shoes."

Before the Civil War, arsenic had also been used as a tonic as well as the poison strychnine, which was mistakenly believed to produce heart stimulation when given in small doses.

But the most widely used tonic was alcohol, usually in the form of whiskey or brandy. As an aid to digestion, alcohol was recognized as a stimulant to the mucous membranes of the stomach as well as to the heart. Alcohol was sometimes used as a remedy for snakebite. It was even thought to be a germicide when taken internally. This belief was popular after the bacteriological discoveries and may explain why alcohol was given in large doses for diphtheria. Some people mistakenly believed that alcohol had food value, another belief which enhanced its use.

Alcohol was used to treat typhoid, pneumonia, and even diphtheria in children. The recommended dosage was large enough to produce considerable intoxication on the part of the patient. One physician said he "would not hesitate to give children ill with diphtheria ten to twelve ounces of whiskey a day if necessary, but the more usual dose was from one-half to two teaspoons every three hours for infants and young children."

Indeed, alcohol was a very popular tonic — so popular, that in the last two decades of the nineteenth century, the medical profession and the temperance movement clashed over the value of alcohol as a medicine. Some physicians even considered the temperance movement a threat to medical therapeutics.

Opium, its alkaloid: morphine, and its tincture: laudanum, were the chief pain-reducing drugs in the second half of the nineteenth century. At that time, patients could have their own hypodermic syringes. There was even experimentation with cocaine during the Civil War period.

Opium was used extensively for almost any type of illness, particularly for any form of diarrhea. Opium killed pain and made the patient more comfortable, but physicians did not recognize opium's addictive characteristics. There were many victims of opium treatment. One source states that nearly all the inhabitants of one western town were given so much opium that everyone became addicted. The *Taylor County News,* of April 1885, reported that the "wife of a well-known Connecticut traveler died from effects of opium at Dallas, Texas on the 10th."

Morphine given by hypodermic needle became popular during the Civil War. Doctors did not know of its addictive properties, but as the dangers of opium and its derivatives became more apparent, the use of cocaine grew more popular. Only toward the end of the nineteenth century did addiction to drugs become a recognized social issue.

Even though surgery had been performed in Texas since the first reported operation by Cabeza de Vaca in the sixteenth century, surgical treatment in the early part of the nineteenth century had not greatly improved. Doctors often made their own emergency surgical instruments from turkey quills, hairpins, twigs, and other sharp objects. Using ingenuity, doctors devised instruments which were often used to extract imbedded objects.

Before the use of anesthetics, many patients had to be held or tied down during surgery, a practice that generated much fear and trembling. James Buckner Barry, of Bosque County, described such medical conditions in the 1850s:

> Injuries, deaths, and murders were to be expected by the frontiersman but, nevertheless, they always came as a shock. I had the experience of narrow escapes from death but received only serious injuries, and had my smaller son, Willie, seriously gored by a wild cow. Medicine and surgery were crude. It was my lot to help hold some patients for the doctor when he was amputating limbs without anesthetic. Both men and women had falls from horses, accidents at the hands of stock, tame and wild, and other injuries too numerous to record.

Around mid-century, some doctors began to use anesthetics. Using ether, Dr. Ferdinand Herff became well known among the Indians as a "medicine man," when he performed bilateral cataract surgery on a Comanche brave.

Part of the success of the operation may have been due to Dr.

Dr. Ferdinand Herff. Photo by Lungkwitz and Iwonski.
Courtesy James P. McGuire
Copy from U.T. Institute of Texan Cultures, San Antonio

Herff's fastidiousness. The doctor scrubbed his hands before surgery, a personal habit not based on knowledge of the germ theory.

Since ether is highly flammable, surgery could not be performed near candlelight or kerosene lamps, the only sources of artificial light. Dr. Herff solved the problem of adequate light by performing the surgery outdoors. A dozen or more attendants waved large palm leaf fans to keep the flies away.

Dr. Herff's surgery restored sight to the Indian, and word spread quickly about the doctor's healing magic.

Many other cases of early surgery in Texas, were performed on the kitchen table in the home of the patient, usually with the assistance of various friends and relatives. If the home did not have sufficient light, patients were moved outside, and surgery was performed on a large table in the open air and sunlight.

Toward the end of the century, Dr. James William Nixon of San Antonio, related that he saw his father, a country doctor in Gonzales, amputate a woman's leg above the knee. He said that the pa-

Dr. Adoph Herff, son of Dr. Ferdinand Herff. Photo by Cone's Studios.
Courtesy of San Antonio Conservation Society

tient received chloroform, the amount determined by the patient's breathing. He went on to say:

> There was no operating table, no sterilizers, and . . . he removed the side boards from a wagon bed and used them for the operating table. He placed them on two carpenter sawhorses. He then placed a mattress upon the side boards for the patient's comfort. He brought the kitchen table out into the yard for an instrument table. He always insisted it was safer to work out in a clean yard than in an utterly dirty house.

Misconceptions and half-truths about fevers abounded into the nineteenth century. Dr. William McCraven expressed an opinion common among physicians in 1849:

> . . . I cannot bring my mind to the conclusion, that intermittent, remittent, and yellow fever, are identical in origin, and only differ in degree. Intermittents are often as malignant and fatal as yellow fever; so too, remittent. Mild cases of yellow fever are gen-

Fever: The Unsolved Mystery

". . . fever is Nature's engine which she brings into the field to remove her enemy."

— **Thomas Sydenham**
Seventeenth century English physician

erally, less severe, and more evanescent, than either of the others. There may be the same affinity between them, that exists between influenza and catarrh, or cholera and diarrhea. Intermittent or remittent fever, may possibly constitute an element of yellow fever, but in my judgment, something else must be superadded; and then we have a new disease. What that something is, or whether it be simple, or compounded of two or more morbific elements, remains as yet, concealed among the unsolved mysteries of nature.

Autumnal fevers occurred anytime from late summer until first frost in October or November. A fragment of a letter from Galveston, in October 1853, illustrates the notion that frost will put an end to illness:

> We have had an awful time of it, have had largely over 2,000 cases of sickness and over 400 deaths since Sept. 5, and tho the number of deaths per day is now smaller compared with the past, yet this abatement is only for want of material for the fever to feed on. We have no hope but in frost and when that will occur the Lord only knows.

Dr. Ashbel Smith in his treatise on yellow fever had also noted a connection between the first frost and the end of epidemics.

Dysentery and malaria, common infectious diseases, were associated with autumnal fevers. Malaria, sometimes called intermittent fever because it peaked in cycles of so many hours, was the most widespread endemic disease in the early nineteenth century.

The word malaria literally translates "bad air," reflecting the belief that the cause of the disease was blamed on heavy dews or mists which rose from low-lying swamps. As a preventive of malaria and a protection against such poisons during the period of the Republic of Texas, Dr. Alexander Wray Ewing recommended drinking early morning coffee.

Dr. James Addison Abney reported that his professor at Galveston, J. D. Rankin, taught: "the malarial germ was a product of heat, moisture, and decaying vegetable and animal matter, hence, during the long summer droughts we did not have malaria because the moisture was eliminated from the combination."

By 1879, J. D. Hall, Assistant Surgeon, reported: "I have seen only one case of malarial fever that proved intractable, and that was in a woman much reduced by hard work and nursing her child in hot weather; one of these cases where change of air and surroundings is called for imperatively."

Fevers had many names. Brazos fever was another name for a form of malaria. Ague was also a fever, sometimes malarial. Falciparum malaria was often called blackwater fever.

Influenza or catarrhal fever, sometimes called lung fever, was the cause of a series of epidemics in the first part of the nineteenth century. 1808 was a bad year at Bexar; over one hundred of the one hundred forty-four soldiers were ill with fever and malaria. Women often suffered from a puerperal infection called childbed fever.

Typhus and typhoid fever were threats in later years. Patients having typhoid fever supposedly smelled like hot bread, a fact which aided the diagnostician. Typhoid was a "slow, nervous fever," while typhus was a "putrid, malignant, petechial fever."

Another perplexing illness was milk sickness. This fever, *morbo loacteo*, was caused from cows which ate white snakeroot and rayless goldenrod. The cause of this mystifying fever was not discovered until the twentieth century. Cattle were often affected as well as people. The fever was often fatal, as in the case of the mother of Abraham Lincoln.

Rocky Mountain spotted fever was transmited by the bite of wood ticks, and became epidemic in the town of Aurora, in the 1890s. Marking the gravestone of a six-month-old victim of spotted fever were the words:

Don't see what I was begun for
Since I was so quickly done for.

Yellow fever, popularly called Yellow Jack or Bronze John, was another puzzling fever. Opinions varied as to who was immune from this terrible disease, which was sometimes diagnosed by the butcher-shop odor of its victims. Dr. McCraven stated, "I believe an opinion generally obtains, both in and out of the profession, that children, native to the soil, are not subject to yellow fever." He went on to say that later observations caused him to believe that this was not true; instead he came to the conclusion that persons who had mild attacks were then later immune to the epidemic.

Chart of Yellow Fever along the Texas coast, giving elevations above Sea Level of Localities where yellow fever has appeared since AD 1668. (Figures accompanying names of localities indicate elevations above sea level in feet.)

From Greenville Dowell's *Yellow Fever and Malarial Diseases,* published in 1876. University of Texas Health Science Center Library in Dallas.

Among a variety of treatments, Dr. McCraven described his method:

> . . . My principal means of combatting this formidable malady, were a small dose or two of castor oil; and from thirty to fifty grains of quinine; with the addition of hot mustard baths, mustard cataplasms and poultices, cold affusion of the head, and sponging other parts as indicated, anodynes pro re nata, and brandy or wine in the last stage. The nurse was minutely instructed, and warned of the importance of diligently attending to her duty. If called early, a hot mustard bath was ordered, at least for the feet and legs; a cataplasm to the epigastrium, and red pepper tea, or other hot drinks administered till the chillness had abated. As soon as the stomach was in a condition to bear it, four to six drachms of castor oil were given, in mint water, toddy, or some other agreeable drink, in as small bulk as possible; it was seldom rejected.

Nothing much helped the victims of yellow fever or Asiatic cholera, but some believed the sufferers fared somewhat better under homeopathic treatments as opposed to the harsh measures of heroic treatments. This probably accounts for the fact that there were more homeopathic physicians in areas where there was a lot of yellow fever, such as along the coast.

The comments of Dr. William McCraven, a Houston physician in 1849, however, dispute the success of homeopathic methods. He said:

> Mercurials have probably been more extensively employed in the treatment of yellow fever than any other class of remedies. That they have been successfully employed in some epidemics, I cannot doubt. . . . Is mercury the proper remedy for this condition: If I were a homeopathist, I would answer yes; for it induces that same, or a very similar condition; consequently it must cure it. But I am not one of that school, who think that the more you weaken an article the stronger you make it; or that quinine will produce intermittent fever, and must therefore cure it. I believe then, that mercury, under such circumstances, increases the mischief, and acts rather as a poison, than a remedy.

Quinine was sometimes used in the treatment of yellow fever in the belief that the fever resembled malaria. Dr. McCraven made the following observations about the use of quinine:

> . . . I believe it is used by all our physicians; but they differ ma-

terially in the mode of administration. Some give it freely from beginning to end. Some in small, frequently repeated doses, after the fever has subsided; some combine it with purgatives, capsicum, etc., and give it throughout. I think it only adapted to the early stage, before adynamia predominates.

The fear of yellow fever was greatest in tropical, semi-tropical, and temperate parts of the world. Southern Texas was no exception. People feared an invisible poison that rose from the warm swamp areas and permeated the air. The unseen, unknown killer indiscriminately chose victims despite pathetic precautions.

The Surgeon General of the United States succeeded in completely frightening the populace with his official decree published in papers all over the country:

> The weight of scientific evidence seems to warrant the conclusion that yellow fever is produced by an invisible poison capable of self-multiplication outside the human organism, which it enters through the air passages . . . When a wharf or a spot of ground or a house becomes infected, the poison at once commences to spread, creeping slowly in all possible directions, continually enlarging the area around the center of infection. . . .
>
> [signed] Jno. M. Woodworth, Surgeon General.

In mid-century, uninfected cities posted quarantines, refusing to permit people, mail, or supplies to enter from "infected" areas. Incoming trains were inspected; passengers were questioned and required to produce travel credentials. Incoming supplies on trains and vehicles were closely scrutinized for any source of infection. Transportation, communication, and commerce bogged down when an epidemic threatened.

For months in 1878, Houston papers had a daily front-page "Fever Report." While the Houston Health Department worked desperately to enforce quarantines and to instruct people in preventive measures, they were severely criticized for what they did and did not do.

People had many theories about yellow fever. Some thought that city folk were more apt to take the fever than those who lived in the country; they believed that the poisonous air was more prevalent at night than in the daytime. Consequently, people who came to town from the country during the day made sure they were home before nightfall. In Galveston, popular misconceptions associated the causes of fevers and sickness on the island with the time of year (summertime), the climate (the heat of the day and the dampness of the night), and the foul vapors that arose from a swampy area on the island.

Health notices were issued for individuals to freely use "prophylaxis by the internal use of small doses of sulphate of quina at regular intervals, and tincture of iron and chlorate of potassia." Believing the poison entered the system through the air passages, nasal spray with a quinine solution was also considered an effective measure to prevent the fever.

Everyone was cautioned to stay out of the "poisonous night air," and to "bathe and change flannels daily." A Houston city ordinance in 1854, decreed that tar and sulphur be burned in the streets of Houston after dark to disperse the poisoned air. A resulting amber glow settled over a fearful city, and even if the air smelled ghastly, the people felt safer. They closed their doors and windows to the night air, sprayed their noses, took hot mustard water baths, and changed clothes often.

Unidentified at that time, the killer mosquito, *Aedes aegypti,* was in the air; all the nasal spray in the world was powerless against indiscriminate injections of lethal organisms that produced the dreaded yellow fever. By 1881, the mosquito was suspect; the proof came in 1900, resulting in the eradication of the *Aedes aegypti* mosquito.

Yellow fever strangely retracted its mantle of fear over much of the entire country after the big epidemic of 1867. Epidemics occurred only once in the state thirty-three years before the mosquito was discovered as the carrier and the resulting fever from a mosquito bite was noninfectious. The sudden cessation of epidemics was due probably in great part to better sanitary regulations by city officials, screens on houses, and generally improved living conditions.

The ability to distinguish between the various types of fevers was a mark of progress toward the end of the century. When dengue fever and yellow fever both occurred at the same time in Galveston in 1897, Dr. H. A. West was able to differentiate between the two. For his clinical perception, he was commended by Osler and the United States Public Health Service. Dr. West was the first professor of medicine at The University of Texas Medical Branch.

A poignant account of illness and death was revealed in the letters of Lucy P. Shaw who, as an early settler with her husband on the sparsely populated island of Galveston, wrote to her mother in Eastport, Maine, in 1839. She pleaded with her to write news of home

Yearly Fever Report

In 1837 fever was imported into Texas;
1838, it prevailed;
1839, it was fearful;
1840, not noticeable;
1841, the same;
1842, the same;
1843, it increased;
1844, it was again epidemic;
1845, it was bad;
1846, not prevalent;
1847, it reappeared;
1848, there was fever;
1849, fever;
1850, doubtful conditions;
1851, doubtful;
1852, none;
1853, a plague;
1854, bad. . . .
1855, the fever was bad again;
1856, none;
1857, again prevalent;
1858, the same;
1859, the same;
1860, 1861, 1862, and 1863, no fever;
1864, a blockade runner brought the fever to Galveston, and it reached Houston;
1865, no fever;
1866, no fever;
1867, a terrible scourge visited Texas, and the last she has had of great consequence.

— Robert Rutherford,
First State Health Officer, in 1888

more often and to send various and sundry items: seeds, herbs, and medical supplies. Exchange of mail took months in transit. Lucy told her mother that the ten pounds of arrowroot they purchased for twenty cents a pound and brought to Galveston, was nearly gone. Used as a popular medical remedy, it cost nearly ten dollars a pound on the island.

At that time, the island had ten resident physicians: two at the garrison and one on board each man-of-war ship in the harbor.

Lucy described her firm belief in a Dr. Hamlin's medical attention when she and her child became sick with diarrhea. He gave Lucy an emetic and the child castor oil. Lucy expressed the belief that:

> . . . we shall be much better for the medicines we have taken and if we only take proper care, we shall not suffer from sickness through the summer. This is a very healthy place and it is only necessary to avoid the night dews and exposure during the heat of the day.

Lucy was distressed when Dr. Hamlin later became ill and died. She also spoke of a Dr. Jones, "a good physician" who treated her child, Emily, who had asthmatic fever. Such fevers sometimes lasted three to six weeks.

Later a Dr. Smith was attentive to the medical needs of Lucy's family. When her child was sick, the doctor required that the child wear flannel next to his skin. He consoled Lucy when she had a stillborn child, and she wrote to her mother: "it was occasioned by sitting the night but one before on a low seat and washing my feet and cutting my nails, and was sensible all the time that I was hurting myself very much."

Lucy graphically described the island's many mosquitos as much larger than those in Maine. Annoyed at their pesky bites, she writes: "My left eye is very much swollen and very lame in consequence of a mosquito bite on the upper lid."

Lucy wrote of the first yellow fever epidemic that plagued the island but hastened to reassure her mother that it was not contagious. She attributed it to:

> . . . a strip of low marshy land, which extends almost the whole length of the city, running parallel with the shore. It is a perfect mud hole, never dry, the filthiest part of the city, and the smell from it dreadful. It was the bad air which occasioned the sickness. It lasted about six weeks and there were 205 deaths. Among them no one was sick with the disease except those who lived in the vicinity of the mud hole or whose places of business were near there and there were only four females who died of it. Some of the best and most valuable men in the city were its victims, but the majority were people who led irregular lives and their habits were bad (not vicious or intemperate), but carpenters and mechanics who lived in sheds and cooked, ate, and slept in them or in the open air, as many do here.

Lucy was not alone in worrying about the Galveston mud hole. Dr. Ashbel Smith, who was Surgeon General of the Texas Army during 1837–1838, had strong feelings about the mudhole that was the town health hazard, and he advised city authorities to have the low spot filled up with sand and lime. Some disbelieved the mudhole caused yellow fever, however, and others thought that the thousand dollar cost of filling the mudhole excessive.

In a later letter to her mother, Lucy observed that they "had weather cold enough to make ice about ten days ago, so shall probably not have more yellow fever."

Actually, yellow fever was considered the most manageable of the hot weather fevers. Even though Ashbel Smith did not understand the cause of the disease, some of his recommended treatments were effective. All doctors, however, dreaded congestive fevers.

In a heart-rending account of the death of her son, Lucy wrote her mother of a Dr. Wynne and a Dr. Monk, who devoted time and attention to the small boy with the hoarse croupy cough. They tried every treatment they knew, giving him antimonial wine for the inflammation of his bowels and thirty drops of paregoric, then holding him in warm bath water, then wrapping him in flannel, alternately repeating the treatment for hours. Having remittent chills and fever, the boy seemed better, then worse. Once more he got better, then finally succumbed.

In her letters, Lucy mentioned a Dr. Work who went to trade on the Neches, a Dr. Forrest who returned to Baltimore, and a Dr. Desmond, or Desmont, who was an English doctor.

Lucy recounted that Dr. Smith opened up nine bodies, victims of yellow fever, and had several phials of the black vomit. Perhaps Dr. Smith was a man ahead of his time or ahead of the discovery of scientific detection by autopsy. Smith, who had begun his practice in Galveston the previous year, was determined to find the cause of yellow fever. Unfortunately, he was unable to learn the cause, but he did make many accurate observations, and he was convinced that yellow fever was not passed directly from one patient to another. He was willing to taste the black vomitus of patients to prove his point. Undoubtedly he convinced Lucy, as she had so written her mother.

In 1853, Dr. S. P. Moore reported 245 cases of yellow fever and fifty deaths at Fort Brown on the Texas–Mexican border. He treated his patients with nitric acid and salt instead of quinine.

Year after year, the fever took its toll. And twenty-nine years later in 1882, another surgeon, William Crawford Gorgas, had occasion to treat yellow fever at Fort Brown. The illness was first thought to be dengue fever, sometimes called breakbone fever, then the spectral yellow fever. The soldiers believed the wind carrying the odor of oranges and bananas from Mexico brought the yellow death. The soldiers' efforts to immunize themselves by drinking whiskey and chewing mustard seeds proved of little prophylactic value. Soon there were over two thousand cases of yellow fever around the fort.

Feeling helpless, Dr. Gorgas did what he could for the yellow fever patients, one of whom was Marie Doughty, a beautiful girl whom he had met and courted previously. He tended her and kept vigil at her bedside.

Fearing to lose the fort doctor to yellow fever, Gorgas's commanding officer ordered him to stay away from the fever patients. But Gorgas felt a keen need to find out more about the sickness. Observed doing an autopsy on a yellow fever victim, he was punished for disobeying orders and was ordered to live in the yellow fever ward at the fort. There he treated the living, cared for the dying, and read burial services for the rest.

When Dr. Gorgas saw a freshly-dug grave and was told it was for his beloved Marie Doughty who was even then in the black-vomit stage of yellow fever, he despaired. But miraculously, she survived, only to discover Dr. Gorgas himself had contracted the fever. He too was spared, however, and the two convalesced together and were later married.

Marie's recovery and his own intense experience in surviving yellow fever perhaps later contributed to Dr. Gorgas's determination to eradicate yellow fever in the Panama Canal Zone in 1904.

The first case of Asiatic cholera in America was diagnosed in 1832. During this period, New York experienced a devastating epidemic. Talk of this disease may have been the stimulus for Dr. Ashbel Smith to write a book on Cholera Spasmodica while he was studying in Paris.

Waterborne, Asiatic cholera spread from Quebec down to the Great Lakes, and then on to the Mississippi ports. In Texas, there were early accounts of cholera epidemics in Goliad, Victoria, and San Felipe. In Brazoria, over eighty people died while Stephen F. Austin was in Mexico in 1833. One colonist wrote to Austin that he would find "a great vacuum" of his friends upon his return.

Burgeoning Texas towns often fought panic and waged all-out

efforts against the phantom sickness, cholera, in 1833 and 1834. The Asiatic scourge would suddenly appear and, weeks later, suddenly disappear. Just the mention of cholera paralyzed a town; talk of an impending epidemic made people fearful to assemble anywhere. Many fled their homes in panic, camping in wagons or out in the open in spite of weather or inconveniences.

Cholera broke out in Santa Anna's army after defeat at the Battle of San Jacinto in 1836. Santa Anna was taken to Orozimbo, the Brazos plantation of Dr. James A. E. Phelps. Santa Anna, who was despondent over being held prisoner, asked Dr. Phelps the best way to take cholera. Refused an answer, he tried unsuccessfully to contract cholera by eating fruit, a popular misconception. He also reportedly swallowed poison. To be on the safe side, the doctor pumped out Santa Anna's stomach. At any rate, Santa Anna survived without contracting cholera.

The second wave of Asiatic cholera reached epidemic proportions in the United States between 1848 and 1853, and was found to a lesser extent in some places until 1854. Indianola had such a severe cholera epidemic in 1846, that for a time dead bodies remained in the streets.

As the frontier spread south and west during the migrations to California around mid-century, large numbers died from cholera and diarrhea. Some calculated that the cholera epidemic of 1849 lasted about eight years, probably resulting in more fatalities than the smallpox plague. In 1866, there was another national epidemic of cholera, but the disease had been reported in San Antonio two years earlier. The mystery of cholera was not solved until several decades later in 1883, when Dr. Robert Koch discovered the bacillus of cholera in India.

Cholera Infantum was the leading cause of infant mortality. Dr. Notson of Fort Concho grievously lists the cause of death of his infant son as Cholera Infantum.

In 1833, an early treatment of cholera consisted of administering compounds of laudanum, peyote, tea, and slaked lime. Another mixture was recommended by the Abbe Domnenech on recovering from cholera in 1849: "a glass of camphorated alcohol, laudanum, unground pepper, and 'eau de Cologne.' " Later in the century, during the nationwide epidemic of 1866, calomel was faithfully used in line with the "heroic" treatments popular with Texas doctors. Other treatments included bloodletting and plasters.

Commonly called consumption or uncommonly, phthisis, or

Dr. Labadie's Cholera Remedy

When looseness of the bowels begins, take a teaspoonful of Cooking Soda, dissolved in a cup of cold water; add a few peppermint drops and sugar; give one tablespoonful every hour when all has been drank mix another teaspoonful soda & c: Take a teaspoonful of common chalk dissolve it in a tea cup of water. give one tablespoonful of it with 5 drops Laudenum {sic} every 2 hours, till well, If vomiting is severe apply mustard to the pit of the stomach and between the shoulder blades, if the feet, arms or legs are cramped, apply mustard by rubbing the parts with it well. Take a little lye, lime, or copperase disolved & keep a wine glass full in the chamber utensil so as to destroy the poison from the stools bury each stool in the sand and keep none in the chamber give the sick a spoonful of water often keep him in bed quiet, Peppermint Tea is good for the stomach if the tongue is coated give 10 grains of calomel to the chalk, for one day then chalk and laudenum {sic} every day till well.

— Papers of Dr. Labadie,
Rosenberg Library, Galveston

"the white plague," tuberculosis caused twenty percent of the deaths in Texas in the period following the Civil War. Nationwide, tuberculosis only accounted for fourteen percent.

As there was no known medicinal specific for the malady, the only hope of cure for many with the disease was to move to a dry area. Doctors believed that consumptives had a better chance in climates free of dust, which had little moisture and a great deal of sunshine. Southwestern Texas had such a climate.

One doctor from Arkansas, Dr. J. B. Garrison, sent his wife, who had the disease, to that area. Her improvement "proved the doctor's firm belief that tent life in the dry, pure air of Texas would benefit even the most delicately-constituted consumptive."

Toward the end of the nineteenth century, beliefs about consumption and its treatment changed. From Koch's experiments, which isolated the tubercle bacillus, the contagious nature of the disease was recognized. Tent cities sprang up due to the fear of contagion, and many hotels and inns refused to accommodate consumptives. Still, science had found no means of cure, but a better informed public was less apt to place its hopes in worthless remedies.

Dr. Frank Paschal of San Antonio, was noted for his work in tuberculosis prevention and control. After the turn of the century, Dr. Paschal was even instrumental in the founding of the Tuberculosis Sanitarium at Carlsbad, Texas, which opened in 1912. This institution is now the McKnight State Sanatorium.

Meningitis, pneumonia, measles, influenza, syphilis, scurvy, and smallpox were also known in nineteenth century Texas. Some called pneumonia, "Captain of the men of death," and the disease regularly took its toll of frontier settlers. Measles, which had devastated the Indians, was also a dreaded disease. The *Taylor County News* of April 24, 1885, reported that "a malignant type of measles is raging in Sherman. It is said to be very fatal."

Scurvy was a common problem in early Texas. In Austin's colony this disease occurred only in winter when pokeweed greens were not available. The leaves of "scurvy grass" were boiled and eaten by many of the early settlers as a preventive. "Scurvy greens" included horseradish leaves, sorrel, and dandelion — greens which science has indeed confirmed are rich in Vitamin C. Sassafras tea was also taken for scurvy. The common prickly pear and the juice of the maguey or other agave plants were additional remedies. Lime juice, when available, was another preventive.

Soldiers on expeditions suffered from scurvy. William W. McCullough, in his book on Dr. William Dennis Kelley, reported on John Pope's 1857 Expedition:

> By July, scurvy had broken out in the camp. No supplies of antiscorbutics could be procured except on the Rio Grande, 170 miles distant, and 'they completely spoil before they can be brought to camp. The command has been without supplies except the bare ration for nearly a year.' Plenty of activity for the poor physician!

Conditions were not much better at remote military posts. Dr. J. V. DeHanne, assistant surgeon at Fort Concho, wrote on April 2, 1879: "The rations are of fair quality in general; tho' there exists a scarcity of vegetables most of the time; to the latter circumstance is due a tendency to scurvy observable among the men who come on sick report."

More serious was the still-present threat of smallpox. *The Texas Republican,* of Brazoria, included this warning in February 14, 1835:

> The schooner *Santiago,* arrived at the mouth of the Brazos with several cases of small-pox on board; we would advise all those who have not been vaccinated, to have immediate recourse to that prevention.

Even though vaccination for this disease was a proven measure, the failure to vaccinate still resulted in much needless illness. Sometimes the vaccine was not available; other times its cost was prohibitive; occasionally the vaccine was inert and ineffective.

The Texas Republican of March 14, 1835, reported:

> We have been informed by a Medical gentleman of this place that a doctor arrived today from Matagorda, having in his possession Vaccine matter, which he refuses to furnish our Physicians unless they will pay one hundred and fifty dollars for a single scab; and also that he charges five dollars for vaccination. We are not in the habit of being personal in our remarks, but we think such imposition in the present crisis ought to be held up to the public notice.

In a letter from Dr. S. L. S. Smith at Camp Charlotte to his mother on April 28, 1879, he tells of unusual circumstances regarding vaccination on the frontier:

> At one ranch we came across on the South Concho, I rode up to the house with my orderly to obtain some milk and eggs, and while Ross held my horse I crossed the acequia — the irrigating ditch, and made overtures. The woman said she could give me a canteen of milk, but no eggs, but upon my insisting she went out and brought in one dozen with the remark that, that was all she had. I said granto — how much — and gave her forty cents, and was just turning to leave, when her 'Ole man' came in, and blurted out, 'Hello Doc, how is ye.' I talked with him a few minutes about the news at the post, for he resided only 18 miles from Fort Concho, and was going to take my departure with many thanks for the milk and eggs, when he casually remarked that a boy standing in the door-way was about half sick from a vaccination — and of course my curiosity led me to examine it. It was just at the right stage to revaccinate from, and as the mother said he was healthy and that she was afraid of the small-pox getting among her progeny to calm her excited fears, I whipped out my pocket case of instruments and vaccinated them — six children from two years old up — in less than no time; combining pleasure with business.

Despite precautions, epidemics occurred, and many doctors unselfishly fought the disease. Dr. Paschal of San Antonio did not hesitate to go to the aid of Presidio, a town of 3000 people, which was struck in 1874 by a smallpox epidemic. He stayed four months, until the epidemic was over.

Born in San Antonio in 1849, Dr. Paschal studied medicine first with Dr. Cupples and then at Louisville Medical College.

After completion of his studies, he went to practice in Mexico. First he had to pass a difficult examination in Spanish to receive a medical license. For fourteen years, he was Physician to the City Hospital at Chihuahua. He did not return to San Antonio to practice until 1892.

In San Antonio, Dr. Paschal became president of the West Texas Medical Association, president of the Board of Health of the city, city health officer for four years, in charge of City Hospital, and a member of the State Board of Examiners. Dr. Paschal also served on the committee which reorganized Texas medicine according to the plan of the AMA in 1903.

The memoriam to Dr. Paschal, which appeared in the February 26 issue of *The Pioneer,* shows the high esteem in which this doctor was held:

> *Farewell, dear friend, A knightlier man ne'r buckled belt nor sword about his loins nor sheaved a purer spear. Beneath a banner where but true men march the silken glory of the radiant past in all its warp and woof of circumstance, shall live in the palace chambers of our hearts.*

Many frontier communities remained apathetic to vaccination. Records from the medical history of the post at Fort Concho note:

> I am informed that three cases of Smallpox in San Angelo resulted fatally last week, and that three cases still exist there. The Commanding Officer, on my recommendation, has endeavored to quarantine the town, and with apparent success. This will at least arouse the townspeople from their past neglect and sluggishness in regard to the disease.

Other communities did not take heed. In 1882, thirteen persons died in Albany from a smallpox epidemic. All the afflicted were isolated in a log house.

Only time and better communication convinced doctors and others that prevention as well as treatment of some of these diseases was within their grasp.

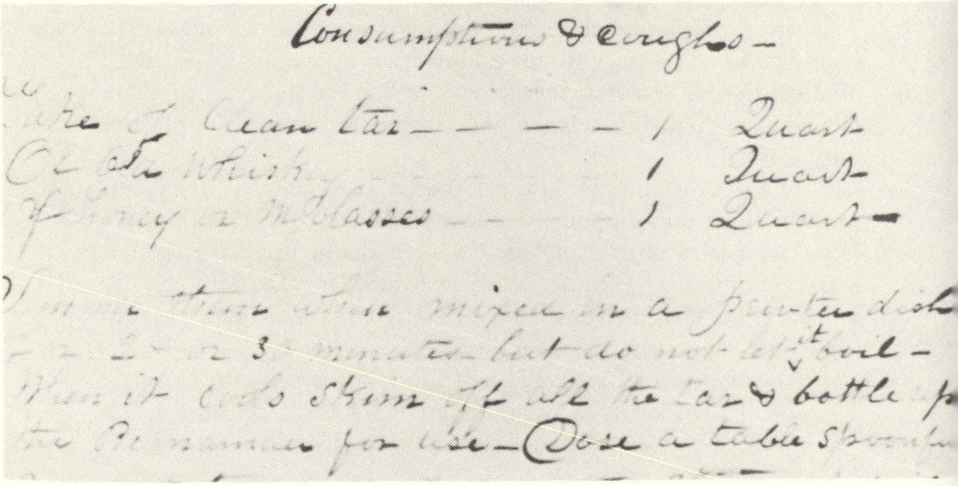
Consumption & coughs—

...ke of clean tar — — — 1 Quart
Of ... whisky ... 1 Quart
of honey or Molasses — — 1 Quart

... these mixed in a pewter dish
... 2 or 3 minutes but do not let it boil—
When it cools skim off all the tar & bottle up
the remainder for use—Dose a table spoonful

Photocopy of early remedy for consumption and coughs. Location of the original unknown.

Courtesy Archives, University of Texas Health Science Center, San Antonio

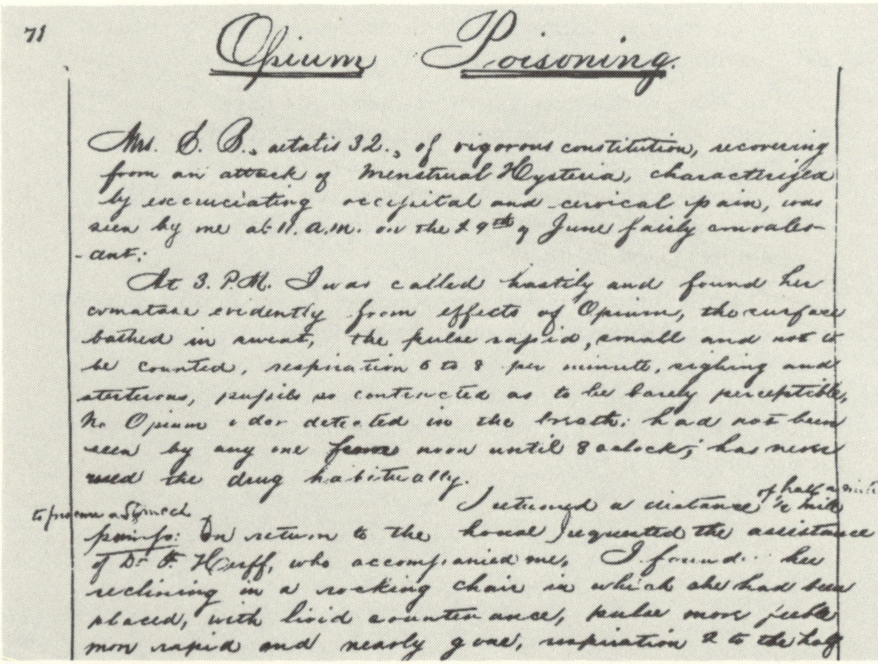
71

Opium Poisoning.

Mrs. S. B., aetatis 32., of vigorous constitution, recovering from an attack of Menstrual Hysteria, characterized by excruciating occipital and cervical pain, was seen by me at 11. a.m. on the 29th of June fairly convalescent:

At 3. P.M. I was called hastily and found her comatose evidently from effects of Opium, the surface bathed in sweat, the pulse rapid, small and not to be counted, respiration 6 to 8 per minute, sighing and stertorous, pupils so contracted as to be barely perceptible, No Opium odor detected in the breath: had not been seen by any one from noon until 8 o'clock; has never used the drug habitually.

I returned a distance of half a mile to procure a stomach pump: On return to the house I requested the assistance of Dr. F. Herff, who accompanied me, I found her reclining in a rocking chair in which she had been placed, with livid countenance, pulse more feeble more rapid and nearly gone, respiration 2 to the half

A page from the casebook of Dr. George Cupples, San Antonio.

Courtesy Archives, University of Texas Health Science Center, San Antonio

6

Healing in Wartime:
Scalpel and Sword

Indeed it was the custom in those days: the physicians would use their rifles during the battle and their scalpels afterward.

— Dr. P. I. Nixon

The Texas Revolution of 1835–1836 developed out of tensions between the government of Mexico and the residents of Texas. At that time, Texas was a part of the single state of Texas and Coahuila in the Mexican Republic. The Texans, dissatisfied with the government's attempts to regulate immigration and collect taxes, petitioned in 1832 for separate statehood and other reforms. This petition was signed by fifty-nine men, seven of whom were doctors.

The petition availed little, and the Texan's distrust of the Mexican government continued. In 1835, President Santa Anna discarded the Federal Constitution of 1824 and imposed a centralist dictatorship. He sent General Cós, his brother-in-law, to Texas to keep the residents peaceful.

Fighting began, however, at Gonzales in October 1835, when Mexican soldiers demanded the surrender of a cannon, which the Mexican government had loaned for Indian protection. Several days after this skirmish, all able physicians in the area of Gonzales volunteered their services.

Among the first volunteers were Dr. Amos Pollard, Dr. Thomas J. Gazley, and Dr. Thomas Kenney. Dr. Pollard became Surgeon of the Regiment. Other early volunteers were Dr. Joseph E. Field who was later with Fannin at Goliad, Dr. William P. Smith who was appointed Surgeon of the Army, and probably Dr. William Richardson who was appointed Surgeon of the Staff soon after San Antonio was besieged. Dr. George M. Patrick, Dr. T. Martin, and Dr. T. F. L. Parrott were other physician volunteers in the Anahuac and Velasco encounters, earlier incidents of the conflict.

As well as volunteering to take arms, some Texans were delegates to a Consultation at San Felipe in the autumn of 1835. Dr. Branch Archer presided over this convention. The names of Dr. Archer and Dr. John Sutherland were among the signatures of the document called the Declaration of 7 November 1835. At that time, a provisional government was established as well as a volunteer army.

But no clear-cut government of the new Texas immediately took shape because military and political figures clashed over strategy. Chaos ruled. Many worked on plans, but few knew what others were doing.

Despite the weak provisional government, the volunteer army emerged, three hundred strong. The fact that men of high calibre gave support to the cause induced many others to volunteer also.

The earliest doctors submitted the following statement to Colonel John H. Moore as they joined:

> You are hereby requested to accept the medical services of the undersigned, who without any distinction of grade, have with a special eye to the good of their country, constituted themselves a board for the volunteer army of Texas . . .

Late in 1835, the volunteer army defeated General Cós and his 1200 men who were forced to take leave south of the Rio Grande and never return to Texas. Nevertheless, the Texans feared that it was only a matter of time until Santa Anna and his army returned. In the meantime, they did what they could to increase the number of patriots.

Many professional men came to Texas at this time in addition to the local doctors who had already volunteered their services. These men answered pleas for help and willingly fought, sometimes losing their lives for a cause they had only recently encountered.

Dr. Albert Moses Levy was one such volunteer who joined the

Dr. Albert Moses Levy at the Siege of Bexar, San Antonio, 1835. Watercolor painting by Bruce Marshall.

Courtesy U.T. Institute of Texan Cultures at San Antonio

fight. His career illustrates the amazing ambivalence of many physicians of the day, who were armed with both scalpel and sword. "I have crossed a street when more than two hundred muskets were shot at me, our men begging me not to expose myself as I was a double man, being both soldier and surgeon." So wrote Dr. Levy to his sister, 20 December 1835.

Although Dr. Levy's date of birth is unknown, he was raised in Richmond, Virginia. He earned a degree from the University of Pennsylvania. His wife died while his only daughter was quite young, and soon afterward, Dr. Levy went to New Orleans where he heard much talk about the state of affairs in Texas. There he joined the volunteer group known as the New Orleans Grays. He also volunteered as a Surgeon in the Volunteer Army of Texas.

Dr. Levy explained some of his reasons for volunteering in the same letter to his sister:

> . . . I am engaged for the first time in my life in the real, stirring and precarious struggle of man with man, & should I succeed, I

> shall at once be elevated to such a standing in society as must ensure me independance, . . . aye even a fortune, & an immortalized name. Should we fail, my life falls a sacrifice to outraged liberty.

Dr. Levy was involved in the storming of Bexar in December 1835, at the time Texas forces captured the Alamo from the Mexicans. Afterwards, he was cited for serving "with exemplary bravery." Receiving a new assignment in February 1836 as Surgeon on the schooner *Brutus,* he departed San Antonio before the March siege of the Alamo. He was later transferred to the Texas Naval vessel, *The Independence,* which was attacked by two armed Mexican brigs in April 1837. After a stormy battle, he was captured along with the crew and taken to Brazos Santiago.

Gifted in the art of persuasion, Dr. Levy not only escaped after three months' imprisonment, but he coaxed his jailer, Captain Thomas, into coming with him. Captain Thomas later enlisted in the Texas Navy.

Upon returning to Texas, Dr. Levy married, settled in Matagorda, and became actively involved in community affairs. He was elected December 1837, to serve on a Board of Medical Censors representing the district of Matagorda, Victoria, and Jackson. This board, created by both houses of Congress, was an early step toward regulating medicine in Texas. Dr. Levy also ran for a Senate seat in the 1840s but was not elected. Despite this defeat, he lived to enjoy some of the benefits of Texas independence.

In early spring 1836, fifty-nine Convention delegates assembled at Washington-on-the-Brazos, and on 2 March 1836, they issued a Declaration of Independence. Seven doctors were among the signers of this document: Doctors George W. Barnett, Stephen H. Everitt, Thomas J. Gazley, Benjamin B. Goodrich, William Mottley, Charles B. Stewart, and Lorenzo de Zavala. The delegates then began work on drafting a constitution for the new government.

Meanwhile on 23 February, Santa Anna's troops had begun the siege of the Alamo which was defended by Lieutenant Colonel Travis and his men. On a chilly pre-dawn 6 March 1836, with their ammunition, food supplies, and medicines all but exhausted, the men committed to die inside the Alamo heard the Mexican buglers sounding the dreaded *Deguello* — no quarter to the defenders. They then saw hundreds of Mexican soldiers attack while they sustained an inexorable tide of rifle and cannon shot. Finally, the remaining

Dr. Amos Pollard, surgeon who died at the Alamo, 6 March 1836.
Courtesy Archives Division, Texas State Library

defenders were put to death with grapeshot, musket fire, and bayonets.

Of the approximately 190 patriots who chose to make a stand with Travis, there were six physicians. Little is known about some of the six who gave their lives in the cause for freedom.

Dr. Amos Pollard was chief-surgeon in command. Pollard, age thirty-three, came to Texas from Massachusetts in either 1834 or 1835. For a short while before the war, he was a land prospector in Gonzales. After assuming his post at the Alamo, Dr. Pollard wrote letters to Governor Henry Smith stating: "Things have been in the worst possible state here as you are aware. . . . I am interested in this you will see for the Hospital is in great want of a little money."

Less than a month before the fall of the Alamo, Dr. Pollard wrote:

> It is my duty to inform you that my department is nearly destitute of medicine and in the event of a siege I can be very little use to the sick under such circumstances . . . I have plenty of instru-

ments with the exception of a trephining-case, some catheters and an injection syringe which would complete this station.

Dr. John H. Forsyth, age thirty-nine, was the senior captain in command under Travis and Bowie. Forsyth was from Kentucky and had command of a company of volunteers. Forsyth studied medicine but never established a career practicing medicine. Indeed, he cared little about anything after his wife died on Christmas Day 1828. His abiding grief seems the reason he left his baby son with his father in upstate New York and fled to Texas.

Dr. Edward P. Michison (Mitcherson, Mitchusson, or Mitchasson), age twenty-nine, was from Missouri or Virginia. He arrived in Texas just prior to the battle and served as a surgeon.

Dr. John W. Thomson, was one of Crockett's Tennessee company. He was a surgeon with the rank of private.

Dr. John Purdy Reynolds, age twenty-nine, was a well-trained surgeon with the rank of private. He held no official position at the Alamo. He was graduated from Jefferson College in Philadelphia in 1827, and he had practiced medicine for seven years at Mifflin, Tennessee.

William D. Howell, age forty-five, and on the Alamo death list, held rank of surgeon, and came to Texas from Massachusetts and New Orleans.

A chosen career ended before it began for William D. Sutherland, eighteen-year-old nephew of Dr. John S. Sutherland. William had only begun the study of medicine before he died in the Alamo.

Heroes of the fight for Texas independence, these physicians and other soldiers of the Alamo fought valiantly to the end. According to legend, the soldiers had earlier signified their willingness by crossing a line Travis carved on the dirt floor with his sword.

Dr. John Sutherland, messenger and scout, played an important part in the story of the Alamo. Sutherland came to Texas in 1835, arriving at the Alamo in January 1836. He brought a small quantity of medicine with him because Dr. Pollard had run out of many needed items. Both food and medicine were in short supply.

When a sentry reported Mexican cavalry approaching, Dr. Sutherland, accompanied by John W. Smith, offered to act as a scout to see if the rumor were true. They did see the Mexican cavalry, and then spurred their horses in a run back to the city. When the sentry saw them coming, he rang the bell to alert the garrison.

Dr. John Sutherland, one of the Alamo couriers
Courtesy Archives Division, Texas State Library

Because it was raining, Dr. Sutherland's horse slipped in the mud and fell to the ground. The doctor's right leg was caught under the horse which did not move. His knee injured, Dr. Sutherland was unable to walk. Utilizing the injured doctor as a messenger, Travis sent Dr. Sutherland and Smith to Gonzales to rally the people for support and reinforcements.

Thus Dr. Sutherland and Smith escaped the fate of those in the siege of the Alamo. Later, Dr. Sutherland was given other important messages to relay. He was sent by Houston to Harrisburg with dispatches for President Burnet.

Three weeks later the victorious Santa Anna erred grievously when he ruthlessly ordered the massacre, at Goliad, of more than three hundred prisoners taken at the Battle of Coleto Creek, 20 March 1836.

Colonel J. W. Fannin and his men had earlier taken refuge in La Bahia at Goliad. While there, orders came from General Sam Houston to fall back to Victoria. Fannin, however, postponed the move, a delay with disastrous consequences. He was forced to stage a retreat upon learning the overwhelming number in the approaching Mexican army. On the morning of March 19 under cover of a dense fog, he began to march with his men and wagons. In the confusion of leaving, most of the provisions and water were left at La Bahia.

Fannin and his men had not gone far when they encountered Mexican cavalry. Although they attempted to reach the wooded area which lay ahead, they were detained on the open prairie by the breakdown of the ammunition wagons. Anticipating a battle, Fannin gathered his men with the wagons and teams in the center. The Red Rovers were among the soldiers who fought valiantly. The battle lasted until dark when the Mexicans drew back.

Dr. Barnard related in his journal:

> . . . on account of the excessive darkness and our having no lights, I found no chance to attend to the wants of our suffering men to any extent. The want of water was most severely felt, for all had become thirsty, and more especially the wounded, whose misery was greatly aggravated by it.

The next morning the Texans saw enemy reinforcements arrive. With little hope of aid from outside and with no water or provisions, the position of the Texans was precarious. After consultation among the officers, the question of surrender was submitted to each company. Dr. Barnard, a member of the Red Rovers, described the dilemma:

> It was finally agreed that we would surrender if an honorable capitulation would be granted, but not otherwise, preferring to fight it out to the last man in our ditches, rather than put ourselves in the power of such faithless wretches without at least some assurance that our lives would be respected.

Not long after that discussion, a white flag was raised by the Texans, and Colonel Fannin with a few of his men went out to discuss the terms with the Mexicans in command. Some believed that Fannin received some form of assurance from the Mexicans that the wounded would receive proper attention. Later events did not bear this out.

The prisoners were marched to the fort where they were confined until Palm Sunday, 27 March 1836. Then the Texans were marched out of the fort and the infamous massacre took place. Before this tragedy occurred, the doctors were asked to treat the Mexican wounded at Mission La Bahia, which had been turned into a hospital. The accounts of three of the doctors, as well as adding to the historical information about the incident, indicate their dedication and service.

Dr. Pollad wrote:

> Now that our fate was decided I gave all my attention to the wounded. I was assisted by Dr. J. E. Fields [*sic*] who joined us about ten days before, also by Dr. Shackleford [*sic*], Captain of the company; of "Red Rovers," who was a surgeon and physician by profession, and by Dr. Ferguson, a student of his, who had come out with his company.
>
> The prisoners were not marched back to Goliad, the wounded being left on the field until carts could be sent (back) for them. The loss of the enemy in the engagement I never could learn with precision. They had above a hundred wounded badly that we (the surgeons) were afterwards obliged to attend to.
>
> Carts came out (March 21, 1836) and took in a portion of our wounded men, attended by the other surgeons, while I remained on the ground with those left. This day, while dressing the wounds of our men, some of the soldiers stole my pocket case of instruments, and thus deprived me of the power of properly attending (to) them.

Dr. Barnard described his arrival at the fort:

> My first effort was to see Colonel Fannin, and if, by any possibility through him get hold of some of our surgical instruments and hospital dressings for the wounded, we having been robbed of everything of the kind. . . .
>
> We were politely requested by the Mexican officers as a favor that we should attend their wounded, as their surgeons had not yet arrived; which we, not to be outdone by them in politeness, told them we would do so with the greatest pleasure. We, however, found we were not to be permitted to visit our own wounded until we had attended to all of theirs. We remonstrated with them, but to no purpose. A Mexican surgeon had at length arrived, but we had not assistance from him. It took us nearly the whole day to get through with the Mexicans before we could be allowed to see our own men and then we had so little time we could only dress some of the severest wounds and leave the rest altogether; some of them up to this time had not had the first dressing. We resolved to refuse attendance altogether on the Mexicans, at all risks, unless we could be allowed time to attend our own, at least once a day. . . .

After the battle, Dr. Shackelford wrote:

> It has been often asked as a matter of surprise, why we did not retreat in the night. A few reasons, I think, ought to satisfy every candid man on this point. During the engagement, our teams had all been killed, wounded, or had strayed off; so that we had no possible way of taking off our wounded companions. Those who could have deserted them under such circumstances, possess feelings which I shall never envy. I will mention another reason, which may have more weight with some persons than the one already given. We had been contending for five hours, without intermission, with a force more than seven times larger than our own; had driven the enemy from the field with great slaughter; and calculated on a reinforcement from Victoria in the morning, when we expected to consummate our victory.

Speaking of the imprisonment, he wrote:

> Our situation at this time was truly deplorable; having everything stolen from us but the clothes on our backs; without any of the comforts of life; — compelled to labour in the Hospital day and night; — exposed to a piercing March-wind, and no blankets to cover us during the night; having little or no food, and that of the most revolting kind — covered with vermin, worn down with fatigue, and a prey to the most heart-rending forebodings. But still, under every discouragement, we sustained ourselves with becoming fortitude. The officers, in their intercourse with us, evinced great politeness, which they seemed to consider the sum total of their duty. On one occasion they invited Dr. Barnard and myself to eat with them; but we gave them such a demonstration of American appetite, as to admonish them in future of the bad policy of extending to us such acts of hospitality.

Dr. Barnard described the scene the night before the massacre in an optimistic vein:

> Fannin asked me to dress his wound, and then talked of his wife and children with much fondness until a late hour. I must confess that I felt more cheerful this evening than I had since our surrender. We had reiterated assurance of a speedy release, it is true, by the Mexicans, though we replaced little reliance on them. Yet we had at least got our wounded in a way they all could be attended to each day, which was very satisfactory. Our fare had been of the hardest, being allowed no rations but a little beef or broth. Now we had been able to purchase from the camp-follow-

> ers some coffee and bread, more grateful to me than any luxury I had ever tasted, and, after sleeping on the ground without a blanket from the time of our capture, I had at least succeeded in getting an old worn-out one, upon which I laid down to rest this evening with more pleasure and happier anticipation than I before had allowed myself to indulge in.

Daybreak, Palm Sunday, Dr. Barnard and Dr. Shackelford were summoned to the gate of the fort. There they were led to Colonel Guerrier's quarters in a nearby peach orchard some three or four hundred yards from the fort. Soon they heard volleys from the fort, at first not realizing their significance. They were told the Mexicans were cleaning their rifles, but upon hearing screams and shouts, they became aware that their worst fears were true. The Mexicans, needing the services of the two doctors, spared their lives but did not spare them suffering and misery. Two of the other doctors escaped.

A survivor described the anguish of Dr. Shackelford:

> . . .Imagine the feelings of a father whose only son and beloved nephew came to such a horrible and traitorous end. At every volley, at every shot the unhappy father groaned: "My son — my son — my brave Red Rovers, all, all are murdered — Oh, it is horrible! Shackleford has robbed the citizens of Alabama of their sons — Alabama is bereft of its sons! . . ."

Dr. John (Jack) Shackelford, born in 1790 in Richmond, Virginia, had practiced medicine in South Carolina, participated in the War of 1812, and then served in the State Senate in Alabama for several years. Upon hearing of the fight for Texas independence, Shackelford made the fateful decision to respond to pleas for help.

According to Sam Houston, Dr. Shackelford was a true friend of Texas, sometimes called "the first friend of Texas in Alabama." He earned this esteem by organizing a select group, seventy neighbors and friends from Alabama, who joined the Texans in their fight for freedom. Shackelford as Captain organized this group of red-jeaned volunteers into a unit known as the Red Rovers, arriving in Texas early in 1836. They were ordered to serve under Colonel Fannin, the Commander-in-Chief, whose forces were in Goliad.

Although Shackelford and his companions were law-abiding citizens, some of his men became boisterous and quarrelsome on the way to La Bahia. One account relates "such was the power of his influence and the great esteem in which he was held, that he soon succeeded in allaying the excitement and soothing the angry feelings of (most of) the men into peace."

Dr. Joseph H. Barnard, who enlisted as a private, joined the company of Red Rovers as they made their way to Goliad. He was later appointed by Fannin as Surgeon to the Garrison. He had come from Chicago in answer to the call of Dr. Archer and Stephen F. Austin for volunteers to fight for the freedom of Texas. His journal of the happenings of these days is considered one of the most accurate reports. His account from December 1835, to 5 June 1836, was published in 1875 as, *A Journal of the Massacre of Fannin's Command.* Dr. Barnard, in addition to his medical skills, was later known as a surveyor, state representative for his county, and one of the founders of Richmond, Texas.

Dr. Joseph E. Field, a physician and surgeon, claimed to be the first member of his profession to volunteer his services to the army. He also claimed that all the medicine used at Gonzales and San Antonio was supplied by himself and other doctors.

Field had settled in Brazoria and Matagorda upon coming to Texas. After the Siege of Bexar, he was allowed to treat the wounded Mexicans but not the Texans. Due to his successful care, the Mexicans became very fond of him and tried to persuade him to return to Mexico with them. He was able to escape, however. After traveling over 100 miles on foot, he learned of Santa Anna's capture. He wrote an account of his war experiences called *Three Years in Texas.*

Following Texas independence, he practiced at Brazoria and Corpus Christi. His later years were spent in Florida, where he became blind and destitute. He petitioned the Legislature for some support which was denied, although he was given a small pension from 1858 to 1881.

Dr. John Walker Baylor also served at the Alamo, Goliad, and San Jacinto. He narrowly escaped death in these encounters only to die later from a wound received at the Battle of San Jacinto.

Dr. Joseph G. Ferguson, a medical student, was not spared to treat the wounded as were the other doctors. He was kept in the same room with Fannin and supposedly shot at the same time, his death causing much grief to his uncle, Dr. Shackelford.

Several other doctors also were among the group at Goliad, including a Dr. Hall, making the total number of physicians at least eight.

At least eleven physicians' names are indelibly written on another page of Texas history, the Battle of San Jacinto, 21 April

Dr. Alexander Wray Ewing
Courtesy Archives Division, Texas State Library, Austin

1836. This siesta-hour battle, lasting only eighteen minutes, ended the fight for Texas independence.

Dr. Alexander Wray Ewing, an Irishman who came to Texas in 1830, was appointed Surgeon General of the Texas Army. He had studied surgery at Edinburgh, and was considered a "profound scholar."

Acting in the best interest of one of his patients, General Sam Houston, Dr. Ewing received an unlikely reward. He treated the General for gunshot sounds received during the Battle of San Jacinto. The General sustained a compound fracture of the right tibia and fibula; small bone fragments were removed. Complications developed, however, and Dr. Ewing believed that Houston should be sent to New Orleans where better medical facilities existed. Although President Burnet did not give his permission, Houston, accompanied by Dr. Ewing, was placed on the schooner *Flora,* destined for New Orleans. For his dedication and insubordination, Dr. Ewing was dismissed from service.

Probably due to his friendship with Houston, Ewing was rein-

Dr. Nicholas Labadie.
Courtesy Barker Texas History Center, University of Texas at Austin

stated as Surgeon General, a position he filled until 7 June 1837. His later dismissal from the service a second time was the result of political considerations. Dr. Ewing then established a private practice in Houston.

The stormy military career of Dr. Ewing contrasts sharply with his later career as a respected professional leader. In 1838, he became first President of the Medical and Surgical Society of Houston, the first society which attempted organized medicine in Texas. Serving on many civic and business committees, he played an active role helping develop the city of Houston. For some unexplained reason, Dr. Ewing did not receive payment for his military service for fifteen years, but he was then given 1280 acres of land for service in the Battle of San Jacinto.

Dr. Nicholas D. Labadie, a Canadian of French descent and Catholic background, wrote his account of the famous San Jacinto battle. He had studied to be a priest in Missouri, but in 1829, he decided instead to read medicine in St. Louis, financing his studies by working as a clerk part of the time.

When he heard about Texas, he went to Nacogdoches where he gave his letters of introduction to the commandante there. He soon went to New Orleans to bring a supply of medicine. When he returned, Colonel Bradburn hired him as surgeon of the Mexican garrison at Anahuac, which housed three hundred soldiers.

When Santa Anna invaded, Dr. Labadie joined the Second Regiment of Texas Volunteers which reported to Houston at Beason's Ferry on 20 March 1836. When the retreat to San Felipe began, Dr. Labadie was on a scouting mission, but he rejoined the army at Groce's Ferry, acting as a surgeon to the Texas army.

On 6 April 1836, General Houston appointed Labadie Surgeon of the First Regiment of Regulars. He was in charge of the medicine chest which was hauled by ox wagon on the retreat.

In the Battle of San Jacinto, he fought as a volunteer private in Captain Logan's Company, the Liberty Volunteers, in the left wing of the army. According to Labadie, he and two other doctors had a discussion on what posts they would assume in the battle. As a result, Dr. Labadie took the left, Dr. Davidson the right, and Dr. Fitzhugh the center.

After the battle, Houston requested him to treat the wounded Mexicans which he refused to do until he was promised the $300 owed to him by Bradburn. Later Labadie said he was not paid.

In his account, Labadie describes the scene when Santa Anna was brought before Houston. After this fateful meeting, Labadie returned to treat the wounded who were brought to the Zavala place. Seeing a scarcity of bandages, Labadie searched through the plunder from the battle looking for material which could be used in dressing the wounded. There he found sheets, beeswax, and tallow which could be used for making a salve. To his dismay, he was later billed fifteen dollars from the Republic for sheets for bandages.

He was ordered by Secretary of War Rusk to Galveston. On the way he stopped at Anahuac to see his family. There he learned the sad news that one son had died. Dr. Labadie subsequently became very ill, also suffering a loss of hearing which he never recovered.

Labadie was very much opposed to General Houston after the war. He wrote many articles opposing Houston's policies.

Later Labadie moved to Galveston where he built one of the first frame homes on the island, and there he also opened a drugstore. In 1859, when yellow fever, the dreaded *vomito*, came to the island, his wife died leaving him with the care of three little girls.

Dr. Labadie was involved in many ventures in Galveston. He

established a line of sailing vessels between Pensacola and Galveston. He also built a wharf which was named for him. He was active in many civic affairs. He established and helped build the first Catholic church in Galveston. Even though he could not serve in the Civil War, he was on the examining board of the First Brigade of Texas troops. He died soon after the war in 1867.

There were other doctors at the Battle of San Jacinto. One was Dr. Thomas J. Gazley from New York, a signer of the Texas Declaration of Independence from Mina Municipality, which is now Bastrop. Gazley responded to the call for help from Gonzales in 1835, as did four other doctors. He fought at San Jacinto as a private. After the battle, he practiced law in Houston in partnership with John Birdsall. Gazley became a member of the House of Representatives in the Second Congress, September 1837 to May 1838. He settled in Bastrop County (near present Smithville), where he became a Mason and practiced medicine.

Some other surgeons who served at the Battle of San Jacinto had barely arrived in Texas in time to be a part of the army, such as Dr. William Francis H. Davidson from Tennessee, Dr. John P. T. Fitzhugh from Virginia, and Dr. Shields Booker from South Carolina.

Dr. Booker was promoted to surgeon in the army after the battle. Later he attended court in San Antonio when the Mexican General Woll captured the entire court and carried the attendants to Mexico as prisoners. He was held in the famous old prison, Castle Perote, where many were jailed and mistreated. In prison he was accidentally shot by a drunken man aiming at a Mexican officer. Booker was buried there in the prison yard.

Another doctor who fought in the Battle of San Jacinto was Dr. Charles Bellinger Stewart, who had come to Texas with Baron De Bastrop's party. He had helped draft plots of land for the Midway Colonists, and he established a drugstore in Brazoria when he first came to Texas. He later lived in San Felipe. During the time of the provisional government, he was Governor Henry Smith's secretary. His linguistic skills probably made him one of the interpreters between Santa Anna and Sam Houston after the Battle of San Jacinto.

When the provisional government was negotiating a treaty with the Cherokee Indians, Dr. Stewart improvised the first Texas seal upon the Indians' demand for an official marking. This eight-point star seal was used for a treaty on 28 December 1835, the first

Drawing of Button Seal. Dr. Charles Bellinger Stewart was responsible for this seal used 28 December 1835.

Courtesy Artist John Heslip

time a star was used as an emblem on a Texas seal. Dr. Stewart gave the following account:

> A mother of pearl button that had been in our family a long time, brought from England and preserved by my father as a relic of an ancestor. It had a star about 3/4 inch dia on it cut in deeply and when issuing and countersigning commissions (it was) utilized as a fitting emblem of a new star arisen in the Galaxy of States.

Although this seal was probably used but once, Dr. Stewart served on a committee to recommend both a seal and a flag for the Republic of Texas. He made suggestions for the first seal which was officially adopted 25 January 1839. Artist Peter Krag sketched the drawing. Dr. Stewart also made drawings for the first flag which was adopted at the same time.

Another doctor who fought in the Battle of San Jacinto as an Orderly Sergeant with the Cavalry Corps was Dr. Robert K. Goodloe. He joined Sidney Sherman's Kentucky Volunteers, coming to Texas in January 1836. Goodloe was also a member of First Regiment of Texas Volunteers until March 20, 1836, when he transferred to First Company of Texas Cavalry. In 1846, Goodloe commanded Company K., Second Regiment Texas Mounted Volunteers.

Also in the battle was Dr. Samuel Stivers, a man six-feet-four, who was called "Big Doctor." Fighting at the front on his great Kentucky horse, he was a colorful figure wearing a bright red sash that he had taken from one of the Mexicans at San Jacinto.

Stivers came from Amsterdam, Holland, and settled in Philadelphia when he first arrived in America. The United States Government had sent him to Mexico on a "secret mission." As he traveled through Texas, he liked what he saw and determined to settle and fight for the new country's independence.

Stivers became a messenger from General Houston to the Alamo carrying instructions for retreat. Four hours before reaching the fort, he heard news of the fall of the Alamo. Heartsick, Stivers returned to General Houston with the sad news.

Before the Battle of San Jacinto, Dr. Stivers ordered his wife and children to cross the Sabine River for safety. During her journey, Mrs. Stivers encountered the Indian Chief Nose, who advised her to return home. Perhaps out of regard for the doctor, the chief promised to send his best warriors to guard the family. He reassured her: "No matter what happens we will take care of you for the Big Doctor."

The only doctor who died during the Battle of San Jacinto was Dr. William M. Mottley, aide-de-camp to Secretary of War Rusk. Only twenty-four years old, Mottley was treated like a son by Rusk. Mottley studied medicine at Transylvania University, graduating only two years before the fatal battle.

He arrived in Texas late in 1835, with over $100 worth of surgical instruments. He soon offered his services to the Texans, and early in 1836, General Houston appointed him surgeon to the military command at Goliad. His loyalty to his newly-adopted country prompted him to sign the Declaration of Independence — the seventh doctor to sign. Elected from the municipality of Goliad, he was one of two delegates to the Constitutional Convention which met 1 March 1836 at Washington-on-the-Brazos.

Colonel Rusk expressed his sorrow at Mottley's death at San Jacinto in these words:

> My aid-de-camp Dr. William Motley [*sic*] of Kentuckey, fell near me mortally wounded and soon after his spirit took its flight to join the immortal Milam and others in a better world.

Following the Texas Revolution, most doctors resumed practice of medicine and other occupations in the life of the Republic of Texas, an independent state for nine years. After prolonged negotiations, Texas was annexed by the United States in 1845.

Annexation brought problems of its own. Soon the United States and Texas were involved in a war with Mexico, but fortunately, the conflict was not long-lasting. Many doctors saw Texas for the first time, when they served with the United States Army during that period.

Quiet then settled on the state for more than a decade, as settlers went about the business of living in mid-century frontier Texas. Prospects for a permanent peace were shattered, however, by the growing tensions between North and South. Texans were caught between the two factions, and loyalties were divided. Many doctors became involved and spoke out on the issue of secession.

When the final vote was cast, however, a majority wished to secede. Regardless of their former stand, many doctors now joined with others to once again take up arms.

Although the state was not involved in much actual conflict, Texans had to protect the Gulf Coast and the frontier against Indians and be prepared to resist a threatened invasion by Union forces. These tasks were difficult since many men had left the state to go to war. The loss of manpower affected business and agriculture, causing disruptions in normal activities.

The Union blockade of the Gulf Coast caused shortages of supplies, not the least of which was medicine. One account says: "Commodities readily available before the war — purgatives, opium, whiskey, turpentine, quinine, and calomel — had completely disappeared by the spring of 1864."

Medical care during the Civil War was inadequate, even according to the standards of the day. Confederate medical departments were not only ill-equipped, they were understaffed. A lack of surgical instruments and supplies also brought about many improvised treatments. Military conditions made cleanliness difficult — even instruments were often not cleansed between cases. Wounds frequently became infected resulting in gangrene.

Although use of anesthesia had become widespread, chloroform became unavailable toward the end of the war. Many major surgeries were performed without any anesthesia. Amputation was the standard treatment for open fractures, but the mortality rate for primary amputation of open fractures was fifty percent. The percentage was even higher for secondary infections.

Disease took an even greater toll than the actual battle casualties. During the four years of the Civil War, 164,000 soldiers died of disease; 94,000 Confederate soldiers were killed in battle. Disease flourished due to many factors, including poor sanitation, inadequate shelter and clothing, impure water, and the presence of parasites. Army rations were inadequate, and soldiers suffered from poor diets and malnutrition.

Dysentery was the largest killer, followed by malaria. Diarrhea, virulent erysipelas, and digestive disorders were common. There were also epidemics of typhoid fever, typhus, and smallpox. Few soldiers had been vaccinated. Epidemic measles were frequent in both camps, since many of the soldiers from rural areas had not been exposed to children's diseases. Pneumonia was also a threat to many of the injured. Morphine addiction, known as the "soldier's disease," became a problem during this period.

One of the few medical contributions made during the Civil War was the mobile hospital unit. There were also contributions made in the field of nursing. Physicians gained valuable training, particularly in surgery. Repair of war-wounded necessitated new and different procedures and instruments. These were small compensations, however, for the untold suffering brought about by the war.

Texas supplied men for the Confederate army, among them many physicians. There were only forty-six medical officers from Texas in the Confederate armies, a small percentage of the 3000 total medical officers. Eleven Texas physicians joined the Confederacy strictly as soldiers.

Prior to the Civil War, Dr. Jerome Bonaparte Robertson practiced medicine in Kentucky before coming to Texas along with other volunteers to fight for Texas Independence. The group arrived, however, too late for the fighting. Dr. Robertson settled in Independence where he established the practice of medicine and led raids against Indians and Mexicans.

Dr. Robertson was a delegate to the Texas Secession Convention from Washington County. When the Civil War began, he organized a group of infantry called Texas Aids, which became a part of Hood's Texas Brigade. Robertson was soon appointed in charge, becoming the commanding officer of the Texas Brigade of the Army of Northern Virginia, succeeding General Hood. This unit has been called "one of the most effective infantry units in Anglo-Saxon history." Robertson led the Brigade into battles at Fredericksburg, Chickamauga, and Gettysburg. In 1864, the doctor was sent back to Texas to recruit for the Army of Northern Virginia. He later resumed private medical practice. Dr. Robertson organized and became president of Hood's Brigade Association of Texas in 1872.

Another Civil War doctor, Dr. Richard Montgomery Gano, organized two companies of Texas cavalry known simply as Gano's Squadron. They established an awesome reputation when they reported for duty with General Morgan at Chattanooga, with more Yankee prisoners than men in the squadron.

Closer to home, Dr. Robert Locke Harris, who was graduated with a medical degree from Tulane University just prior to the Civil War, served with Captain Dick Dowling protecting the Texas coast. Dr. Harris was among the group who took possession of the Union boat, the *Harriet Lane.* The Confederates enjoyed unexpected luxuries with this capture. The loot included excellent surgical instruments, which were appropriated by Dr. Harris, the first he had ever owned. He later used his spoils of war in a long and successful medical career in Fort Bend County.

One doctor who served with Dick Dowling in the famous battle at Sabine Pass, 8 September 1863, was Dr. George H. Bailey. He was caring for wounded soldiers in the hospital when the enemy began attacking the fort. Carrying a roll of bandages with him, he ran the distance to the fort under heavy shelling to join the fight. Although greatly outnumbered, the Confederates achieved the final victory. Dr. Bailey's deeds show valiant service as both soldier and surgeon.

One famous medical doctor turned soldier was Dr. John Salmon Ford, better known as "Rip." The nickname evolved naturally enough. Ford, as Adjutant of Colonel John Coffee (Jack) Hays's First Regiment of the Texas Mounted Volunteers in the Mexican War, signed official death notices and thoughtfully added the words, "Rest In Peace." With circumstances and pressures of war, the words were shortened to "R. I. P." The nickname stuck with him. As Captain of the Texas Rangers, he fought Indians as well as the Mexican General Cortina. As a Confederate Colonel, he commanded the Rio Grande Military District, capturing Forts Ringgold, Davis, and Brown, which the United States was abandoning.

Ford had some success in driving Federal troops away from Texas. The numbers diminished as Ford pursued them with his ragamuffin army. Without supplies, his men had little food and they

Texas Torpedo Boats

During the Civil War, Dr. William Richardson is credited in the annals of Texas History with the idea of building torpedo boats to patrol the waters between Texas and Louisiana. He sold Texas governor Murrah on the idea. The governor authorized a $20,000 draw on the Texas Treasury for the project, if the Governor of Louisiana would likewise back the project. Before plans were complete, the need for the boats ended with General Lee's surrender and the fall of the South.

lived without shelter for long periods of the pursuit. Many became ill. At last, Ford was forced to raid Mexico for cotton which was sold to get supplies.

While Ford was winning, his army gained supporters at every stop, including many deserters and refugees. Although he was daring and reckless in pursuit of his duties, he encountered many problems. B. P. Galloway described Ford's hardships:

> . . . the end of May 1864, Ford had almost a thousand tough, dirty, unruly, and surly troops riding under his banner. Suffering from recurring malaria, he often found it difficult to stay in his saddle; but somehow he managed to continue in pursuit of a rapidly retreating enemy.

For over six months, Ford's Second Texas guarded the Federals who were entrenched on Brazos Island. In the spring, the Federals made forays onto the mainland. At last, Ford's soldiers engaged the enemy on 13 May 1865, at the Battle of Palmito Ranch. This Confederate victory was the final armed conflict of the Civil War. When it was all over, Ford received word that Lee had surrendered about five weeks earlier.

ERA OF FRONTIER FORTS

The United States Army established military forts after Texas annexation, primarily to protect the expanding frontier from interior Indian menace as well as invasion at the border. These forts, far from settlements, depended upon periodic shipment of supplies. Late shipments caused privations of food and medicine.

Difficulties in transporting supplies to the forts were caused by many factors. Heavy rainfall at times made the streams impassable for wagons, miring the wagon wheels in mud. Prairie grass died or

Fort Concho Hospital: construction was begun in 1869, and was completed in 1872.

Courtesy National Library of Medicine,
Copy from Fort Concho Museum

disappeared seasonally, leaving oxen or mules in supply trains with little forage. It was unprofitable for wagonmasters to use payload space to carry grain for the oxen. Wagon trains were also sometimes delayed by Indians or outlaws.

Generally, forts had a building or buildings designated as a hospital with twelve or more beds. The structures were usually primitive. At Fort Belknap, the post surgeon complained in 1855 that the hospital roof leaked, while the doors and windows were covered with muslin which kept out neither rain nor cold.

Construction on a new post hospital building was begun in 1868 at Fort Concho. Although only one ward was completed by November, some patients were moved from the deteriorating hospital tents. By the end of December, the entire hospital was set up in the new building, the remainder of the construction postponed until spring.

When ventilation and lighting were pointed out as deficiencies

Dr. David Hershey, Assistant Post Surgeon at Fort Concho from April to July 1876, was age thirty-eight when he died at Fort Concho Hospital in September 1876 of toxemia.

Courtesy Fort Concho Museum

in the new hospital in 1870, the post surgeon reported with a dry sense of humor that those things were being gradually and abundantly supplied "thanks to shrinking windows and doors" constructed of green pecan lumber.

An unnamed post surgeon was responsible for having the first hospital constructed at Fort Davis. Not officially sanctioned by the Army, there were no funds for construction. The post surgeon, however, struck a bargain with the civilian workmen: if they would construct a temporary hospital using their own labor and money, he would assure them free medical care when needed.

In the summer of 1868, they finished an adobe structure with a mud floor and cotton curtains at the windows, which cost the government only $120. In 1869, a more permanent structure of native limestone was begun, but it was never completed. The old adobe hospital stayed in use, but crumbling and leaking became part of a gradual deterioration process.

Post Surgeon's Quarters in foreground at Fort Concho ca. 1876.
Courtesy Fort Concho Museum

Whatever the reasons for delay, the War Department approved in 1874 the construction of a twelve-bed hospital at Fort Davis, not to cost over $7,500. Designed as a more permanent structure, it was adobe with a tin roof, seven rooms, a storehouse, and a ward. It was built on the site of the old hospital in a canyon, which became known as hospital canyon.

Many of the fort hospitals had some type of ambulance. At Fort Davis, the post surgeon noted that "the post has one old dilapidated ambulance, which is always broken down when used [needed] and requires days for repair." Sometimes, in a large patrol with several wagons, one covered wagon was utilized as a horsedrawn ambulance. On other occasions, if a soldier were injured on a mission, he was tended by other soldiers and returned to the fort on a travois, if necessary. The post surgeon did not usually accompany such patrols or scouting parties.

The military surgeon stationed at each post had many duties, including treating the wounded and ill. He might be a weatherman,

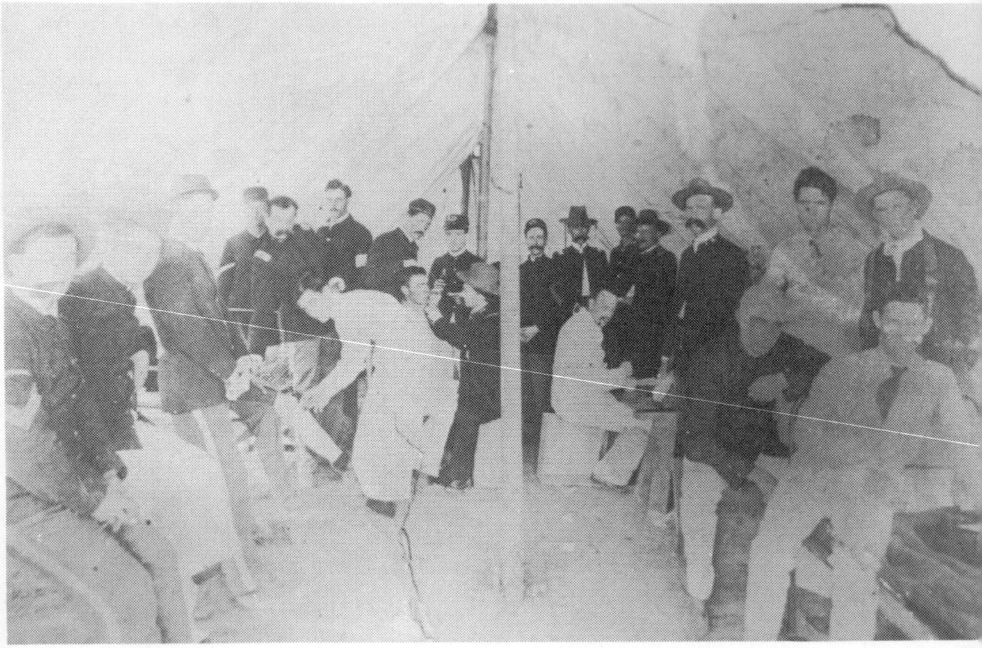

Sick call at Fort Concho Hospital Tent, ca. 1868, before the hospital was built. The man with the mustache is Lieutenant McHenry, Post Surgeon.

Courtesy Fort Concho Museum

scientist, or commander; he could also be counselor, chaplain, mapmaker, or veterinarian.

Military surgeons reported on conditions at the fort to their superiors in more civilized areas. Much of what is known of life on the frontier comes from the reports of the post surgeons.

These military doctors were responsible for the health of the post. They inspected the living conditions of the troops. One time, Assistant-Surgeon Henry McElderry at Fort Griffin recognized and reported the inadequacy of quartering six enlisted men together in small one-room picket huts. He pointed out those in tents during the winter months had "no means of heating except from kettles or pans of hot coals." This inadequate form of heating was a fire hazard as well. The doctor's requests were noted, but no improvements were forthcoming.

In a similar vein, Dr. Rufus Choate, a post surgeon at Phantom Hill, reported in 1872 about the poor ventilation in the sleeping quarters at the Mountain Pass station. Whenever a fire was built,

Dr. Southworth, First Texas Cavalry, Union Army
Courtesy Estate of Emmie Braubach Mauermann.
Copy from U.T. Institute of Texan Cultures, San Antonio

smoke kept the men from remaining in the room. He also said the roof leaked when it rained. In spite of Dr. Choate's report which resulted in the immediate requisition of building materials for better accommodations, little was done to the sub-station.

Dr. Notson, a military surgeon at Fort Concho, was much concerned with fire prevention measures at the hospital, particularly after someone took a shot at the belvedere one night, almost causing a fire. The belvedere, a structure on top of the hospital, was the highest point for miles on the prairie; a beacon was kept lighted there for those in sight of the post. For protection of the hospital building, Dr. Notson had eight large water buckets placed on a rack on the first floor, second floor, and loft. Axes and detailed instructions on fire fighting were provided. Even so, Dr. Notson expressed his concern about fire prevention to the Quartermaster General, who suggested that Dr. Notson requisition fire extinguishers. Dr. Notson did just that, and the fire extinguishers arrived nearly a year later.

The military surgeon made other recommendations for the welfare of the troops. Assistant Surgeon D. G. Caldwell noted in December 1874 at Fort Griffin, that at least half of the peacetime surgical cases were occasioned from the use of whiskey. Building a school-library building on the post proved to be a simple solution: it reduced drunkenness, while also providing "good readable novels" for the soldiers to read in their spare time.

The post surgeon, additionally, had to determine which soldiers had legitimate health complaints and which ones were guilty of malingering. Some used this path to avoid arduous frontier service, which required more from a soldier than carrying a weapon.

Of necessity, the soldier labored with axe, hammer, shovel, and saw. Engaged in hard labor in extreme daylight heat, a soldier then retired, usually in perspiration-soaked clothing, as in some parts of the state, the Texas temperature dropped with bone-chilling nightfall. Sometimes these conditions led to illness.

Little trauma was sustained due to enemy action. Troops were engaged in a more defensive role than offensive, and military doctors probably treated fewer battle casualties than other medical problems.

One such problem was scurvy. The post surgeon recognized the need for fresh fruits and vegetables and made recommendations on diet. These items were in short supply at all the forts. Procurement was difficult if not impossible. To compensate, Dr. A. Taylor at Fort Phantom Hill recommended adding pickles to the soldiers' rations to compensate for the lack of vegetables.

Post surgeons frequently recommended that soldiers plant gardens, especially onions, which were the easiest thing to grow. Wild onions were eagerly sought in the spring. With the limited supply of antiscorbutics, Dr. Notson of Fort Concho arranged for some watercress plants he obtained at Kickapoo Springs to be taken and planted along the Concho River.

Concerned with preventing other illnesses, the post surgeon reported on food spoilage and contamination, which often resulted from lack of refrigeration. Food poisoning was often a problem.

Another probable source of gastro-intestinal infections was a fort's water supply. The post surgeon was responsible for reporting and examining this source. For instance, he might recommend that wells and creeks be kept free of human and animal excretions, a sound and wise policy not always followed. Some soldiers believed that if water turned over five times at the site of contamination from a dead animal, it was "purified."

Examining the water supply at Fort Concho, Post Surgeon Notson in 1870 thought the post water barrels might be a source of contagion for many cases of fever, diarrhea, and a number of typhoid fatalities. Since these containers had become lined with fungoid growths and slimy decay of minute vegetable structures, Dr. Notson ordered the barrels partly filled with hay, and the hay fired until the interior was lined with a thick coat of charcoal.

Typical of other reports from the period, Dr. Choate at the Sub-Station at Mountain Pass reported in 1872 that the spring water was threatened with pollution from accumulated debris and trash.

In other sanitary measures, Dr. Daniel Weisel of Fort Davis tried unsuccessfully to get orders issued requiring every soldier to bathe at least twice a week during the summer months. The soldiers apparently thought they had cause to regret their failure to observe Dr. Weisel's warnings: the entire post suffered a smallpox epidemic in 1861.

Infectious diseases as we now know them were the post surgeons' most frequent problem, and most were generally classified in the broad category of "fevers." Giving a wide choice of diagnosis, Dunglison's medical dictionary listed 134 kinds of fevers, including depuratory fever, gastroangiotenic fever, singultus fever, tragic fever, and even erotic fever.

Fever differentiation was hardly necessary unless the patient had an obvious rash or diarrhea. All else was considered "malarial fever." The post surgeon used quinine so frequently his supply was often depleted. His only effective antimicrobials were mercury inunctions and calomel.

During a ten month period at Fort Richardson in 1868, out of 688 cases of sickness, the post surgeon treated 289 cases of "malarial fever" and 163 cases of "diarrhoea and dysentery." Two cases were designated phthisis, and one typhoid fever. Tuberculosis was diagnosed twice, but more cases may have been misdiagnosed as "catarrhal affection."

Post surgeons also treated venereal disease and, less frequently, delirium tremens and insanity. Sometimes they treated self-inflicted wounds, more rarely a suicide. The majority of wounds treated by post surgeons were from peace officers keeping the peace, barroom brawls, or kicks from mules and horses.

Health conditions and percentages of illnesses were not too dissimilar among the forts. For instance, at Fort Phantom Hill near Abilene, Dr. A. Taylor treated 363 cases of illness during a seven-month period of 1853. Of those, the most prevalent were ninety-one cases of intermittent fever.

According to the belief popular during the time of the forts, post surgeons relied on climate factors to explain a cause-and-effect relationship between environment and disease. A Fort McKavett doctor stated, "constant exposure to the hot sun is a prominent cause of disease and especially fevers." At the other extreme, Texas northers as far south as the Rio Grande were believed to cause winter diseases.

When the inevitable makeshift towns of camp followers established themselves just outside military forts, treating civilian medical problems in military medical facilities was not always clear-cut. Sometimes the post surgeon undertook this responsibility as well.

Apparently the frontier town near Fort Griffin in the early 1870s became so wild and rowdy that it was not safe for the fort's officers and enlisted men to go to the town unarmed. An admixture of saloons, gambling, cowpunchers, Indians, prostitutes, bowie knives, firearms, and little law and order led the post commander to declare the area within the government reservation. Further, he ordered transient gamblers, outlaws, and women to leave. The low-life, gambling, and drinking establishments rapidly disappeared.

Assistant Surgeon Rufus Choate was glad to see one desperado in particular, go: a barkeeper named Peppert (alias "Joe Bowers"), who had murdered two men and had not been brought to justice. Peppert had twice tried unsuccessfully to kill another man named Cockrell.

Cockrell and other wounded civilians were treated in the Post Hospital, anywhere from five days to seventy days. Dr. Choate expressed a criticism of this policy to his commanding officer: he felt the government was losing money because, as patients in the Post Hospital, they were paying less than they would pay for boarding in town.

Dr. Choate did not have to concern himself long with Cockrell's hospitalization: Peppert gunned him down on the third try.

Dr. Albert J. Myer, riding with his cavalry unit across the Texas plains in the 1850s, was far more fascinated with the Indians' smoke signals and beacon lights than fearful of the Indians' observations of the military unit.

He studied the Indians' communication methods and devised a system of signalling with flags by day and flaming torches by night. He perfected his system and was so confident of its success that in 1858 he took a seven-months' military leave of absence to demonstrate his signal system to authorities at Fort Hamilton, New York, and Old Point Comfort, Virginia.

Signaling rather than surgery must have been an overriding interest for Dr. Myer, as he became the chief signal officer of the U.S. Army. He set up the Signal Corps and was responsible for having military telegraph lines strung throughout the West to help troopers fight Indians. Dr. Myer successfully endeavored to make weather observations an official requirement in 1870, and he persuaded Congress to pass legislation which stated:

> That the Secretary of War be and is hereby authorized and required to provide for taking meteorological observations at the other points in the states and territories of the United States, and for giving notice on the northern lakes and on the sea coast by magnetic telegraph and marine signals of the approach and force of storms.

The United States Weather Bureau began its service to the public under the direction of Chief Signal Officer Myer.

Dr. William Notson, a veteran of the Battle of Gettysburg in the Civil War, was thirty-two years old when he arrived on the Texas frontier for duty at Fort Concho in December 1867. A graduate of Jefferson Medical College in Philadelphia, Dr. Notson was Chief Medical Officer at Fort Concho.

He chronicled data with many detailed observations in his monthly Medical History Reports to the Surgeon General's Office, from 1869 to 1872. While Dr. Notson was not a naturalist by education, his zoological observations are a contribution to the history of the Fort Concho area. He told of the large herds of buffalo nearby, white-tailed deer, antelope, wild cattle with long thin horns, wild horses, pumas, wildcats, lynxes, coyote, gray wolves, red foxes, beavers, prairie dogs, ground squirrels or gophers, mule-eared rabbits, and peccaries, muskhogs, and black bears twenty to thirty miles away from the fort. He identified many species of birds, and there were many he could not name. He found the rivers abounded in fish, and turtles and snakes were plentiful.

Dr. Notson also made many comments about the shortages at Fort Concho. After moving into the unfinished hospital in January 1869, the Medical Department was out of nearly everything including castor oil, iodide of potassium, chloroform, and stimulants. The next year, still wanting medical supplies, Dr. Notson carefully notated his correspondence and requisitions for the past seven months. By December 1870, he was bitter: the storeroom was vacant — bottles were empty.

Several Post Surgeons followed Dr. Notson at Fort Concho. They saw conditions improve by 1882 at Fort Concho, which were perhaps better than some of the other frontier posts.

After his marriage to Maria Brace in 1892, and a honeymoon in Italy, Dr. (Colonel) James P. Kimball and his bride arrived at Fort Clark. The doctor was obliged to assist military personnel, traders, travelers, and ranchers. He was also surgeon, dentist, and general practitioner.

Dr. Kimball's first notable case was officially reported as "a case of maggots in the nose." While taking a nap in the sun, a fly indigenous to the tropics deposited its larvae in the nostrils of a sleeping soldier. Dr. Kimball's astute treatment with chloroform destroyed the maggots and saved the man from suffocation.

In her diary, Mrs. Kimball records that Dr. Kimball was absorbed with many serious cases of "Texas Fever," which turned out to be typhoid, caused by a contaminated water supply. The doctor also was stricken, hovering at length between life and death, but finally recovering.

During the early years of Fort Mason, Post Surgeon Lafayette Guild enlisted the help of Colonel Charles Augustus May of the Second Dragoons at Fort Mason to perform some "medicine man" magic at a powwow with the Indians. Colonel May was a colorful, flamboyant character, his reputation and appearance equal to his size. Described as six feet, four inches tall, he weighed over two hundred pounds. His coarse brown hair hung well past his waist, and his beard was nearly as long.

Post Surgeon Guild had received a shipment of chloroform, the chemical whose anesthetic qualities had just been discovered. At the behest of the post commander, he apprised Colonel May of those qualities. Colonel May, in turn, was introduced to the Indians at the next big powwow as a powerful "medicine man." Colorfully garbed, awesome in size, he announced with much ceremony that his "med-

Dr. Joseph H. Barnard was one of the survivors of the Goliad massacre in 1836. Location of the original unknown.

Photocopy courtesy Archives, University of Texas Health Science Center, San Antonio

icine" was so powerful, he would demonstrate the power the Great White Father had given him to restore life to the dead.

When the braves refused his invitation to participate in a demonstration of proof, he took a small dog at his feet and announced he would prove his power with the little dog. Retiring to his tent with the dog, May quickly put the dog to sleep with the chloroform and then carried the apparently lifeless dog back outside. Then Colonel May made big medicine. While the Indians watched incredulously and the dog slept peacefully, May sliced off pieces of the dog's tail which he handed to each chief. May then announced that he would restore the dog to life. Soon he returned from the tent with the dog barking and running around very much alive.

Afterwards, the Fort Mason post commander had little trouble with the marauding Indians. Colonel May established a lifelong reputation as a great medicine man and possessor of "magic powers." Post Surgeon Guild became knowledgeable in the uses of chloroform; the Indian chiefs prized the pieces of the dog's tail as "big medicine," and carried the trophies in their medicine bags for a long time; and the little dog lived a dog's life, untroubled by a shorter tail.

Many doctors who came to the state as temporary Texans and served as soldiers, in time became permanent settlers. Putting down their guns and sabers, they practiced medicine, using scalpels, medical skills, and assorted talents to combat frontier foes in many guises.

Dr. Jack Shackelford who with other physicians was spared at the Goliad massacre to treat wounded Mexican soldiers.

Photocopy courtesy Archives, University of Texas
Health Science Center, San Antonio

Dr. James Webb Throckmorton, governor of the State of Texas, from a painting by Huddle.

Courtesy Archives Division, Texas State Library

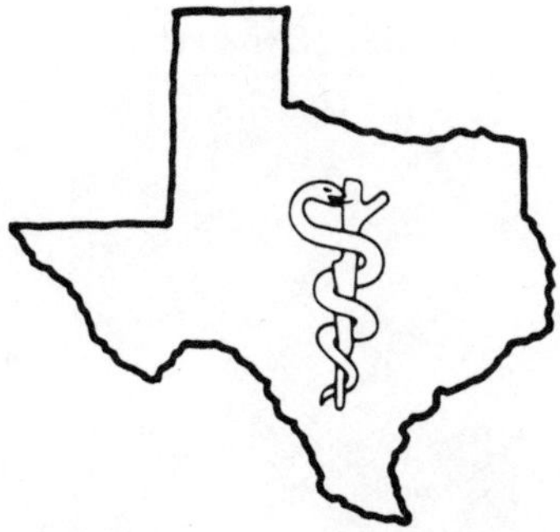

7

Building A State:
Medical Statesmanship

I have made it an invariable rule never to seek office, or to decline it when there appeared to me a necessity for my accepting public trust.

— Dr. Anson Jones

Better educated than most of their contemporaries, some doctors were leaders in frontier politics; some were rightly called "statesmen." The public turned to them for advice, particularly in running their government.

At various times doctors filled the following positions of prominence: president of the Republic, treasurer of the Republic, secretary of state, minister to England and France, governor of the state, legislator, and many other civic and county positions. In these capacities, they served their state well, sometimes at the expense of their medical practice. Despite various forms of self-sacrifice, their contributions to government added immeasurably to the growth and development of Texas.

Ashbel Smith, an outstanding man of medicine in the last century, was born in 1805 in Hartford, Connecticut. A versatile and talented man, he was a Latin and Greek scholar who later studied both law and medicine. He was graduated from Yale at the age of nineteen with a B.A. and an A.M. degree. To pay for his studies, he

Ashbel Smith: Known as "the Regent who bellowed fire," Dr. Ashbel Smith was a man of diverse talents: a Greek and Latin scholar, an early educator, an astute statesman, and a distinguished physician.

Courtesy Moody Medical Library of The University of Texas Medical Branch, Galveston

went to North Carolina for two years as a schoolteacher. He was highly regarded by both his students and the community.

Ambitious to broaden his horizons, however, he returned to Yale to study medicine. For further training, he went to France where he learned fluent French. In Paris, he became acquainted with notables of the day, including the Marquis de Lafayette. Upon his return to North Carolina, he established a medical practice and became part-owner and editor of a newspaper, the *Western Carolinian.*

Hearing about the Texas Revolution in 1836, he went to Texas in 1837 soon after the Battle of San Jacinto. He was appointed the Surgeon General of the Texas Army, for the Republic of Texas. He soon became a close friend of Sam Houston.

The new Republic needed the help of able men, and his diverse abilities were recognized. He was a leader in negotiating the first treaty with the Comanche Indians. After the completion of this task, he resigned from the army to settle in Galveston.

During the yellow fever epidemic of 1839, Dr. Smith treated many inhabitants there. His observations were later published, one of the first significant medical contributions printed and published in Texas.

In 1842, Dr. Smith became the first Minister Plenipotentiary to England and France for the Republic of Texas. In that position, he was able to promote the best interests of Texas. Due to his diverse diplomatic talents, the Republic of Texas remained on good terms with these countries during the uncertain years of the Republic.

As Secretary of State of the Republic under President Jones, Dr. Smith also negotiated a peace treaty with Mexico. Texas wanted to take steps to guarantee its independent state from Mexico, and Dr. Smith was responsible for negotiating with Mexico the Smith-Cuevas Treaty. The United States Congress, however, passed at this time a joint resolution offering annexation to Texas, an offer which was soon accepted, and Dr. Smith signed the preliminary treaty for annexation in 1845. His attempts to make peace with Mexico were misunderstood. He was even twice burned in effigy: once the result of his stand on the annexation of Texas and once the result of his coming out against the party tenets of the American or Know-Nothing Party, which caused much debate in the 1850s. This party discriminated against both Catholics and those foreign born, and Dr. Smith saw the dangers of such prejudices.

In the Mexican War of 1845, Dr. Smith was surgeon under General Zachary Taylor in Mexico. After this duty, he served in the Texas Legislature of 1855. He served both in the House of Representatives and the Senate in his later years.

Dr. Smith became quite noted as a speaker after the war. Because of his abilities and achievements, he was asked to address the United States Military Academy at West Point as well as the Phi Beta Kappa Society of Yale. He served in a variety of public service positions, such as American Commissioner to the London Industrial Exposition of 1851. The President of the United States asked him to be chairman of a board which reported on the condition of West Point.

Always involved in political issues, Dr. Smith, a slave owner, spoke openly against secession. Even so, after the Civil War developed, Dr. Smith became a soldier in the Confederacy and earned the rank of brigadier general with the Second Texas Infantry. Before this promotion, he served as colonel. At Shiloh, he was seriously wounded in the elbow.

After returning to Texas, he was given the task of defending Galveston Island as well as the Texas coast from an invasion by Federal forces. When the war was over, he was appointed commissioner along with William P. Ballinger to go to New Orleans to surrender Texas. By opposing the Ku Klux Klan in the Reconstruction period, he again adopted a far-sighted position.

One of his charitable endeavors involved treating the children in an orphanage in Harris County. Although Dr. Smith never married, he became a surrogate father to one small child. To facilitate treatment of her eyes, he lodged her in his home called Evergreen. Though he intended to take her back to the orphanage when her eyes were well, man and child developed a father-daughter affection. The young girl grew up in his bayside home as his daughter. After his death, the discovery of oil on his land made her wealthy.

Always a scholar, Dr. Smith was a collaborator of the American revised version of the *Bible* published in 1885. Despite his many obligations, he did not neglect his medical ties. He became President of the State Medical Association in 1881. He had been active in the organization of the State Medical Association of Texas in 1853, and he published many articles on medical procedures in the *American Journal of Medical Sciences*. Most of these appeared in print between 1835 and 1858. Dr. Smith was also influential in the passage of laws regulating the practice of medicine.

All of his endeavors were not successful. An attempt was made to establish a medical school in Houston in the 1850s. Even though $20,000 was raised, the institution never opened.

Much was accomplished, however, by this doctor who had ably served Texas and his country in so many capacities.

Two other leading physician-statesmen of the Republic of Texas shared much in common. Both Dr. Anson Jones and Dr. Branch Archer settled in Brazoria, and became active leaders of the Masons and other organizations.

They clashed, however, on more than one occasion. Dr. Archer at one point challenged Dr. Jones to a duel, a challenge that Dr. Jones declared was invalid because no personal wrong had been committed. Dr. Archer, secretary of war at the time, let the matter drop. More important challenges awaited them.

Anson Jones, whose mother had blood ties with the English Protector Oliver Cromwell, was the thirteenth child of a Massachusetts family. His family had decided that he should be a physician, and even though he seemed to prefer a career in printing, he became

Anson Jones, the "architect of annexation," was the last president of the Republic of Texas.

Courtesy Archives Division, Texas State Library

an apprentice under a physician at the age of eighteen. He also attended lectures at Jefferson Medical College, where he received the degree of Doctor of Medicine in 1827.

In 1832, he moved to New Orleans, a city of many temptations. There he developed bad habits from too much drinking and gambling. He came to Texas in 1835.

Dr. Jones settled in Brazoria where, with several friends, he established the first lodge of Freemasons in Texas. In December 1835, he was chairman of a committee which drew up resolutions in favor of Texas independence, the first resolutions of the kind.

After the fall of the Alamo, Dr. Jones enrolled in the army as a private. He was appointed judge advocate to consider cases of insubordination. By request, he later became Surgeon of the Second Regiment.

He disobeyed an order to assist Hospital Surgeon Phelps in order to join the army moving toward Santa Anna prior to the Battle of San Jacinto. After the battle, he was promoted to Apothecary

General. In the line of duty, he was sent to New Orleans to obtain medical supplies for the new Republic.

After the war, Anson Jones returned to Brazoria where he planned to practice medicine, but being keenly interested in public issues, he was persuaded by his friends to run for Congress. During his campaign, Anson Jones wrote letters protesting the charter for the Texas Railroad, Navigation, and Banking Company promoted by some of his fellow townsmen from Brazoria, including Dr. Branch Archer. He signed these letters "Franklin," hoping Texans would recognize a scheme that he considered not in the best interests of thrifty citizens. His election to the Second Congress in 1837 affirmed his stance. The next year, he married Mary McCrory. Their license was the second issued in Travis County.

While Lamar was President of the Republic, Anson Jones became a Senator. Because of his diplomatic experience, he became chairman of the committee on foreign relations, a committee composed of several other doctors, including Francis Moore, Jr., editor of the *Houston Telegraph and Texas Register.* During Sam Houston's second term as President of the Republic, Jones served as Secretary of State. Then Dr. Anson Jones became the last President of the Republic of Texas in 1844.

When the Congress of the United States passed resolutions desiring the annexation of Texas on 1 March 1845, President Jones called for a popular vote on the matter. After the mandate from the people, he surrendered the government of Texas on 19 February 1846. In his final address, he declared, "The Republic of Texas is no more."

Dr. Ashbel Smith commented on President Jones's position:

> What was President Anson Jones's opinion on this cardinal matter. I was clearly of the belief that he would have preferred independence to annexation. He subsequently declared himself the most decided friend and promoter of annexation. In conducting affairs during this critical period, he never for a moment forgot that he was the representative of the people, not their ruler.

Dr. Smith declared in later years:

> . . . I look back with admiration on the sublime calmness of Mr. Jones, who pursued the unruffled tenor of duty amidst threats, denunciations and falsehoods in newspapers, in public speeches, amidst insiduous plots to betray him into fatal measures and to overturn his administration.

Dr. Smith went on to say:

> In these trying and difficult times Anson Jones indulged in none of the cheap sentimental Americanism then so rife — he made no professions, he was carried away by no false enthusiasm — he did not despair of the fortune of Texas — he was not blown about — he did not falter — and, with consumate wisdom, he did not precipitate action. With him it was at all times the calm transaction of business. Peace offered he would present it to the people. But within reach at the same time, he would present both to the people for their option, for their selection, for their determination. His personal preference for annexation or for peace did not mould, did not bias his action as chief executive officer of Texas. The foreign ministers believed him lukewarm on annexation — they did not err — he manfully and honestly did his duty.

After retiring from service to the Republic of Texas, Dr. Jones spent most of his efforts on a business venture: the growing Atlantic and Pacific Railroad.

In 1844, he built a home called Barrington after his hometown in Massachusetts. This was located on his property near old Washington-on-the Brazos. In 1857, he sold his home with the intention of moving to Galveston to practice.

He was despondent, however, by the seemingly ingratitude of the people of Texas who did not choose to send him to the Senate of the United States, a position that he felt he had earned. He committed suicide at the Capitol Hotel in Houston 9 January 1858. At the time he told a friend, "Here in this house twenty years ago I commenced my political career in Texas, and here I would like to end it."

Branch Tanner Archer, known to some as the Father of the Texas Revolution, was a Virginian by birth, his family linked with some of the most prominent in the Commonwealth. He attended the College of William and Mary and received his medical degree in 1808 from the University of Pennsylvania. After finishing his training, he practiced medicine in Virginia. He served as captain in Colonel Thomas Randolph's Virginia Militia in the War of 1812, and in 1819 and 1820, he served two terms in the Virginia House of Delegates.

Archer's interest in politics led to an unfortunate duel in which he killed another man, James Otway Crump. Archer had tried to prevent the duel, and he was later acquitted from the charge of murder on 21 May 1828. Whether the turmoil caused by this affair was the cause of Dr. Archer's move to Texas is not known, but he arrived in Matagorda in 1831. After walking to San Felipe to see Stephen F. Austin, Dr. Archer settled in Brazoria.

He was not destined to peacefully practice medicine. With his political background, he soon became involved in the unrest of the times. In December 1831, Dr. Archer was present at a mass meeting in Brazoria to protest the hated customs regulations set up by Mexico. Dr. Archer was one of the first to advocate separation from Mexico, loudly proclaiming the cause of liberty. At the same time, Dr. Archer sent a circular to the United States hoping to arouse the people against the tyranny which existed in Texas. His words claimed:

> The war dogs are unkennelled. The scent of blood grows upon the breeze, and the cry of 'Liberty to the rescue' lingers upon the tongues of the heroic. The Goddess of Liberty has been barbarously violated in these realms and we feel that we have a right to call our brethren of the North to aid us in rescuing her from further pollution.

Dr. Archer was involved in the Convention of 1833, when grievances were drawn up against Mexico. A Consultation was held in November 1835, and he was elected President. He was in favor of Independence but the majority of delegates were not ready. The Consultation also voted Branch Archer, Stephen F. Austin, and William H. Wharton to act as commissioners to go to the United States seeking aid in money and supplies for the Texan cause. The men did not leave until the end of the year, and due to illness and other delays, the journey took them many months. They found support in Washington and wrote back on 3 March 1836, that the Texans should declare their independence. But one day earlier, the declaration had already been made thousands of miles away in Texas.

Dr. Archer did not arrive back in Texas until 13 July 1836. The long journey had been a success, and the events which transpired in his absence proved the validity of the mission.

In appreciation for Dr. Archer's role in promoting independence, he was elected to the House of Representatives of the First Congress of the Republic of Texas.

Dr. Archer was one of the chief promoters of the Texas Railroad, Navigation and Banking Company, chartered by the First Congress. This venture was not successful.

An able politician, Dr. Archer was chosen Speaker of the

House of the second session of the First Congress, June 1838. Dr. Archer worked for the election of Mirabeau B. Lamar, 1838–1841. After Lamar took office, he appointed Dr. Archer secretary of war. During this time a ship, the *Archer,* was named for him, one of four vessels turned over to the United States after the annexation of Texas.

In spite of his active political career, Dr. Archer continued to practice medicine until several years before his death in 1856. One of his sons followed his father's footsteps, not only by graduating from his father's school, the University of Pennsylvania Medical School but also by practicing medicine in Velasco. This son was killed in the Civil War.

Both Archer County and Archer City were named for Branch T. Archer. An editorial from the *Northern Standard* of 11 October 1856, shows something of his character:

> He is gone and we shall see few like him — with a gentlemanly simplicity of character, combined with a Roman nerve, and stern high sense of duty. . . . He was a part of the old Republic, and a fixture of Velasco.

Dr. James Harper Starr, a native of Connecticut, educated in Ohio, opened his first practice in the state of Georgia. There he settled his father-in-law's estate and became involved in various financial enterprises. When some of these ventures did not work out as planned, he and his wife came to Texas. They traveled overland in a covered wagon, accompanied by one faithful slave, Tempie.

Dr. Starr became land commissioner in Nacogdoches. In 1839, he was appointed Secretary of the Treasury by President Lamar and came to be called Financier of the Republic. Dr. Starr resigned after one year to return to the practice of medicine in Nacogdoches.

As a family physician, Dr. Starr was in demand. He had a hard time, however, making his practice pay. Many patients did not settle their bills, even though he charged according to the distance he had to travel and the cost of the medicines prescribed. To keep solvent, he began a real estate business on the side. Since this profitable business took much of his time, he reluctantly gave up his medical practice.

Dr. Starr also became a banker, the first in Nacogdoches. Through many business ventures, Dr. Starr accumulated considerable wealth.

Dr. Starr was active in political matters, an enemy of Sam

Houston and an active supporter of Lamar and David G. Burnet. He favored annexation to the United States, using his influence in support of this move. He also influenced the coming of the railroad to Nacogdoches.

Prior to the Civil War, Dr. Starr opposed secession from the union, even though he owned slaves himself. When it became obvious that the South had little choice, however, he did what he could to support the southern cause. He was too old to serve in combat, but among other services, he turned his home into a workshop where cloth was spun.

During the war, Dr. Starr moved to Marshall to serve as postal agent for the West. After the defeat of the confederacy, he lost this appointment and moved back to Nacogdoches. There Dr. Starr fought against injustices regarding the civil rights of Negroes, particularly the unfair practice of assessing severe penalties for minor crimes.

The Reconstruction period was a hard time for Dr. Starr. He lost many of his holdings because of debts. Despite these difficulties, he continued in real estate, and many people relied upon his business acumen. He handled the land for Nacogdoches University. Many of his friends named him executor of their wills. In 1870, continued hard times prompted another move to Marshall where he and his son established the first bank.

Dr. Starr had long been interested in higher education. Early in his career, he raised money for the establishment of Nacogdoches University in 1845, one of the earliest universities in Texas. He was later appointed trustee for the University of Eastern Texas. He worked to establish The University of Texas at Austin and was asked to serve on the first Board of Regents. Poor health forced him to decline this appointment.

Dr. Starr died in Marshall in poor health in 1890. His contributions to the development of Texas were numerous, and a county named in his honor is a living memorial to his various efforts.

Dr. Richard Roman, a Kentuckian with a degree from the University of Transylvania, came to Texas as many others in 1836. He enlisted in Sam Houston's army as first lieutenant and was later elected Captain of Company C. During the Republic, he was elected to a seat from Victoria County in the House of the First Congress. He also served in the Third congress. In the Ninth and last Congress, he was a Senator.

During the Mexican War, Dr. Roman enlisted in the United

States Army as a private, and attained the rank of major by the end of the war when he was wounded in the Battle of Monterey. Dr. Roman later moved to California where he held several state offices.

Dr. Lorenzo de Zavala, a native of Merida, Mexico, was one of seven doctors who signed the Texas Declaration of Independence. His loyalty to the Texas cause may be explained by his family connections as well as his personal experience serving with Santa Anna. While connected with the Mexican Legation at Washington, he married a charming American woman.

Dr. de Zavala served the Mexican government in many capacities: legislator in the Mexican Congress, Governor of the State of Mexico, National Minister of Finance, and Minister to France. Believing Santa Anna a tyrant, however, he resigned and moved to Texas in 1835.

He acquired land on Buffalo Bayou near Harrisburg. It was his nature to be involved in political matters, and he soon became a friend of Stephen F. Austin, Lamar, and other men of influence. He chaired a committee of public safety, the purpose of which was to secure men and arms for the Texas cause.

Following the Battle of San Jacinto, many of the wounded soldiers were carried to the plantation home of Dr. de Zavala near the battlefield.

As an elected delegate to the Consultation of 1835 and the Convention of 1836, he was one of the men who drafted the Texas Declaration of Independence. His compatriots also designated him to help write the Constitution of the Republic of Texas. Dr. de Zavala also became Vice-President of the *ad interim* government of the Republic of Texas. Lamar referred to him as "the gentleman, the scholar, and the patriot."

The physicians who signed the Texas Declaration of Independence written by George C. Childress at Washington-on-the-Brazos on 2 March 1836 were:

(1) George W. Barnett (never practiced in Texas)
(2) Stephen H. Everitt
(3) Thomas J. Gazley
(4) Benjamin B. Goodrich
(5) William Mottley
(6) Charles B. Stewart
(7) Lorenzo de Zavala

The Texas Declaration of Independence was signed by seven

physicians who risked their lives for the future of Texas. The *Medical Record and Annals* of March 1965, had this about the man:

> . . . They were an interesting lot. Two never practiced medicine in Texas at all. Two more practiced medicine in Texas for less than three years. Five had been in Texas less than two years. Only one was born west of the Alleghenies and he was a former Mexican citizen. Most of them were accomplished politicians. One was a lawyer; one was a farmer; one, a captain of the Texas Rangers; four served in the Texas Legislature; one was a vice-president of Texas; one was killed at the Battle of San Jacinto; one was a former governor of the state of Mexico; one was a liquor merchant who recommended his 40 cents per gallon whiskey for those who only professed to be friends, and for those seeking public office; one was killed by Indians; one provided the original star for the seal of Texas; and one had a country named after him, but the name was misspelled. It is from cloth such as this that freedom is fashioned.

Dr. George Barnett served in the Senate of the Republic of Texas 1837–1843. He later lived in Gonzales until his death by Indians on the Guadalupe River fifteen miles from his home.

Dr. Benjamin B. Goodrich, one of the signers of the Texas Declaration of Independence, had a brother who died at the Alamo. Goodrich wrote a stirring letter home to his relatives about the death of his brother.

Dr. Charles Bellinger Stewart was a member of several conventions, first at San Felipe de Austin in 1832 and 1833, then at Brazoria in 1834. He was a member of the central committee of vigilance at Velasco, and perhaps because he spoke fluent Spanish, he became secretary to the Mexican Supreme Court in 1834. He also served on a committee which issued a protest against the policies of the Mexican government in 1835. Dr. Stewart was appointed secretary of a Council organized by Stephen F. Austin which was called "the Committee of Safety and Vigilance of San Felipe."

Just prior to independence, Dr. Stewart was a delegate from Austin to the Convention 1 March 1836. He also served on the committee to draft a constitution.

After the war, Dr. Stewart became a Senator in the Republic of Texas from 1837 to 1843. With such experience as a delegate, it was not surprising that Dr. Stewart was again a representative to the convention in Washington in 1845 when annexation was discussed.

Dr. Stephen H. Everitt will be remembered for his words as he signed the Declaration of Independence. "This is the proudest act of my life. By it I may have forfeited it, but I will die like a freeman should die, battling against tyranny."

Dr. Everitt later served in the Senate of the Republic in the First, Second, Third, Fourth, and Fifth Congresses. He was appointed mail contractor in 1836, quartermaster for the Eastern Division of Texas, and commissioner of public property for the Jasper District.

Following annexation, many doctors served the State of Texas. Dr. James Throckmorton, who was born in Tennessee in 1825, was one of these. During the Mexican War, he was a surgeon with the Texas Rangers. After the war, he settled in Collin County where he practiced until 1859.

Dr. Throckmorton was elected to the Legislature in 1851, and again in 1853, serving six years followed by eight years in the State Senate. While there, he was in agreement with Sam Houston that secession was not the answer to the problems of the nation.

As an elected representative, he attended the Secession Convention in Austin in 1861, casting a vote against secession. His was one of seven opposing votes. After his action, the gallery responded with both applause and hisses, causing Dr. Throckmorton's famous statement: "My President, when the rabble hiss, well may patriots tremble." This comment spoken so quickly brought the whole convention to applause.

In spite of his opposition, he served four years in the Confederate Army, being promoted from captain to brigadier general.

Following the Civil War, Dr. Throckmorton became Governor of Texas in 1866, by a vote of four to one. He dispensed his duties in a sensible manner, making every effort to restore harmony to the state and national government. However, authorities of the federal government were determined to replace him with their own candidate. He was deposed by General Sheridan in 1867, after one year's service to the state of Texas.

Dr. Throckmorton did not resume the practice of medicine after his retirement from public service. Instead, he studied law, becoming a successful and respected attorney. Although Throckmorton County was named for his father, Dr. William Edward Throckmorton, the naming probably intentionally honored the politically prominent son, Dr. James Throckmorton.

Dr. David C. Dickson served as Lieutenant Governor in 1853.

Dr. James Webb Throckmorton

Biographical Souvenir of Texas.
Chicago: F. A. Battey & Company, 1889

This physician, who was one of the charter members of the Texas Medical Association, lost his race for Governor in 1855.

Dr. Beriah Graham served as State Treasurer in 1872. He was chairman of the Sixth Ward. This graduate of Transylvania and St. Louis Medical College had also served as Superintendent of the State Lunatic Asylum in 1859 and again in 1865–1868. After serving in public office, Dr. Graham opened a drugstore in 1874, as did many physicians of the time.

Dr. W. G. W. Jowers of Palestine was defeated in a bid for Lieutenant Governor in 1855. He was another charter member of the Texas Medical Association.

Dr. John R. Simms, who arrived in 1852, was a candidate for senator from Williamson County, 1857.

Dr. M. A. Taylor, an Austin physician who arrived in 1851, was actively involved in the fight to oppose secession. Others who opposed secession were General Sam Houston, Dr. Ashbel Smith, and Dr. James Throckmorton. Nevertheless, the people of Texas voted for secession on 2 March 1861.

Dr. Taylor was chairman of the commission for Relief of Soldier Families, 1856–1865, as well as a trustee of the State Lunatic Asylum during 1856–65, 1870. He served as alderman in 1874, in 1876, and in 1877. He was also on the Board of Health for Austin.

On the other hand, Dr. George Bickley (Brickley) was pro-secession. He was appointed to the faculty of the Eclectic Medical Institute of Cincinnati before the Civil War. In the four months after he joined the faculty, he wrote a book on botany, several thousand pages of manuscript lectures, hundreds of pages of newspaper correspondence, and a three hundred page novel, which was translated into French and German.

While at the school, he was one of the organizers of a secret society known as the "Knights of the Golden Circle," an organization which had 17,000 members at one time. Many of the members were slave-owners and they dreamed of an extension of slavery from the southern states through Central and South America. There was talk of invading Mexico and setting up a military government there. While the Mexican leader, Benito Juarez, was in exile in the United states, he offered the Knights grants of land and other gifts in exchange for their support. President Lincoln did what he could to suppress the organization since he felt the Knights were pro-Southern. In Texas, the Knights had a major part in the secession movement.

Some physicians served as ministers abroad. Dr. Ashbel Smith was Minister to England and France during the days of the Republic of Texas, as noted earlier. Dr. Ralph Steiner of Austin became consul to Munich, Germany, late in the century.

Other physicians actively served political parties. Dr. John G. Chalmers organized the Democratic Party in Austin. He gave a keynote speech, probably the first such speech at a convention in this state.

Dr. A. H. Parrish, who had arrived in Texas in 1855, was chosen as delegate to the National Democratic Convention in 1860. He also was involved in the Rump Convention in Baltimore that same year. Four years earlier he cast the Texas vote in the electoral college for John Cabell Breckinridge who became Vice-President of the United States under James Buchanan. Dr. Parrish died in 1873.

Dr. J. W. McComb of Jacksboro made a contribution to strengthening the organization of the Democratic Party by becoming Chairman of the Democratic Executive Committee in 1888.

Daring Doctor

In the tense political situation following the Civil War, a Democrat, Dr. W. H. Wilkes, member of the Waco Medical Association, assisted at the polls in the congressional election of 1871. At that time, the radical element in the Republican administration following the assassination of Lincoln, did not make it easy for members of the Democratic party to cast their votes. Dr. Wilkes, disregarding personal danger, guarded the polls with pistol in holster for four days and nights, only alternating with a fellow Democrat for short snatches of sleep. The box did go Democratic, an indication that the threats and intimidations of the radical scalawags had failed.

Dr. David Wallace believed in encouraging independent thinking and voting. While he was Superintendent of the Insane Asylum, he refused to follow the custom of voting the employees as one slate. When one employee asked Dr. Wallace how he should vote, he replied: "I want you to vote just like I vote." The employee then asked how that would be. Dr. Wallace quickly replied, "Just as I damn please."

Often active in community affairs, many doctors served as mayors. In 1856, the first mayor of Dallas was Dr. Samuel Pryer, "Old Doc Pryer."

Dr. Samuel G. Haynie, mayor of Austin for two terms, 1850–1852, was prominent in the affairs of the Capitol City. He served as postmaster as well as legislator. Enterprising as both druggist and merchant, he owned a general store for almost ten years from 1856 to 1865. Although he practiced until his death in 1877, he was also Commissioner in charge of the construction for the State Capitol, and he was active in the building of St. David's Episcopal Church. He served as a leader of the temperance movement as well.

Dr. J. H. Lyons was mayor of San Antonio in 1865. His term was interrupted by the provisional government. He was later reinstated, and in 1867, Dr. Lyons was elected mayor and served until November of that year. Dr. Lyons commendably carried out his duties, even during these difficult years of Reconstruction. Dr. Lyons was a charter member of the Texas Medical Association.

The duties of some mayors consisted of more than presiding at gala affairs. In 1899, Dr. A. W. Fly, the mayor of Galveston, took charge of the police force, with pistol in hand, to overcome a labor riot.

Dr. W. P. Burts, the second civilian doctor to practice in Fort

Worth, became in 1873 the first Mayor after the city had incorporated. Dr. Burts, who had practiced there since 1858, had given up his practice in 1872 to engage in the mercantile business. His long interest in health care was evident, however, in one of his first official acts as Mayor. He promoted an ordinance to establish a Board of Health. He returned to his medical practice after serving his term as Mayor. Surprisingly, his office was located between the White Elephant Saloon and a gambling establishment.

Dr. John S. Rip Ford served as Mayor of Austin. In 1854, he called a meeting to discuss protecting the slave owners whose slaves were running away to Mexico. Vigilante committees were organized to prevent slaves from associating with Mexicans who were thought to encourage them.

Earlier, Dr. Ford had been elected to the Congress of the Republic of Texas. While there, he helped frame the bill annexing Texas to the United States in 1848. At the Democratic Convention of 1856, Dr. Ford and J. M. Steiner apologized for their brief defection to the party of Know Nothingism. Dr. Ford also served as a Senator from Brownsville in 1876.

Physicians served in other public offices. Dr. J. B. Robertson, an Austin physician, was elected Superintendent of the Bureau of Immigration.

Dr. John Sutherland became the first postmaster at Sutherland Springs, the town he founded.

A Dr. Howard was the Postmaster of San Antonio after a varied career. He was a soldier in the Civil War and then he became an associate in the large mercantile establishment of Howard and Ogden.

Ever ready to serve their country and community, patriotic physicians helped lead Texas to independence. Some then guided the Republic; others led the path toward annexation. Later, as Texas became a part of the United States, physicians in a variety of public service offices added to the growth of the new state which emerged strong in the Union.

8

Leaving a Mark:
Vocations and Avocations

Wanted for a family who have had bad health, a sober, steady person in the capacity of doctor, surgeon, apothecary and man mid-wife. He must occasionally act as butler, and dress hair and wigs. He will be required sometimes to read prayers, and to preach a sermon every Sunday. A good salary will be given.

— From an old advertisement referred to in a speech
by President Coleman to the TMA in 1896.

Many nineteenth century physicians had diversified careers in addition to their practice of medicine. By having other interests and engaging in other occupations, they made significant contributions to science, culture, education, and business. More often than not, these other careers unrelated to medicine necessarily supplemented a doctor's medical income.

Many early doctors with a natural curiosity and background in science conducted laboratory experiments to determine causes and cures of illnesses. Others who traveled with expeditions or who were stationed at military forts on the frontier observed, selected, and recorded natural data. They collected fossils and specimens of plants and animals to send to the Smithsonian for use in the Pacific Railroad Reports. There, the data and specimens were analyzed and studied, arranged, classified, and cataloged. These scientific observations became valuable records for posterity. Many doctors also made scientific contributions in other fields of science, such as geology, horticulture, and meteorology.

Dr. T. C. Osborn of Cleburn was a doctor who leaned toward scientific investigation. Lifelong, he searched for the cause of malaria. For sixty years, on most days, Dr. Osborn would ready his horse and saddlebags or wagon and team to make calls around the countryside on patients who were hurt or ill.

But most nights during those sixty years, Dr. Osborn worked in his homemade laboratory, seeking the cause and cure of malaria. While that success eluded him, he discovered in his experimentation the use of bichloride of mercury solution in the treatment of smallpox rash.

Curiosity also enabled Dr. Ferdinand Herff, a prominent physician and scientific researcher, to discover the hookworm in 1864 because of his knowledge of similar conditions in Europe. Herff also recorded observations on parasites of entozoa. His additional interest in botany stemmed from his student days in Bonn, Germany.

Sometimes early settlers were suspicious of science and scientific endeavors. This attitude affected a doctor's activities as in the case of Dr. Weidemann.

A fight between Indians and settlers outside San Antonio in 1840, required the dual skill of Dr. Eduard Weidemann, an assistant surgeon in the Texan army. He was later praised for his use of rifle and scalpel.

After the battle, however, the doctor's bent for scientific research received, perhaps, unjust attention. Much to the consternation of the townsfolk, Dr. Weidemann brought into town two severed Indian heads and two Indian cadavers. The people did not understand why a compassionate doctor would want the grisly trophies, but he explained he long had wanted such specimens for research.

That explanation might have passed in time without repercussion, but Dr. Weidemann wanted the bones without the bodies. That night, he prepared a huge kettle of water and boiled the bodies and heads to loosen the flesh from the bones. Saving the precious skeletons for study, before dawn he disposed of the unwholesome liquid in the water of the Acequia Ditch. Little sleep after a hard night's work ill-prepared him for the wrath of an outraged town.

San Antonians customarily laundered clothes and bathed in the river, but they used the clear water of the Acequia only for drinking.

When the people discovered what Dr. Weidemann had done, they thought they had been drinking water polluted with Indian bits. Havoc and hysteria reigned. An angry crowd took Dr. Weidemann by force, and he was then arrested and jailed.

When he was brought to trial, this gentle man was astounded at the furor he had caused. He explained to the judge that the noxious liquid he had put in the Acequia Ditch had quickly washed on downstream with the free-flowing water. He assured the court that no one had ingested "Indian soup."

Convinced for the most part, the court let Dr. Weidemann off with a heavy fine, assuring him that if it were not for his previous good reputation, he would have been run out of town at gunpoint.

Dr. Weidemann's bent for scientific research was undeterred. He often sent collected materials to a museum in St. Petersburg.

Dr. John Milton Bigelow (1804–1878) was a botanist of the U.S. and Mexican Boundary Survey 1850–1853. He gave up his practice in Boston to serve in this capacity. He made an extensive botanical collection during his travels. A specific scientific name for a type of glasswort was named for Dr. Bigelow, *Salicornia bigelowii.*

Dr. Jean Louis Berlandier (d. 1851) collected plants and animals in south Texas and northern Mexico in the first part of the nineteenth century. Originally a botanist, Berlandier arrived in Mexico in 1826. He was commissioned by scientists in Europe to bring back specimens of flora and fauna from the new world. Joining the Mexican Boundary Commission, he traveled over sections of Texas in the late 1820s. In later expeditions, he also gathered material in the San Saba River area and around the city of Goliad. Bad weather, insects, and malaria were only some of the obstacles he encountered.

In spite of these problems, he collected over 50,000 specimens, as well as many sample insects and small animals. Nevertheless, the ingratitude of his sponsors caused Berlandier to break ties with them. He settled in the city of Matamoros and became a respected physician and chief of hospitals in that city. Now he is best remembered for his natural history contributions, which early added to the knowledge of a sparsely settled country.

Dr. Edwin James (1797–1861), surgeon and naturalist, was a part of Major S. H. Long's second expedition to the Rocky Mountains in 1820. He is credited with beginning "scientific exploration in Texas." During this adventure, Dr. James and others traveled down the Canadian River, now part of the Texas Panhandle, making a collection of fossils and various plants native to the region. These were later described by Dr. John Torrey in the Pacific Railroad Reports.

Some doctors chronicled their scientific explorations. The first to write about the exploration of Callahan County was a Dr. H. C. Connelly, of the Chihuahua Expedition in 1839.

Dr. Josiah Gregg's training included law, mathematics, astronomy, and the classics. He made eight journeys over the Santa Fe Trail from 1831 to 1841. He reported his experiences in a journal published in 1844, which overnight became a classic.

Many army doctors stationed in the numerous forts of frontier Texas had sterling opportunities to collect specimens of plants, animals, fossils, and flowers — in largely unexplored, and unrecorded areas.

Dr. Samuel Wylie Crawford (1829–1892) was an army surgeon in Texas from 1851 to 1860, at Fort Clark, near the present Bracketville. While there, he sent to the Smithsonian Institution large collections of vertebrates from the vicinity of Fort Clark and Las Moras Springs.

Dr. W. L. Diffenderfer was a part of Captain John Pope's expedition as a surgeon in 1854. The findings of his collection of plant and animal life were later published by Torrey and Gray in Volume II of the Pacific Railroad Reports.

Dr. Andrew Jackson Foard (d. 1867), was attached to Fort Davis as an army surgeon. He sent mammals and other materials to the Smithsonian Institution from that area. He also sent large collections of Texas vertebrates for Volume IX of the Pacific Railroad Reports.

Dr. S. Hays was probably an army surgeon at Fort Belknap and sent material from that region to the Smithsonian Institution in 1859.

Dr. William Shakespeare King (d. 1895) was another army surgeon who sent mammals to the Smithsonian Institution. His specimens were later used in the Pacific Railroad Reports.

Dr. Zina Pitcher (1797–1852) collected fossil and plant material along the Red River in 1833. He sent them to a Dr. S. G. Morton of Philadelphia. These specimens were used in Dr. Morton's *Synopsis of Cretaceous Fossils of the United States,* in 1834. Later Dr. Pitcher was instrumental in founding the Medical School of the University of Michigan.

Dr. Henry McElderry (d. 1898), another army surgeon in the

late 1860s with the troops on the Upper Brazos, collected fossils and sent them to the Smithsonian Institution.

Also making scientific observations was Dr. Wilhelm Remer who came to Texas with the German immigration of 1845. He was one of the famous Breslau family of scientists.

Dr. Ebenezer Swift (1819–1885), stationed in charge of Fort Chadbourne from about 1853 to 1856, sent material from that area to the Smithsonian.

Dr. Heinrich Poselger collected plants during the period 1850–1856 for the U.S. and Mexican Boundary Survey on the lower Rio Grande, and near Corpus Christi. He sent his collection of cacti to Dr. David Dietrich, custodian of the Jena Herbarium. Poselger's descriptions of cacti are listed in the 1859 report of "Cacti of the U.S. and Mexican Boundary Survey."

Dr. Adolphus Schlottmann studied medicine in Germany and came to Texas in 1853. He was an apothecary and physician at Round Top in Fayette County. He sent his collection of insects to the Smithsonian in 1872.

Dr. Redfield Sharp, while stationed in San Antonio as an army surgeon, collected insects and reptiles in alcohol. He sent them to the Smithsonian in 1866.

Dr. James Cushing Merrill (1858–1921) was an army surgeon who sent many specimens to museums. He also wrote "Notes on the Ornithology of Southern Texas."

Dr. Louis Joseph Frederic LeClerc (b. 1810), a Frenchman associated with the medical school and hospital of Tours, evidently came to Texas in the summer of 1838. He was the first to describe the famous San Felipe deposits of Pleistocene mammals. Later he wrote an article, subsequently published in book form, on the Texas Revolution.

Dr. Rudolph Menger (1851–1921) made observations on nature and recorded his reminiscences, which were later published in 1913, as *Texas Nature Observations and Reminiscences.* He was listed in the first directory of San Antonio. He had studied at Leipzig, and received an M.D. degree there.

Dr. E. M. Walker (d. 1868) graduated from Medical School at the University of Louisiana. After intense study of the agricultural ant of Texas, Dr. Walker presented a widely acclaimed paper on that subject to the New Orleans Academy of Sciences in 1854. He practiced medicine in Yorktown, Texas.

Dr. Francis Moore (d. 1864), the well-known newspaper editor, became State Geologist of Texas in 1860. Dr. Moore was the author of many natural history articles relating to Texas as well as a book, *Map and Description of Texas* published in Philadelphia in 1840. Early in his career, he served as a surgeon in the Texan Army of 1836.

In 1885, several officers of the Central Texas Horticultural Society were doctors. Among the vice-presidents were Dr. B. Miller of Dallas, and Dr. Stewart of Fort Worth. In 1884, the Pilot Point Horticultural Society was organized under the leadership of Dr. A. M. Ragland, President, and Dr. T. N. Wylie, Treasurer.

Dr. Ragland, who practiced medicine at Pilot Point, was also the originator of the San Jacinto apple and Dayton plum. Dr. Ragland had a medical degree from Tulane and also had practiced at Shelbyville, Texas. For his achievements and fruit exhibit, he received a bronze medal at the Louisiana Purchase Exposition of 1904. He was also involved in commercial canning and preserving.

Journalism was another field of interest for Dr. Ragland who was the horticultural editor of various publications. With John Howell, he edited the horticultural news of *Texas Farm and Ranch,* published in Austin from 1884 to 1896. Dr. Ragland was also editor of the *Horticulturist* organized in 1888 at Pilot Point. Some of his articles were "Pear Growing for Profit" and "Our Insect Enemies."

A graduate of the University of Berlin, Dr. Eduard Friedrich Becker was interested in many scientific fields when he arrived in Texas in the 1850s. When he settled in Frelsburg to practice medicine, he built one of the first brick houses in the county. He planted a vineyard and also enjoyed gardening and beekeeping.

His interest in horticulture was not the only thing Dr. Becker brought with him from Germany. He brought some tiny apple seeds; the Becker apple was subsequently developed. In Dr. Becker's later years, when he no longer practiced medicine, he moved to Brenham to live with his son. Science continued to fascinate Dr. Becker, and he devoted much of his time to horticultural experiments involving asparagus cultivation.

Dr. Edwin L. Burton, a physician of McKinney in Grayson County, originated the Burton peach. He was a graduate of the University of Louisville in 1889.

Another doctor interested in the culture of peaches was Dr. A. S. Lipscomb of Montgomery. He developed the Lipscomb Pride peach, a fine early variety which was exhibited at the Houston State Fair in May 1871. Dr. Lipscomb, his interests not confined only to the medical field and the horticultural field, also served in the Thirteenth Legislature.

Dr. J. T. Whitaker, a well-known nurseryman from Smith County, introduced the Tarbell and Governor Hogg peaches.

Dr. J. N. B. Guinn was involved in horticultural experiments with blackberries, plums, grapes, and peaches. A native of South Carolina, he settled in Alto, Cherokee County, in 1854.

One of the better known Texas horticulturists was Dr. William Rapp Howard. Born in 1848 in Arkansas, his boyhood was spent in Missouri and Rhode Island. He later returned to Missouri, graduating from St. Louis Medical College in 1873. It is probable he earned another degree from the College of Physicians and Surgeons in Baltimore.

When he came to Texas in 1876, he settled in White Rock, in Hunt County, and practiced medicine for ten years. During 1894, when Dr. Howard was a member of the first faculty of the medical department of Fort Worth University, he found time to enjoy a sweet hobby, experimenting with honeybees. He became a member of the National Society of Apiarists as well as first secretary of the Texas State Beekeepers' Association. Additional merit was given to the results of his work published in *The American Bee Journal.*

Dr. Michael Perl, who practiced medicine for many years in Houston, was born in Vienna, Austria, in 1835. He had an extensive education, studying medicine in both Vienna and Budapest. His military career in Europe included one year as assistant-surgeon in the Austrian army; he was also connected with hospitals in Hungary.

Before coming to Houston in 1866, Dr. Perl lived for several years in Mexico. He grew foreign exotic varieties of various fruits and tropical plants, placing them side-by-side with native specimens. According to one description,

> . . . pineapples were growing beautifully; cherries, domestic and Japanese plums, quinces, peaches, apricots, figs, chestnuts, walnuts, almonds, filberts, pecans, and Japanese persimmons were in his orchard . . . he had many varieties of orange trees, one particularly noted for its dwarfish proportions and not over six inches high, but bearing mature oranges.

Dr. William Wynne Stell from Kentucky came to the area near Paris, Texas, at the age of six in 1839. He returned to the east to attend Jefferson Medical College in Philadelphia. Due to health problems, he did not practice for long. He started a nursery business with a partner and introduced several varieties of fruits including the Texas Belle, the Tudor, and Bonner plums. He spent much time writing horticultural articles, many of which appeared in *Texas Farm and Ranch.* Some records also give credit to Dr. J. T. Whitaker for introducing Texas Belle or Paris Belle plums.

Dr. Isaac Monroe Cline was a climatologist who forecast the Galveston hurricane of 1900. He wrote a book in 1894 on the effects of climate and weather changes on persons suffering from various diseases. He lectured in medical climatology at The University of Texas Medical Branch.

Dr. Franklin L. Yoakum was at one time a college president, meteorological volunteer, nurseryman, author, goat-raiser, and country physician. He also entered the ministry of Cumberland Presbyterian Church.

A close observer of nature in many forms, Dr. Yoakum became a Smithsonian Institution volunteer reporting meteorological observations from 1858 to 1860. While President of Larissa College in Cherokee County, he promoted extensive field trips into Indian territory and the frontier areas of Texas in the late 1850s. He was further able to develop a geological museum for the college.

Pursuing his interest in horticulture, Dr. Yoakum established a large nursery in Cherokee County about 1864, later moving the nursery to Palestine. He became a corresponding member of the St. Louis Academy of Science, as well as secretary of the First Texas Academy of Science. An additional writing talent enabled him to complete many articles on horticulture and agriculture, which appeared in *Texas Farm and Ranch* and his own journal, *Texas Journal of Horticulture.*

Dr. Yoakum's interest in science prompted collaboration with Dr. Quintius Cincinnatus Smith of Austin and another individual in the founding of the Texas Academy of Science on 27 October 1880. They asked Governor O. M. Roberts to be President of the Academy and other state officials to serve. According to Dr. Yoakum, "This was a mistake. . . ." The Academy was moved from Austin to Palestine and then to Tyler. At one time there were over one hundred members throughout the state, but the organization apparently disbanded around 1887. The second Academy of Science was organized at The University of Texas by Everhart and others in 1892 and continued until 1912.

Frequently, doctors' additional careers followed natural aptitudes in writing, editing, or publishing. These abilities to communicate often informed and influenced others in many ways. In medical journals, newspapers and books, some doctors described the results of scientific research. Others recorded history or aired political views. One even penned pornography.

Communicating in other ways, doctors sometimes became educators, philosophers, or ministers.

Dr. Theodore Leger's essay, the *Particular Influence of Prejudices in Medicine, over the disease most common in Texas, Intermittent Fever; Preceded by a Few General Observations on Medical Theories,* is considered the first medical publication in the English language in Texas. The essay was published by the People Press of Brazoria in 1838. Listed on the cover page were Dr. Leger's credentials: "Late Professor of Midwifery of the Faculty of Paris, Member of the Medical College of Mexico, and Ex-Vice-President of the Medical Society of New Orleans."

Dr. Ashbel Smith wrote a book called, *An Account of Yellow Fever in Galveston, 1839,* which was the second medical work in the English language published in Texas. At the time it was considered a significant medical contribution. Smith also wrote on cholera and published articles in the *American Journal of Medical Sciences* on various surgical procedures including rectovaginal fistula and cancer of the breast.

Dr. J. Cameron Massie wrote a 720-page treatise at the request of physicians on *Eclectic Southern Practice* which was published in 1853 in Philadelphia. It is the third known medical book in the English language written by a Texas doctor. At the time the book was written, physicians believed disease produced different symptoms in Texas. In contrast to the opinions of some of his older contemporaries, Dr. Massie gave support to the use of the newly invented stethoscope, saying: "there seems to be an innateness in the human mind to reject the light of science in regard to new discoveries."

Dr. F. C. Wilkes wrote a book entitled *Manual of Practice for the Diseases of Texas,* published in 1866 at Chappell Hill [Institute] by Wilkes and Stone.

Dr. R. H. L. Bibb served as Secretary of the Tarrant County Medical Association in the 1890s before he moved to Saltillo, Mexico. He wrote a paper on the *Nature and Treatment of Leprosy,* which won the Alvarigo Prize granted by the Philadelphia College of Physicians.

Dr. Gideon Lincecum wrote many newspaper articles, signing his articles "Gid." He had studied Choctaw Indian remedies.

Dr. Berthold Ernest Hadra, a German physician who came to Austin after the Civil War, wrote a book published in 1888, *Lesions of the Vagina and Pelvic Floor, with Specific Reference to Uterine & Vaginal Prolapse.* He described certain conditions which he is credited as the first to recognize. Dr. Hadra was also the first to use wire in vertebral fractures.

Dr. Thomas Jefferson Heard wrote a pamphlet in 1868, *Report on Medical Topography, Meteorology, and Epidemic Diseases in Texas.* This doctor was an advocate of medical progress in Texas, speaking out in 1870 in favor of a state medical college and a state medical journal. Control of devastating epidemics was another of his main concerns. Speaking of typhoid fever, first observed in Texas in 1852, he said, "Nothing of the kind was ever known before in the state." He felt that typhoid and many epidemic diseases were due to hardships, hunger, and the "effects of poor, mean, whiskey."

Dr. George P. Hachenberg was an Austin doctor who wrote many articles for scientific journals. He is better known however, as an inventor of such devices as the lie detector. He is less known for a controversy with Bell over the invention of the telephone. He graduated from New York Medical College in 1851, but it was not until 1872 that he chose Texas for reasons of health, returning to practice in Round Top. He also wrote a book called *The Medial Consultant's Book,* which contains descriptions of a variety of ills and his recommended treatments. His book included diet recommendations also.

Dr. James Wharton McLaughlin, an Austin doctor, wrote *An Outline of the Physical Theory of Fermentation, Immunity, and Infection.* Reviewed by the London *Lancet,* Dr. McLaughlin's work very nearly approximated the modern-day concepts of immunity. He theorized blood proteins were involved in producing immunity; however, he identified albumins rather than globulin fractions which were eventually correctly identified. In 1885, he published an investigation of the bacteriology of dengue fever, entitled *Fermentation, Infection, and Immunity.*

Dr. James W. Nixon, a doctor in Gonzales, wrote a treatise in 1898 on amebic dysentery, the first paper published on a successful cure for that disease. Dr. Nixon chanced to meet a passerby on a donkey loaded down with brush. Upon inquiry, he learned that the brush was used as a remedy for diarrhea.

Dr. Nixon became interested as this was a common malady.

Making infusions from the bush known as bitterbrush, he conducted successful experiments. Finding the substance both safe and effective, he sent quantities of the brush to scientists all across the United States and Europe. Pharmaceutical companies later marketed the resulting product for diarrhea.

Another medical writer, Dr. Warren W. Webster, a Medical Director of the Fifth Medical Military District in Austin, wrote a manual in 1870 for hospital administration.

Not all doctors confined their writing to scientific or textbook material. Dr. John Wesley Carhart (1834–1914) wrote psychiatric fiction and was arrested for sending pornographic material through the mail. He wrote on inversion of the sexes.

Medical journals played an important part in bringing medical practice in Texas up to the standards of practice in more advanced areas of the United States. Some have estimated that Texas was perhaps at least twenty years behind other parts of the country. By reading the journals, doctors in even small communities of the frontier could become aware of the newest discoveries and the most advanced treatments. These journals had a difficult time, however, and the publication of no journal established before 1900 has survived.

Dr. Greensville Dowell established and edited the first medical periodical ever published in Texas, the *Galveston Medical Journal*, from 1866 to 1871. There were five volumes, each containing forty to fifty pages of scientific articles and many pages of advertising. Dr. Dowell wrote editorials as well as many of the articles. He personally invested $10,000 in the publication which nevertheless failed, possibly because of the difficulties of the Reconstruction period.

Dr. Dowell wrote two books on medical subjects, one on yellow fever and one on hernia. In one paper, *Yellow Fever and Malarial Diseases,* he mentioned his belief that yellow fever was transmitted by mosquitoes five years before Dr. Carlos Finlay declared his theory. Dr. Dowell is credited with several original surgical operations, including one for hernia. He is also credited with the invention of various surgical instruments. He lived from 1822 to 1881.

Dr. W. H. Gantt and Dr. J. Boring were editors and publishers of the *Texas Medical Journal* from 1873 to 1879. Dr. Gantt was a professor at Galveston Medical College, having come to Texas from Maryland in 1850. He also served the Smithsonian Institution as a meteorological observer. After his death in 1867, the journal combined with the *Galveston Medical Journal.*

Dr. Ferdinand Eugene Daniel served as editor of the *Texas Courier-Record of Medicine,* which was published in Fort Worth in 1883. After moving to Austin in 1885, this doctor founded *Daniel's Texas Medical Journal,* a publication popularly called the "Red-Back" because of its red covers. He advertised his journal as "a free-lance that goes for the Quacks in as well as out of the profession." After the first eight volumes, the title became *Texas Medical Journal,* in the hope that the publication would become the official voice of the medical association. This did not happen, but as an editor, Dr. Daniel was a powerful voice in Texas medical affairs.

Dr. Daniel, a graduate of the New Orleans School of Medicine in 1862, was a former Judge Advocate General of the Army of Tennessee. He was an educator as well. As professor of anatomy and surgery, he had taught in the first medical school of Texas, Texas Medical College, from 1866 to 1868. He also made a significant contribution to history by writing and publishing *Recollections of a Rebel Surgeon,* his experiences in the Civil War.

Dr. Charles Edmund Fisher was a founder and editor of the *Homeopathic Pellet,* a publication which later changed its name to *Southern Journal of Homeopathy.* Fisher was a graduate of the Detroit Homeopathic College in 1883. Soon thereafter he moved to Austin, and became a partner to Dr. Routh. He also established a homeopathic pharmacy. Later he became president of both the state and national homeopathic medical associations. He also wrote promotional literature distributed by the railroad to entice visitors to Texas. Fisher sold his journal to a Dr. Clifford of San Antonio in 1884.

Dr. T. J. Bennett, Dr. J. W. McLaughlin, Dr. R. M. Swearingen, and Dr. T. D. Wooten were Austin doctors who founded the *Texas Sanitarian* in 1891. By 1894, this journal had become the *Texas Medical News,* and by 1898, it consolidated with the *Texas Health Journal.* Subsequent volumes were entitled *Medical Insurance and Health Conservation.* Dr. Swearingen is accorded some acclaim as "poet," as well as a journal founder.

Dr. A. M. Elmore was a "writer of some distinction" as editor and business manager of the *Texas Health Journal,* a monthly magazine published from 1888 to 1898. Volumes Nine to Eleven were entitled *Texas Medical Practitioner.*

Dr. Francis Moore, Jr., a surgeon of the Texas army, came to Texas from Ohio with the Buckeye Rangers in 1836, even though he was originally from New York. He was founder and editor of the

Houston *Telegraph* in 1837. His association with the paper continued until 1856.

Dr. Moore was involved in politics, serving as a senator in 1839–1840 and from 1841 to 1852. He also served as mayor of Houston several times. A road built during his term from Houston to the Brazos River was known as "Dr. Moore's mud road."

In addition to his political activities, Dr. Moore served as chief geologist of the state of Texas in 1859 and 1860. He pleaded for a geological survey of the state, convinced of Texas's mineral wealth. Toward the end of his career, he worked near the Great Lakes for a copper mining company.

Commenting on this versatile man, one person said: "He was a fine orator, a sincere Presbyterian, and one of the purest men in the country; one in whose nature patriotism was a passion."

Dr. William Carlton, who settled in Austin in 1858, became editor and publisher of the *Rambler.* Published in Austin and Lockhart, this publication supported secession prior to the Civil War.

Dr. R. R. Worrall, (also J. R.), arrived in Texas in 1860 and was temporary editor of his local paper.

Dr. John Salmon (Rip) Ford was one of the more colorful characters of nineteenth century Texas. His talents and accomplishments were many. He was founder and editor of the *Texas Democrat* and editor of the Brownsville *Sentinel* in 1868. He served as editor of the *Southwestern and State Times Ranger Service.* In addition to his journalistic accomplishments, Dr. Ford may have been Texas's first playwright. In 1838, his play, "A Stranger in Texas," was performed by the Thespians of San Antonio.

Dr. J. B. Cranfill in 1881 put out a four-page monthly known as the Turnersville *Effort.* When Dr. Cranfill moved to Gatesville, the paper became the *Gatesville Advance.* Later consolidating with *The Sun,* it became the *Advance Sun.* After another move to Waco, Dr. Cranfill's paper became the *Waco Advance.*

Dr. W. C. Phillips arrived in Texas in 1854, and was an editorial writer under the title "Vesicula Calculus." He became a director of the Austin Gas, Light, and Coal Company. Long interested in public affairs, he attended General Garfield's inauguration. His dedication to politics grew, and he became Secretary of State in 1868.

Dr. John J. Chalmers, another Austin doctor and newspaper publisher, unknowingly met his murderer on a downtown street. For nearly two years Dr. Chalmers had published his weekly paper,

The New Era. Whether it was by chance or whether Dr. Chalmers planned to meet Joshua Holden downtown is unknown. The two were talking opposite the Post Office on West Pecan Street on New Year's Day 1847, when an argument surfaced.

Suddenly Holden, clutching a large bowie knife, struck Chalmers in the temple with an overhand thrust. So swift and forceful was the blow that the knife went through the doctor's silk hat, penetrated his skull, and entered his brain. Death was instantaneous. Holden's reason for taking Dr. Chalmers's life remains unrecorded.

Holden was arrested. Since there was no jail he was confined in a log cabin, but not for long. He engineered his escape by tunneling under the logs. He fled to California and died there several years later. Even if justice was not served, at least the escape made Austinites recognize the necessity of building a more secure jail.

Often trained in scholarly pursuits, many physicians, students of history, became historians. As noted earlier, the eyewitness accounts of various doctors of historical events, such as the massacre at Goliad, are valuable in determining historical fact.

Dr. Joseph H. Barnard, taken prisoner after the Battle of Coleta 1836, wrote an enduring account published in 1875, entitled *A Journal of the Massacre of Fannin's Command.* This remains one of history's most accurate accounts of that period.

Dr. N. D. Labadie wrote an account of the Battle of San Jacinto thirty-three years after the battle, a controversial rememberance perhaps erroneously perceived and personally biased. The account had to do with his military orders and payment he received.

Dr. William Sheppard, in collaboration with Judge Gibson, editor of the Columbus, Mississippi, *Eagle* wrote an history of the Mier Expedition. He later became a farmer, also serving as Superintendent of the Deaf and Dumb Institute in 1884.

Dr. David Cerna, a Mexican, is recognized as Texas's first medical historian. Writing on many subjects, he wrote "Notes on the newer remedies, their therapeutic applications and modes of administration," in 1895. He later taught at The University of Texas Medical Branch at Galveston.

Dr. Greensville Dowell wrote a history of the epidemics of yellow fever and malarial fevers in Texas. Dr. John S. Rip Ford, who was involved in many historical struggles, was a leader in organizing the Texas Branch of the Southern Historical Association.

Dr. W. A. Moore, an Austin octagenarian, wrote *The Writings of Alexander Campbell.*

Physicians were often in the forefront of efforts to promote education in nineteenth century Texas.

Dr. Ashbel Smith was particularly interested in advanced education. He was President of Texas Medical College, as well as President of a committee which received applications for the chair of anatomy in 1876. His work and influence helped bring about The University of Texas Medical Branch, which materialized five years after his death. The original medical school building called "Old Red," is named in his honor.

Dr. Smith had the vision to provide educational opportunities for minorities. Through his efforts, the Agricultural and Mechanical College for Colored Youths was established. He served on a committee which tried to locate the State Agricultural College in 1878.

In addition, he is credited as one of the organizers of The University of Texas. He served many years as a regent, having also served as first President of the Board of Regents. Dr. Smith was known as "the Regent who bellowed fire." With his encouragement, many prominent men were brought to The University of Texas, which helped to establish its reputation for scholarship. He advocated policies for raising standards, as well as an examination system for professorial candidates.

Other prominent educators included Dr. Franklin L. Yoakum, president of Larissa College.

Dr. Greensville Dowell was known as an educator as well as a distinguished surgeon. He was instrumental in organizing the Galveston Medical College, the first medical school in Texas. He served as dean as well as professor; later he became professor of surgery at Texas Medical College in Galveston.

A fellow surgeon described Dr. James E. Thompson as possessing to an unusual degree the qualifications which Guy De Chauliac, fourteenth century surgeon, declared a surgeon should have: "Bold when sure; cautious in danger; kind to the sick; considerate of your fellow workers; uninfluenced by gain."

Dr. Thompson, a man of great personal charm, arrived in Galveston from Great Britain in 1891, the same year the Medical Department of The University of Texas was established. He became the school's first professor of surgery. From that time until his death in 1927, Dr. Thompson worked to improve medical education, particularly the training of young surgeons. He served as professor for thirty-six years. Highly trained himself in London University, he kept his standards high, demanding the same from his students. He spent much time and study on improving operative techniques for cleft palate. His papers on this subject and other studies earned him a place in surgical history. He became a fellow of the American Surgical Association and later, a vice-president. He also was elected president of the Southern Surgical Association. Among his other honors, he was a founder and first president of the Texas Surgical Society. He received the degree of doctor of laws by Baylor University, an unusual honor for a physician, particularly one not associated with Baylor.

After his death one of his colleagues wrote: "It was always a pleasure to see how he attacked what he conceived to be false teachings; if the offending essayist was up in years his language was direct and to the point, but if the essayist was a young surgeon, his remarks were very careful and fatherly; in all instances he was the soul of dignity and courtesy."

Dr. Bacon Saunders of Fort Worth was one of the founders of the Medical Department of Texas Christian University.

Another prominent educator was Dr. Edward Randall. Legend has it that Dr. Randall, professor of the Medical Department of The University of Texas, encountered a student in the library in his bathing suit. His reaction must have been something to behold, because it was said that only after long negotiations was the student allowed to remain at the Medical Branch.

Known as a gentleman of dignified demeanor, Dr. Randall was never seen with his coat off in the presence of a student, and he would have taken it as a sign of rudeness if a student was coatless in his presence. To think of Dr. Randall in sports clothes was unthinkable, so his friends said.

A native Texan born in 1860 in Huntsville, Dr. Randall received his medical education from the University of Pennsylvania. He served an internship in Philadelphia, followed by postgraduate studies in several medical centers in Europe.

Reared by an uncle in Galveston following the early death of his parents, he returned to that city to begin the practice of medicine in 1886. Due to his extensive medical training and other qualifications, he was elected in 1888 to the chair of Materia Medica and Therapeutics at Texas Medical College and Hospital in Galveston. When the Medical Department of The University of Texas was organized in 1891 replacing the other school, he was elected to fill the same chair, a position he held until 1928.

Dr. Randall served the Medical Department in many capacities. Upon his death, Dr. A. O. Singleton, Sr., Chairman of the Surgery Department, said: "He had contributed more than any other man to the success and greatness of the Medical Department of The University of Texas." His contributions were not limited to the school, however. Dr. Randall had a large private practice for many years, and he played an active role in the civic and cultural development of Galveston.

Something of Dr. Randall's character is evident from a speech he gave at the second commencement of the Medical Department of the State University in 1893, printed 3 May 1893, in the *Galveston Daily News*.

> We recognize the general fact that every man stands in relation to the men around him which he cannot avoid or avert. Every citizen strengthens or enfeebles the power of the law in the community in which he dwells. Every individual increases or diminishes the healthfulness of his neighborhood as he observes or neglects the rules of hygiene in his life and in his home. Every man raises or lowers the tone of society as he shows himself upright and honorable, or walks in crooked paths and practices a dubious morality. These things are true of every man but there are some positions in which responsibility is necessarily greater than in others; some callings which in themselves involve less influence on the weal or woe of our fellow man. How may one place himself in the most desirable relationship to the community in which he lives and practices his profession? The answer to this question which so vitally concerns every one of you may be given in a few words — by courtesy, by kindness, by honesty, and by knowledge. I would not have you confine your study wholly to the limits of your profession. Keep abreast of your time, post yourself in all the great political and social questions of the day, that you may be wide awake, patriotic citizens and intelligent companions.

Samuel H. Stout made contributions in many areas. During the Civil War as superintendent of hospitals in the Department of Tennessee, he developed the mobile hospital unit, a notable advance in treating the wounded near the battlefield. He is also credited with establishing isolation wards for diseases known to be contagious, a concept ahead of his time.

Following the Civil War, Dr. Stout became a nationally known educator. He was instrumental in establishing the public school system in Cisco. He was also a founder of the medical department of

Dr. Edmund Montgomery, portrait by Frank Elliott Studio, Hempstead, Texas.
Courtesy Ney Museum, Austin, Texas

the University of Dallas, a school where he became dean of faculty. He died in 1903.

Some scholarly physicians pursued interests in philosophy. Recognizing the need, Dr. Ashbel Smith formed the Philosophical Society of Texas.

Few doctors, however, were able to devote their entire careers to philosophical pursuits. Dr. Edmund Duncan Montgomery followed this path more than most.

Dr. Montgomery, born in Scotland 1835, determined early to "solve the philosophical problems of life and mind by the experimental method." He studied in Heidelberg, Berlin, Bonn, and received his medical degree from Wurzburg. Later he studied hospital practice and technique at Prague and Vienna.

From 1860 to 1863, Dr. Montgomery was resident physician at the German Hospital and Bermondsey Dispensary in London, was demonstrator of Morbid Anatomy and museum curator at St. Thomas's Hospital. He became a member of the Royal College of Physicians of London.

Because of a tubercular infection, Dr. Montgomery vacated his prestigious activities in London, to practice medicine in Mentone, Rome, and thereafter in Munich. There he met and married Elisabet Ney and retired from his medical practice to resume his lifelong passion for scientific research, philosophical reflection, and writing.

When Dr. Montgomery's wife, a famous sculptress, became embroiled in political difficulties in 1870, she and her husband fled to America. They purchased Liendo Plantation in Hempstead and lived in chosen semi-isolation, Dr. Montgomery enjoying the quietude of research, philosophy, and writing, and Elisabet efficiently running the plantation.

Much about the Montgomerys perplexed their neighbors who thought them different and strange. Elisabet strode about the plantation in unconventional clothes, doing a man's work, while her husband stayed in the house; some of the neighbors were not sure that they were really married. The Montgomerys' speech and ways were unlike that of their neighbors. The crowning event that scandalized the community was the rumor that Elisabet had burned her dead son's body in the fireplace of their home. Indeed, she had done so; the child had died from diphtheria, and Elisabet had tried to restrict the contagion.

Based on extensive research, Dr. Montgomery wrote and published many essays and monographs based on his scientific and philosophical views. These were well received and published in the scientific and philosophical journals of America, Germany, and England.

Elisabet Ney's widely acclaimed sculptures of Stephen F. Austin and Sam Houston now stand in the Capitol at Austin. Two months after her death in 1907, Dr. Montgomery suffered a stroke and became an invalid for the remainder of his life, which was to last another four years. His extensive library became the property of Southern Methodist University, Dallas.

Dr. William P. Smith was an outstanding example of a minister-physician. He came to Texas from Tennessee in 1833, and served during the fight for independence as a soldier and chaplain. His text for a sermon to the soldiers at Gonzales in October 1835 was from Isaiah 1:10, 20: "If ye be willing and obedient, ye shall eat the good of the land; but if ye refuse and rebel, ye shall be devoured with the sword. . . ." Dr. Smith was also noted for his bravery during the siege of Bexar. In addition, he served as surgeon of the post at Washington-on-the-Brazos, where he was in charge of caring for the sick and wounded. He later became an outstanding Methodist minister, as well as a farmer-rancher, an editor, and politician.

After the war, he was appointed trustee of Rutersville College, founded in 1840. A generous man, he gave 1111 acres of land to this first college of the Republic.

Later Dr. Smith became editor of *The Monument* in La Grange, a position he said he accepted to honor the memory of the men of the Mier Expedition and those killed with Dawson. Respected by his peers, Dr. Smith was asked to give the prayer at the last meeting of the first session of the TMA. After a life of varied service, he died in 1870.

Dr. A. P. Manley was another Methodist minister-physician, who became a traveling preacher. He was recognized by the Methodist Quarterly Conference in 1838.

Dr. R. M. Gano, who became a clergyman of the Christian Church, abandoned the practice of medicine after the Civil War. A graduate of medical school in 1850, Gano had practiced in Bourbon and Tarrant counties in the decade prior to the war. In addition, he was elected to the Texas Legislature in 1860–1861.

Anxious to enter the conflict, he recruited two companies of infantry which served under General Albert Sidney Johnston. He later commanded the Seventh Kentucky Cavalry of John Morgan's famed cavalry, and in 1863, he commanded the Texas State Cavalry. By the end of the war, he was promoted to the rank of General. After the war Dr. Gano became a clergyman in the Christian Church.

Dr. Franklin L. Yoakum was a minister with the Cumberland Presbyterian Church in Texas. Later he became involved as an administrator in higher education.

Doctors were not only active in their churches as ministers. Some became outstanding laymen, such as Dr. G. J. Starnes of San Antonio. He was a graduate of Meharry Medical College and was quite active in the Methodist Episcopal Church around 1900.

Dr. William H. Boring was an occasional preacher. Professor of Obstetrics and Disease at Galveston Medical College, he was also a good speaker and preached in the Methodist Church on Sundays. Quick-witted when asked whether as a physician he ever prayed that people would get sick, he replied: "No, I simply ask for my daily bread and the Lord knows how it is."

The difficulty of making a living in Texas during the nineteenth century often necessitated diverse business ventures. Limited only by a doctor's ingenuity, these activities ranged from mining to camel ranching. One such venture was begun by Dr. Samuel Stivers and his son, who purchased a salt mine in Angelina County in 1840.

Dr. Johnson Calhoun Hunter was talented in diverse fields. Originally from North Carolina, he completed his medical studies by age nineteen. He married and during the next ten years fathered five children.

The family lived in Virginia, Ohio, and Missouri. They came to Texas in the early 1820s. They were shipwrecked off Galveston Island on their arrival, a portent of things to come. With most of their possessions destroyed, the family survived by eating off the land, which meant, among other things, alligator tail. Their first home in Texas was a lean-to shelter by trees near the mouth of the San Jacinto River.

Needing to earn money, Dr. Hunter secured a license from the Mexican government to skipper the *Adventure*. He also made a living by trading with the Indians as well as trying his hand at farming. He raised crops of both corn and cotton which at that time sold for about five cents a pound. Perhaps these ventures were not as lucrative as he expected, because he soon declared himself a surveyor and was then involved in various disputes over his fees. During this time, he also practiced medicine. His medical fees must have been disputed as well, because his charges to the widow McCormick were brought to the attention of Stephen F. Austin.

Dr. Hunter settled in the Fort Bend County area around 1829. His place, known as the Hunter Plantation, became a landmark for many years. He lost over 600 head of cattle when Santa Anna and the Mexican Army passed through, although part of the herd was used to feed the Texian Army as well. To supplement his income after such a loss, Hunter became a postmaster at Rocky Well, and he lived almost twenty years after the Battle of San Jacinto.

His varied skills and pursuits answered a need in the time and place in which he lived. Few men qualify for such a description:

> He could deliver a baby, ride a plow, go hungry, trade with the Indians, run a traverse, pilot a scow, adjudicate a case, please a woman, cut a bull, teach a school, sire several children, and deliver mail.

Dr. Wade A. Morris was typical of many doctors around mid-century. He had arrived in Austin in the early 1850s, having graduated from the University of Louisville in 1830. Active in civic affairs, he became an Alderman in 1857. He actively practiced medicine, but the profits from a brickyard supplemented his income. He was chairman of the first Board of Medical Examiners and active in the State Medical Association. He was enterprising enough to also own three drugstores in Austin.

Another Austin doctor, Dr. Samuel G. Haynie, was an active building contractor in mid-century Austin. In addition to constructing a new building for his various mercantile ventures, he built a fine new home near the Capitol site. He was one of two commissioners in charge of construction of the new Capitol. When he was postmaster, he built a new post office building. Records indicate he was probably in charge of construction of the new Treasury Building and St. David's Episcopal Church.

Another founder of the Waco Association engaged in an unusual business venture. Dr. David R. Wallace was one of the original directors of a bridge company which built a suspension bridge across the Brazos. Dr. Wallace, a scholarly gentleman, could read and speak Latin.

In Young County, Dr. James H. Swindell was a surveyor, lawyer, and physician. He also was a partner in banking and a stationery business. Dr. Swindell, a Virginian, had arrived in Fort Belknap in the mid-1850s.

In the decade between 1855 and 1865 when many doctors turned to trade to supplement their income, competition was keen for scarce dollars. In order to get an edge, a Dr. Herndon opened a general store carrying such diverse items as carriages, jewelry, and spectacles, as well as all types of food items and liquors. Among his inventory was a good supply of Lediard's "Morning Call."

Dr. C. N. Worthington, a dry goods merchant in Austin after 1870, was another merchant-physician.

Since doctors used pills or potions to heal or ease pain, the drug business was one of the most natural businesses enabling physicians to supplement their incomes. But before 1906, drugs were not standardized, and many contained cocaine, arsenic, and mercury, ingredients which are now controlled by law or recognized as poisons.

Even in Colonial America, educated physicians had opened apothecary shops. At that time, apothecaries adopted the title of "doctor," not so surprising since England had given apothecaries the right to practice medicine. Thus it was not surprising that many

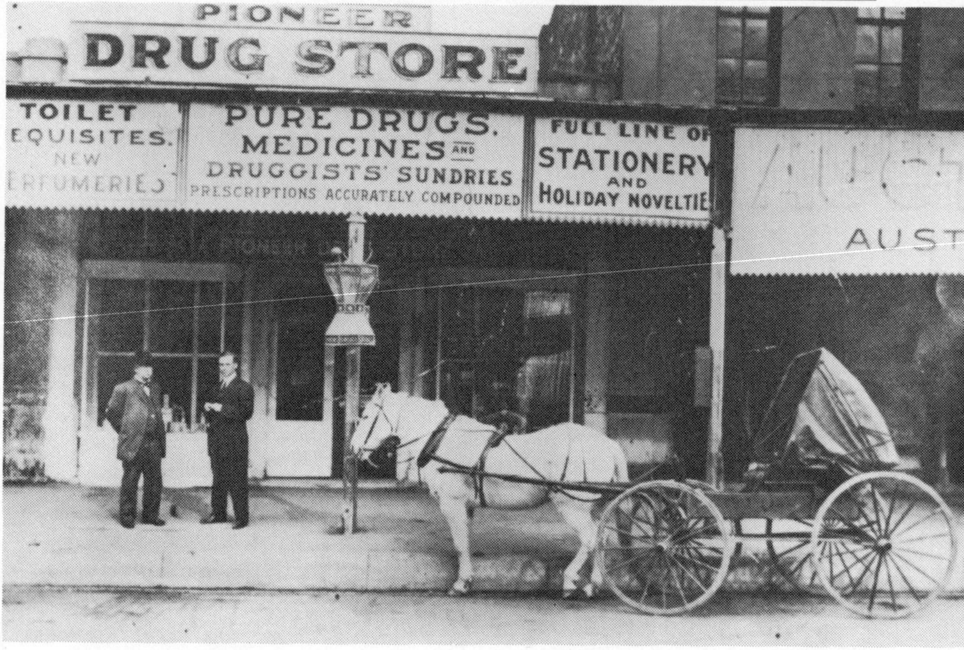

Pioneer Drugstore, San Angelo, opened by Dr. S. L. S. Smith when he left the army in 1882.

Courtesy Fort Concho Museum

doctors became involved in selling medicines, such as Dr. Haynie of Austin who opened an apothecary shop.

One druggist who arrived in Austin in 1871, was Dr. Adam Shirk. He established a drugstore in 1874, and two years later he managed Burrough's Drugstore. He was an assistant physician at the State Lunatic Asylum, as well as engaged in private practice.

Two brothers in Austin, both doctors, found commercial enterprises more profitable than a limited practice. Dr. J. J. Tobin owned and operated the streetcar lines, or the "Street Railway," during the time he was a druggist. He was also very active in civic affairs. He was an Alderman and Trustee of the Blind School. His civic posts included Chairman of the Committee for Charity of the City Council, Vice-President of the Citizens Relief Committee for the Poor, and an incorporator of the Austin Athletic Association. Also an early housing developer, Dr. Tobin built a series of new houses to rent to his streetcar drivers.

Possessing an astute business sense, Dr. Tobin knew a good

Pioneer Drugstore interior where Dr. S. L. S. Smith had an office in San Angelo after 1882.

Courtesy Fort Concho Museum

thing when he saw it, and soon after the new electric lights came on the market, his drugstore had the distinction of being the first store in the city to use colored lights in 1883. He was so delighted with the new invention that he had the grounds of his home decorated with twinkling lights to give a festive touch to his elaborate garden parties. His brother, Dr. W. H. Tobin, developer of the famous product, Hepatazone, was also involved in numerous endeavors.

After arriving in Austin in 1877, Dr. Allen Harn operated two boardinghouses: the Beal House and then the Carrolton House.

Dr. S. A. Owens, one of the founders of the Waco Medical Association, together with others organized a company to build an ice factory, the first in Texas. In May 1871, the first ice was made under patents issued to Mr. A. Muhl. Before this time, ice was brought from Houston, costing about fifteen to twenty-five cents a pound. This factory could sell the same amount for only a nickel.

Dr. John R. Simms retired from practice to open a tanning yard. Perhaps that business was not as successful as he had hoped; he moved to California in 1868. At one time he had been a senatorial candidate from Williamson County.

Dr. Hoyt had previously studied medicine in the office of a St. Paul physician before taking courses at the Rush Medical School in Chicago in 1876. Then financial difficulties prevented him from continuing his education. That in turn prompted him to go west for money to complete his training. Prior to finding a job, unsubstantiated fact indicates he became friends with Billy the Kid in New Mexico.

Dr. Hoyt's manner of supplementing his income was more unusual than usual. As one of the first physicians on the Llano Estacado, he had trouble making ends meet so he worked for a time as a cowboy on the LX Ranch. He could not afford a pair of boots, but his employer decided he was a good risk and gave him a pair with encouraging words, "The valley is full of smallpox and you will soon have all the money you want."

Dr. John A. Veatch visualized an unusual business venture. Originally from Kentucky, he came from Louisiana to Texas in 1834. Prior to his arrival, he married a woman of Spain's royal family. That alliance gave him a grant of half a million acres of Texas land. It also gave him divided loyalties during the Texas-Mexican Revolution.

Although he became an artillery captain in the Texas army, he did not serve. Even as an elected delegate to the Consultation in 1835, he did not attend. His conscience dictated it was impossible for him to give his "personal services to the cause." He did, however, contribute several hundred dollars.

With the annexation of Texas, Dr. Veatch determined his loyalty must go to his native country, and he served in the United States Army. After the war, he had time to pursue scientific interests.

He sought to interest President Lamar in one venture: a factory to extract gum arabic from mesquite trees. Dr. Veatch was enthusiastic about the project, but short of capital. He offered, however, 1000 sheep for wool, and a league of land with adequate water. He anticipated that the same water that ran the machinery could irrigate the land and produce profitable cotton crops.

So enamoured was Dr. Veatch of the idea of the gum arabic factory that he was even willing to turn the proceeds of his medical practice over to a joint account as a further part of the bargain. The factory probably did not materialize, for Dr. Veatch subsequently departed Texas's fields of mesquite trees for California's gold fields.

Farming and ranching have long had a fascination for many in the medical field. Acquiring land led many doctors to become farmers as well as ranchers. Some of the more notable physicians who practiced farming on their land were Anson Jones and Ashbel Smith.

Growing grapes for making wine was among Dr. Ashbel Smith's many agricultural interests. He experimented with various grapes, but he preferred the mustang grape. He commented that though it was not sweet, it made wine which was good taken with food or given as a tonic for "enfeebled health." On his plantation, vinegar was also made from grape juice as well as from persimmons and peaches.

Another farmer, although not as well known, was Dr. Elijah Hays who came to Texas after the Civil War. He farmed in Panola County, but he did not abandon medicine altogether. Having practiced medicine for twenty years in Alabama and Georgia, he brought with him medical notebooks that contained formulas for chills and itches.

Land disputes sometimes had serious consequences. Dr. S. W. Bailey was killed in 1882 in a dispute over cotton territory ownership in North Texas. His wife had previously owned two beautiful plantation homes. One was known as the Jones mansion in Paris, Texas, and the other was Rose Hill. The latter is now in Oklahoma, but at the time of the dispute, the home was in the territory of North Texas.

Dr. R. O. Prideaux, born in 1844 in England, became interested in the cattle and ranching business after moving to Texas in 1871. He explored large areas before settling in southern Archer County, an area with good range land. He was instrumental in the organization of Archer County, which was under the jurisdiction of Clay County at the time.

Because the region was sparcely settled, Dr. Prideaux had ample time for ranching. He bought thousands of acres of land and leased thousands more as his cattle business grew.

Dr. William C. McGoun who moved to Austin from Houston in 1876 was another doctor interested in cattle. He was known for the fine Jersey cattle he raised. He was a graduate of the University of Louisiana in 1854.

Occupations sometimes grew from an enjoyable hobby, such as

raising and racing horses. Dr. R. K. Goodloe, one of the doctors of the Battle of San Jacinto, practiced at Sabine Town, where he raised blooded race horses. He spent a great deal of time racing them as well. He was quoted as saying: "Since 'thirty-six I have served my country in every capacity from Captain to Brigadier General. . . ."

Dr. W. C. Phillips of Austin was another doctor known for his fine race horses. He was quite proud of his horse appropriately named "General Phillips," who won races in such notable places as New Orleans, Charleston, and St. Louis. W. B. Astor, eldest son of famed John Jacob Astor, was so impressed that he offered $10,000 for General Phillips. It is interesting to speculate whether or not Dr. Phillips sold his namesake. Dr. Phillips, however, was interested in things other than horse racing.

Dr. M. A. Taylor of Austin was involved in one of the most unusual undertakings in Texas history: the experiment with camels. The camels were called Jeff Davis's camels because it was his idea to bring the camels to Texas. Dr. Taylor loaned Bethel Coopwood $10,000 (with the camels as security), to establish the camel express from San Antonio to Mexico City.

The venture was unprofitable, and the camels were brought to graze south of Austin about 1878. Later the camels were taken to Taylor's Rambo Ranch near Austin, a model stock ranch with imported sheep. Dr. Taylor was quite concerned about his money. Eventually he became the owner of the camels, even though there is no record that he filed suit. Probably Coopwood readily surrendered title and camels.

Dr. Taylor was also active in the State Medical Association. He was listed as a financier with farming and ranching interests which included acreage on the Neuces River as well as 800 acres south of Austin. While serving as an Austin alderman in 1876–1877, he took a strong stand against excessive government spending. This stance prompted his endorsement for mayor by the Citizens for Good Government.

In these many endeavors, doctors not only supplemented their medical incomes, they also greatly enriched the growth of the state by their scientific curiosity and diversified talents in communication, education, religion, and business.

9

Living the Other Life:
Home and Leisure

With all we think we know about how people lived in the past, there is so much still to be learned, and interpreted, and understood.

— Alice Winchester

Living conditions from rustic to regal varied in frontier Texas. There were as many different types of doctors' homes as there were doctors. Particularly in early Texas, many doctors lived in humble dwellings, often in countrified settings under the crudest circumstances.

As pioneers moved west in the last half of the century, many settlers, including doctors, survived by living in dugouts — shelters literally dug out of the ground. One hazard of living in such a dwelling was that from time to time the roof collapsed, particularly if crossed over accidentally. Accounts of life six-feet underground, note that "in 1886 the leg of a bull shot down over the dinner table of Dr. William Hunt, father of James Winiford, in Crosby County, and of another bull over the breakfast table of Dr. Arthur B. Duncan in adjoining Floyd County." One of the first doctors in Knox County, Dr. John R. Smith, lived in a half-dugout for some time until railroads made lumber available for housing.

Other early living conditions were described by Dr. Cranfill in his *Chronicle* in 1879:

> When my wife and I went over to Turnersville to take up housekeeping, we rented a little two-room weather-boarded house. While this house was weather-boarded on the outside, it had never been ceiled [*sic*], and hence it was not a very comfortable winter home. The rent was three dollars a month. . . . We had no dining table. We took our meals off of the smooth side of a large drygoods box. We had no barn, so we kept the feed for my pony under the bed. It preserved the corn and other provender, and at the same time this feed had its part in keeping out the boreal blasts of the keen north wind.

Typical of Texas at that time, Dr. Benjamin Franklin Young's first home in Marshall in 1846 was a log home, which connected to his office in one corner of the yard. Such homes caused Texas to be called "a log cabin frontier." Even Anson Jones, last president of the Republic of Texas, lived on his plantation in a simple clapboard home called by the grand name of Barrington.

Since the period of the Republic of Texas, however, there was evidence of gracious living on the frontier. One home of Louisiana Creole architecture was built in the 1840s by Dr. Edward Joseph Gillard two miles southeast of Liberty, Texas. Later in the century, some prosperous doctors built larger homes, a number of which are now restored and open to the public. Dr. Theodore Koester's home in New Braunfels, built around 1859 of native limestone, had basement and first floor walls eighteen inches thick. This home was equipped with speaking tubes which connected three floors, a convenience in the days before telephones.

Waverly is another doctor's home, now a Texas Historical Landmark open to the public for tours. This Greek Revival home built in Chappell Hill in 1850, was sold four years later to Colonel William Sledge. Another Greek Revival home is the one built on Mill Creek for Annie McGregor.

Dr. Gregor McGregor came to Texas in 1852 from North Carolina, only a year after graduating from New York University Medical School. Soon he founded a small colony of North Carolinians, composed of many of his relatives and other Scotsmen. In addition to his medical practice, he bought many leagues of land in Austin, Washington, and Fayette counties. According to report, "by 1861 McGregor held land valued at $176,000, making him one of the 250 men in Texas whose total wealth exceeded $100,000 at that time." The town of McGregor, built on land that the doctor once owned, was named for him.

Farr Home in Belton. Dr. Rezin S. Farr bought this house for $2,500 when he moved to Belton from Centerville in 1879. Two years later, Dr. Farr added a "cistern house," horse barn, and tackroom and buggy shed.

Courtesy Greg Korman, Temple, Texas

The doctor married Annie Portia Fordtran, the daughter of a German immigrant, Charles Fordtran, an Austin colonist since 1832. Fordtran became "one of the largest landowners in Austin County." About three miles from Fordtran's house, Dr. McGregor built an imposing home for his new bride in 1861, on a hill overlooking Mill Creek.

The house was built in the Greek Revival style, similar in plan to many two-story homes built across the South. The home may have reminded Dr. McGregor of beautiful homes which were built in North Carolina where he grew up. The home was constructed of native woods; the fireplaces were built with locally-made bricks. The house is noted for its interior fresco painting, thought to be done by the noted artisan, Rudolph Melchior. Among the techniques used on the interior woods of the McGregor house were "freehand painting, stenciling, graining, marbleizing, and pounce-pattern transfer."

Earle–Harrison House in Waco. Dr. and Mrs. Baylis Wood Earle began construction of this Greek Revival house in 1858, the first of its kind in central Texas. Oxen brought the nine cypress columns overland from east Texas.

Courtesy Phil Van Duivendyk, Waco, Texas

Dr. McGregor lived in the home until 1872, when he retired from medical practice. The next year he sold the house to a neighbor. The house, which has since been restored, has now been moved to the Winedale Museum, where it is open to the public.

Through the years, Dr. McGregor had a large, successful medical practice covering several counties. He was one of the founders of the Washington County Medical Association, one of the first organized groups in the state and the group that later issued the call to physicians to organize the state society in 1869.

In 1872, Dr. McGregor suffered frostbite, which resulted in gangrene and the loss of his leg. Subsequently, he retired from active medical practice and moved to Waco, where he became vice-president of the Waco State Bank and continued to add to his land holdings. Still, he was an active member of the Waco Medical Association, serving a term as president in 1878. He also was active in the state medical association, and several times he was a delegate to meetings of the American Medical Association.

McGregor–Grimm House at Round Top. This Greek Revival house was built of native woods in 1861 by Dr. Gregor C. McGregor, one of the Founders of the Washington County Medical Association. This photograph, taken in 1893, shows the house on its original site on Mill Creek near Wesley, Texas. The McGregor–Grimm House is now at the Winedale Historical Center.

Courtesy University of Texas at Austin, Winedale Historical Center

At his request, the only words on his gravestone were:

Here lies a man who tried to do his duty.

Serviceable or stylish, a doctor's manner of dressing varied as much as his circumstances. Doctors on the far edges of the frontier were never seen without their boots, while top hats and Prince Albert coats were worn by some doctors in the larger places. Dr. A. S. McDaniel of San Antonio was one such fashionable dresser; his attire may have been suitable where he lived, but in certain frontier communities further west, his clothes might have been the subject of jest or perhaps even the target of a stray bullet.

Dr. J. F.Y. Paine, first dean of the medical faculty at the Medical Branch in Galveston, was another doctor who dressed in style. The professor was described in this way:

> He always wore a cream-colored beaver hat, an Ascot tie, a Prince

> Albert coat and striped trousers, which with his six-foot-four-inch height and his three hundred pounds of urban dignity must have made him truly a magnificent spectacle.

On the other hand, Dr. J. H. Sears of Waco, a charter member and past president of the Texas State Medical Association, bought a pair of high-top boots once a year when he had his hair trimmed to go to the meeting of the state association.

Earlier, Dr. Francis Moore, Jr., the well-known editor of the *Telegraph,* was described during the period of the Republic:

> In stature, he is a long slabsided, knock-kneed six footer, and . . . sports but one arm. . . . During the intolerably hot weather . . . the same Kentucky jeans pants, the same pair of stichdowns, the same long and flowing green robe, and the same redoubtable ancient drab beaver, adorned the tall and disproportioned outward man. . . .

William O. Wilkes, who wrote *History of the Waco Medical Association*, described the custom of wearing long beards:

> A beard seems to have been almost as necessary to the doctor of the eighteen-sixties and 'seventies as were the tall hats and long-tailed Prince Albert coats to those of the 'eighties and 'nineties — a mark of distinction, setting aside the doctor as some one different from, and really superior to the common herd. . . . By nineteen hundred the beards had shrunken to the dinky little Van Dykes. . . . Soon after the coming of aseptic surgery and obstetrics the lovely germ-catching beards disappeared from the faces of doctors, forever.

Wilkes went on to describe the change in dress brought about by new methods of transportation:

> Many of the early members of the Waco profession abandoned boots for the stylish congress gaiters when buggies began to be used more frequently about 1870; the kind of shoes, you know, with elastic sides that soon lost their elasticity and flopped around the ankles. They could be put on as quickly as boots in hurried dressing.

In a doctor's life, "hurried dressing" occurred frequently.

If doctors, for the most part, had little time for fashion on the frontier, they had even less for leisure. In early Texas, an activity such as hunting or fishing was considered more a necessity than a pleasant pastime. Later in the century, doctors engaged in these activities for sport as well as to offer some variety to the meager fare available on frontier dinner tables.

In Abilene, *The Taylor County News* of March 27, 1885, reported news of one hunting expedition:

> Dr. I. C. McCoy, W. A. Bryant, M. W. Worthington, and G. W. Boyce, returned a few days ago from an extended trip northwest of here, where they went to recuperate and enjoy a few day's hunt. They were on the Salt Fork of the Brazos, where they found turkey, quail, etc. in abundance. They succeeded in killing eleven deer, several quails and, the doctor says, "caught on to a good appetite."

Wild game for the table was not the only pursuit of hunters. Dr. Oscar S. McMullen, a surgeon in Victoria, described a burro hunt which had some surprising sights:

> About 1891, I was out near where Kingsville is now located on the sand dunes hunting burros. The cattlemen of that section wanted the burros killed out as they were there in great numbers and depleting the grass. I was not a little surprised to find two old camels browsing around the sand dunes. Although I was there often after that, I never saw them again.

Dr. Granville Phillips of Kentucky continued foxhunting, his favorite sport, after moving to Tyler, Texas. Certainly a few heads turned as Dr. Phillips, astride a fine horse, raced after his baying hounds while hunting horns sounded in the distance.

A few hours of leisure were not easily obtained in the life of many doctors always on call. Dr. Carroll Peak, the first civilian doctor in Fort Worth, wearied of being the only doctor in town who took patients' calls day and night. To conscientiously solve this problem, Dr. Peak occasionally retreated to a hammock in a grove of trees out of sight of the house. His wife then truthfully told callers the doctor was not at home. Even so, Dr. Peak, who contributed much to early Fort Worth, had little enough time to indulge in this harmless procrastination.

Filling leisure hours was not a problem in the nineteenth century when doctors were always on call. There was hardly time to make a living, much less time to spend on the luxury of leisure.

10

Determining Remedies: *Granny Rags to Tonics*

In early days with rough living, common food and open houses, people were not often sick; and if they chanced to fall ill, they learned to medicate themselves with the indigenous herbs, such as butter-willow, squaw-weed, wild peach; and many other plants and were quite successful, too.

— Dr. J. E. Lay, Lavaca County, *ca.* 1870

Every household on the frontier probably practiced some form of folk medicine or "kitchen medicine." Home remedies were in keeping with the principles of Jacksonian democracy, which emphasized the rights of citizens to take responsibility for their own ills and to choose their own remedies. Since Texas settlers were of necessity self-reliant, they did not hesitate to practice handed-down folk cures.

Various home remedies were based on ancient theories and folk practices used over the centuries. One of these was the doctrine of signatures, the primitive belief that the true nature of an object is expressed in its image. By examining an object's "signature," or image, certain uses could be determined. With this logic, purple and red objects were prescribed for blood disorders. Jaundice was often treated with yellow bark.

Some remedies were based on other applications of this logic.

Many plants were medicinally used because of the shape of their parts. Certain roots and leaves were prescribed if they bore a resemblance to certain ills. For example, pine leaves were used for toothache because the scales of the cone resembled fore-teeth.

Magic and superstition governed other health-care practices such as believing that fern seed made one invisible. Some primitive beliefs concerned removing an illness or symptom through transference by rubbing, touching, or verbal incantation. This was sometimes called "sympathetic and contagious magic." One such remedy required rubbing warts with various objects — anything from a bean leaf to a piece of cloth — and then burying or disposing of the object.

Remnants of primitive practices used on the frontier included wearing some type of charm or amulet around the neck to ward off sickness. Many people wore noxious-smelling asafetida bags of camphor, garlic, and various other ingredients. Some wore "granny rags," flannel cloths rubbed with a variety of "potent" ingredients including turpentine and lard. Various metals, such as copper or silver, used in different ways were thought to have curative powers.

Poultices made of everything from coal oil, cow manure, and various plants were applied for many illnesses. On the frontier, when a person had mumps, a common remedy was a poultice made from prickly pear.

When poisonous bites, such as from rabid dogs, skunks, and rattlesnakes occurred, some people prized a "madstone" as treatment for such emergencies. Not readily obtained, a "madstone" was a stone-like object, usually small and smooth, though sometimes varying in size and shape. These stones were found in the stomach of various animals, generally a deer. Sometimes called "bezoars," these were probably gallstones or alimentary concretions.

The porosity of the "madstone" enhanced rapid absorption of water or milk. After the stone had absorbed a maximum of warm liquid, it was applied to the wound and the process was repeated several times if necessary. Some thought if the absorbed liquid turned green, the poison was being extracted; when the "madstone" no longer clung to the wound, the poison was gone.

Many remedies handed down over the centuries were based on common plants and herbs, particularly from Europe or colonial America. Among these were barks, roots, catnip, slippery elm, saffron, and comfrey. When these were unavailable on the frontier, remedies were improvised substituting whatever was available.

Many early pioneers brought with them seeds to grow herbs and healing plants. Among their favorites were mint, oregano, and anise. Medicinal teas and elixirs were often made from barks and roots as well as from herbs. Sassafras tea, a favorite on the frontier, was made from the dried root bark of the sassafras tree.

The following quote appeared as quoted in *Demorest's Monthly* in the April 10, 1885, *Taylor County News.*

> Those who profess to know, claim that therapeutics, the science of cure, has really made no progress. Galen and Hippocrates, it is believed, were quite as successful in dealing with ordinary complaints as the most advanced physicians of our own day; yet medical science has made marvelous advances in every other department, especially in surgery and the knowledge of diseases; yet with all this it is suspected that the old women of former generations with their "yarb" teas and simple medicines were quite as successful in treating common ailments — colds and the like — as are the usual run of physicians with their powerful mineral drugs and bookish learning. . . . The problem, after all, is not so much how to cure disease as how to avoid being sick.

Black cat tail tea: "Granny" cure for pneumonia

Find the blackest cat that you are able to find and cut off his tail and make a tea and mix it about half and half with good red liquor and have it hot. Give one teaspoonful every ten minutes until the patient goes to sleep. The only times I've known it to fail was when the cat wasn't black enough, the tail wasn't long enough, or the patient didn't get the cure soon enough.

— The Medicine Man in Texas

Dr. William Wolf gave the following account of a cure for tetanus to Judge Frost Woodhull in *A Century of Medicine in San Antonio*:

> I recently went to a place near Fredericksburg on an emergency call. The patient was a young man and I diagnosed the trouble as tetanus. The patient's mother came into the room as I concluded and asked what I thought. I told her with some gravity that I was afraid it was lock-jaw. To my great surprise, she replied in evident relief, 'Oh, I'm so glad it is lock-jaw; I thought it was fits.' I thought that lock-jaw was pretty bad and told her so, but she replied that she wasn't at all afraid of lockjaw, that she could cure that, but that she didn't know how to cure fits. I asked her how she did it and she said that the household remedy for lock-jaw was cockroach tea.

"Nanny tea," made from goat dung, was an unusual tea for fevers. Other teas thought curative were red pepper tea, cocklebur leaf tea, birch bark and wild cherry tea, onion tea, nettle tea, and bitterweed tea.

In addition to the home remedies passed down by word of mouth, many early Texans also relied on domestic health manuals. William Buchan's *Domestic Medicine* was the first manual of its kind published in English. Buchan stated that he wished to clarify medical writings for the general public. He believed that an informed person could better resist quackery, superstition and ignorant practices. For the most part, Buchan recommended practices to assist nature in resisting or overcoming diseases. The first American edition of the book was published in 1795 and included revisions and adaptations for the United States. In 1816, another edition was published in New Haven called *Every Man His Own Doctor.*

The Family Physician by Anthony Benezet was written in 1826 specifically for "the inhabitants of the western country, and for those who navigate its waters." The remedies he recommended were harsher than Buchan's, but Benezet also felt that quackery could best be avoided if the public were well informed on health remedies compatible with professional health care.

Another book of the same title was popular in the South and West. The Georgia druggist, Stoyell C. Parsons, wrote *The Family Physician* in 1891. As the title page claims, it was "Written in Plain Language for Practical Home Use." Included in his book were ads for his "Carbolic Mouth Wash." Carbolic acid, a derivitive of coal tar was an antiseptic, germicide, and disinfectant. Undiluted, it cauterized the skin.

One book which was popular at the time many Americans were making the long journey to Texas was J. C. Gunn's *Domestic Medicine,* or *Poor Man's Friend,* published in 1830. Later the title was changed to Gunn's *New Family Physician* or *Home Book of Health,* a work which reached its 100th edition by 1870. Common sense thinking was considered the backbone of medical practice. Believing that if all the fancy terms could be eliminated, Gunn had great confidence that the common man could practice medicine as well as those who were scientifically educated. For instance, he thought amputation could be performed by anyone with determination and ordinary skills. He claimed that "any man unless he was a fool or an

Gideon Lincecum in bust portrait by H. B. Hillyer of Austin, Texas, ca. 1870.
Courtesy Barker Texas History Center, University of Texas at Austin

idiot, could amputate an arm or leg, provided he had a half a dozen men to hold the victim down."

In contrast to "kitchen manuals" which criticized the medical profession, many books for domestic health simply ignored professionals, including instead, lists of recipes or "secrets" for health care. Such collections were also found in newspapers and almanacs as well as other publications popular at the time. As the public became better educated, more material of this sort was distributed throughout the country.

Books appeared from time to time which expressed the purpose of telling the public what a good doctor would tell his patients if he had the time and ability. One such book written in 1869 was *Our Home Physician* by George M. Beard.

On the Texas frontier, such valued manuals served as sources of comfort and guidance. Their well-worn pages gave reassuring if not accurate advice to those who were unable to obtain the services of a physician as well as to those who chose instead self-treatment.

Some reputable men studied and practiced medicine without

formal training. One such individual was Gideon Lincecum, a self-educated doctor with versatile interests. He was particularly intrigued with native remedies of nineteenth century Indians. He was frontier teacher, Indian trader, pioneer healer, explorer, naturalist, philosopher, musician, and writer. He was born in 1793 in Georgia, but grew up in Mississippi, educating himself by reading a few books. He decided to practice medicine, but finding his own medicine ineffective, he resolved to learn from the Indians. He admitted: "I felt tired of killing people."

Traveling from Mississippi to Texas, for six weeks Lincecum studied under the Choctaw Chief, Eliche Chito. During this time he wrote down the names of all medicinal plants. Not wanting to take advantage of the Indian, Lincecum offered to pay him fifty cents for this instruction every day. When his course of lectures was finished, he owed him $21.00, which he paid. The Indian returned $10.00 of this saying he did not need such sums. The old Indian was pleased that Lincecum was putting all his knowledge in a book and that the book would be in English.

Lincecum traveled throughout Texas with extensive notes on the Indians' medicinal herbs in one side of his saddle bags and a copy of Samuel Thompson's *Guide to Health* in the other. His practice was large, and he was frequently sought in consultation.

For a period of time, he moved his family to Mississippi, but then he returned to Texas in 1848, settling at Long Point, Washington County. During the Civil War, he was too old to fight; instead, he made looms and tools necessary for spinning cloth. After his wife died at the end of the war, he set out on another tour of the wild regions of Texas. Not long after the war, he sold everything to move to Mexico for five years before returning to his home.

Recognized as a writer and naturalist, Lincecum collected many butterflies and other specimens from nature. He compiled a list of over 500 plants in Texas with medicinal uses, much of the information gained from his Indian friends. His descriptions of the natural history of Texas were widely published, and he wrote for many newspapers over the state under the *nom de plume* of "Gid." The Academy of Natural Sciences of Philadelphia published one of Lincecum's papers. Formally trained scientists were amazed and not a little skeptical of his minutely detailed observations and unorthodox conclusions. He corresponded with scientists all over the civilized world and even received a complimentary letter from Charles

Darwin who had sponsored publication of some of Lincecum's research papers in the *London Journal of the Linnaean Society*.

His philosophy is captured in his own words:

> Nature has sowed the remedies for Texas disease in Texas soil and I have put myself to the trouble to familiarize myself with them. You can not imagine how grand I feel, and with what confidence I walk into God's interminable botanic garden and help myself to the pure, fresh, efficient remedies when I need them. Admittance always free, labels very plain and there are no old medicines wrapped up in newspapers to fool the sick man within that grand drug store.

Controversial figure, Gideon Lincecum, was outspoken on issues of the day. As a visionary, he earned derision and laughter in the legislature.

Lincecum wanted to abolish capital punishment. He also firmly believed that legalizing surgical sterilization of mental defectives, criminals, and the criminally insane, was the answer to crime. "Cut and purify the race," he said. He called his castration solution the "Texas Remedy."

Some who dispensed herb medicines, in addition to being formally untrained, were women. Nancy Parker, a widow, arrived in West Texas in late 1870 or early 1871 at Tokeen, later called Content. She chose her homesite about two miles from her brother's dwelling on land that was a tangled mass of cedars, oaks, and mesquites.

She homesteaded a dugout half above the ground and supported herself and her children by sewing. She became known as a fine seamstress.

As civilization pushed the frontier back, Nancy Parker's dugout was near a military outpost established in 1874. Glad for protection from Indians, she earned a little money mending and washing the soldiers' clothes. In gratitude, they built Nancy and her children a one-room log cabin.

Remembering the medicinal teas her mother had brewed, Nancy searched the wild thickets near her dugout for plants and herbs. Experimenting with roots, pods, and leaves, she brewed teas and made poultices. She became known for her knowledge of sickness and healing.

Nancy's reputation as a herb doctor spread as more settlers came into the area. Legend holds that she never accepted any payment for treating a patient; it is also said she never lost a case.

In front of this old log cabin in Runnels County is a metal plaque placed by the Texas State Historical Commission which acknowledges: "The home of 'Grandma' (Mrs. John) Parker, local herb doctor. Here she brewed medicinal teas in a huge pot over an open fire; walked miles in Indian-infested country to visit the sick. Lived here over a decade. Sold cabin after eyesight failed 1888."

Without abandoning herb remedies and self-reliance in health practices altogether, many looked to formally trained doctors when home cures failed or when more severe illnesses occurred. Then, failure by the doctor to relieve or cure disease using "heroic" treatments of bleeding and purging, resulted in disenchanted patients. As regular medical practitioners lost prestige, many patients turned to quacks whose medicines and practices were often more pleasant. According to Voltaire, "Quackery began when the first knave met the first fool."

The Texas frontier was fertile ground for quackery in all its forms. In 1891, Dr. Willis King grouped irregular doctors in four categories: "gentleman quacks, smart pretenders, professional buzzards, and advertising quacks."

Gentlemanly quacks were capable but willfully ignorant of materia medica. The smart pretender was a loudmouthed know-it-all whose failures frequently compelled him to abandon a community in order to escape the wrath of duped patients. The professional buzzard was a "dismal old fraud" who dispensed time-honored but harmless herb teas and vegetable preparations. The advertising quack, guarantor of elaborate and expensive wonder cures for the worst kinds of diseases, was a "cunning, cruel thief, a cowardly robber and merciless pirate, a murderer and a villain."

Add to this list of quacks, the supernaturalists: the spiritualists, clairvoyants, phrenologists, and others who claimed curative powers for cancer and other incurable diseases. Boasting unusual healing powers, these people placed less emphasis on the use of medicines and more on miracles and superstitions.

In Texas, quacks appeared early on the frontier scene. In Austin, a Dr. Persons was known as a Magnetic Healer. In San Antonio, a female quack fortune-teller advertised in 1857 treatment as a Chiromancer (or palmist) for all male and female diseases.

Also Dr. Franklin Stuart Temple, otherwise known as the Boy Phenomenon and the World's Invincible Magnetic Healer, practiced for a time in Austin. Dr. Temple put on a show at Millet's Opera House, charging a quarter admission. He was also privately available to patients in a suite at the Driskill Hotel where he professed to transfer his vital magnetism to the ill.

Other occasional visitors available for consultation at the Driskill Hotel were Dr. R. C. and Dr. A. H. Flower from Boston. They placed an ad in Austin in 1888, both claiming psychometric powers of diagnosis. The older brother, Dr. R. C. Flower, in Austin once every three months, traveled in style in his own private railroad car. Both brothers, graduates of a noted diploma mill, the American Health College of Cincinnati, registered their diplomas to avoid conflict with the established medical profession.

For the gullible in remote areas, the traveling medicine man made rounds of frontier communities. Bringing with him his own cures and particular remedies, he was often as successful as his promotional abilities. If he happened to have some new medicine for female "weaknesses," he prospered overnight.

Since eighteenth century England, patents were sought for medicinal compounds in the belief that a patent implied governmental endorsement. To secure a patent, the ingredients of the compound had to be disclosed. Some "patent-medicine" makers were not willing to make this disclosure; they sold their compounds as "secret" formulas without a patent, but the product was still known as "patent medicine."

As far back as the Revolutionary War, American colonists had preferred English patent medicines, even when they were no longer available, but patent medicines "made in America" grew more popular with growing nationalism. As the populace became more literate, they could also read the ads, many of which attacked the medical professionals and their "heroic" measures. Advertising for the various nostrums grew, and a confused public was soothed by promises for cures.

Always the motivation for patent medicine vendors and other dispensers of packaged nostrums was to maximize sales. Unproven and irresponsibly advertised medicine became an incredibly profitable business for unscrupulous nostrum manufacturers.

Pills that cost a penny to make sold for a quarter; pills that cost a quarter sold for a dollar. Quinine, the best-known fever fighter, sold from six to thirty dollars an ounce, and many compounds, such as Grove's Chill Tonic, included this proven ingredient. When one nostrum was successful, rival companies rushed to produce imitations.

The patent-medicine industry offered to the public an appealing alternative to the regular physician's remedies. Patent medicine advertisements claimed their nostrums contained no mercury or poisons. These were usually mild mixtures in contrast to the harsh, bitter compounds administered by physicians.

There were dangers involved in these mixtures, however. Quack doctors and apothecaries liberally dispensed medicine to a gullible public willing to swallow anything. Most often, these decoctions were pleasantly palatable. Since many nostrums at one time contained alcohol, opium, or other narcotics, excessive use often led to addiction. Opium preparations, used in small amounts as pain killers by orthodox physicians, were peddled indiscriminately by quacks.

In one western town, a large part of one community became addicted to the drug. Likewise bitters (medicinal liquors), which were used moderately in orthodox prescriptions to soothe internal irritations, were excessively used, sometimes leading to alcoholism. Eighty-proof alcohol in some preparations no doubt relaxed users.

Probably the biggest threat to health caused by patent medicines was the delay caused before a patient in critical condition might receive competent care. Certainly the substitution of patent

Collection of Patent Medicines: Dr. Sawyer's Squaw Root Compound for Diseases of Women, Schenck's Mandrake Pills, Motherwort (valuable in female complaint), Dr. Seth Arnold's Indian Vegetable Anti-Bilious Pills, Imperial Granum (the Great Medicinal Food), Oil Stillingia, (45% Absolute Alcohol), Life Everlasting, and Chamberlain's Pain Balm for "Rheumatism, Lame Back, Neuralgia, Sciatica, Sprains, Swellings, Lameness, Cuts, Bruises, Wounds and Lacerations, Burns, Scalds, Chilblains, Frost Bites, Sore Throat, Quinsy, Headache, Tooth Ache, Ear Ache, and All Deep-Seated and Muscular Pains." Photo by Nicky Olson.

Courtesy History Collections, the Museum,
Texas Tech University, Lubbock, Texas.

medicines for professional care was a poor one. The main benefit the patient received from most of these preparations was psychological, a belief that the product was beneficial.

Some of the miracle remedies were Kit's Indian Herb Pad and Blood Medicine, Fannin's Female Regulator, and Salvation Oil, a Remedy for Pain. PPP advertised as, "Spring Medicine for tired men and women, PPP, Prickly Ash, Poke Root and Potassium. Best Blood Purifier in the world." "Indian oil" was sold as a remedy for coughs.

In Austin, a Mr. Radam, who had once grown flowers for a living, concocted a new product called Microbe Killer, which he produced in three strengths. This was developed soon after the germ theory gained credence. Mr. Radam claimed his stronger solutions were capable of curing yellow fever and even cancer.

One group of medicines sold for family use included the following: Dr. Champion's Vegetable Anti-Dyspeptic Pills, Champion's Vegetable Ague Medicine, Dr. Champion's Anti-Bilious Pills, the Plantation Cathartic Pill, Plantation's Anti-fever Pill, The Plantation Expectorant, and the Plantation Cordial. Texas Liniment was also sold at drugstores and by merchants throughout the state by Wilkes.

Elaborate pain-relieving and curative claims were glowingly advertised. The manufacturer of one such elixir cleverly worded its advertisement denouncing quackery. It blatantly pronounced that its product claimed no "magical charms" to cure everything, just lasting cures for three things, "honestly:"

From the *Matagorda Bulletin,* 25 October 1837:

> No branch of science deserves more attention than that of medicine, and every effort made for it against the encroachments of quackery, should be generously countenanced, and rewarded according to its intrinsic value. The discovery of the "Southern Tonic" is claimed as an original and highly valuable discovery, and its inventors are assured that it must rank as one of the most respectable Compounds ever offered to the notice of the public. This medicine does not boast of "magical charms," or venture to insult the good sense of the Public, by assuming for itself the reputation of a panacea for the cure of all diseases, which would be an absurdity; but it honestly claims the credit of effecting a perfect and lasting cure for Fever and Ague, and for being the best Tonic, in diseases of General Debility or Weakness, now known — those medicines which effect a removal of the cause of disease, are alone worthy of confidence — The Southern Tonic, in cases of Fever and Ague, accomplishes this purpose Fully, and therefore makes a perfect cure. It is submitted to the trial of the public with the most perfect confidence, founded upon what it has already accomplished. The certificates which are enclosed are respectfully referred to. Agents are bound to refund the money in case of failure.

Without regulations, advertising was limitless. Many believed Doctor Hoffland's claims for "Celebrated German Bitters:"

> . . . liver complaint, dyspepsia, jaundice, chronic or nervous de-

TEXAN

UNIVERSAL PILLS.

Prepared after a careful personal examination of the diseases incident to this climate, and with a particular reference to the health, comfort, and happiness of the Citizens of this Republic:

By James B. Gilman,

The want of some general Medicine within the reach of every one, and particularly where no physician can be consulted, has often been the subject of much regret in this community.

The scattered settlements and also families residing some considerable distance from each other, and entirely without any medical aid, has no doubt sent many to an untimely grave.

To obviate in a great measure this serious evil, and in some degree to promote the happiness of the citizens of this Republic, these pills are prepared with a particular adaptation to the climate of this country. Perhaps no part of the world possesses the natural advantages for health and happiness which is in the possession of settlers in this country;—but yet, from changes in the season, and especially from cold to heat, the blood becomes sluggish, and humors which, during the cool weather remain in a torpid and inactive state, change their character, and if not removed in season, debilitate the whole system and cause violent diseases; such is the fact with BILIOUS ATTACKS of every kind, and from these remaining for a long time in the system unattended to, they appear determined never to yield to the power of medicine; whereas, if persons in the Spring and Fall of the year would make use of these Pills, say one or two on going to bed at night, to cleanse the system of these humors, they would find themselves far less liable to the attacks of this class of diseases. And the same general remarks will apply with equal truth to the liability to the attacks of CONGESTIVE FEVER, and, in fact, to most of the diseases to which we are subject.

The inhabitants of this country are liable to fewer diseases than in most any other part of the world, and with a general care to health, and when first attacked to make use of means to relieve themselves, would soon cast the foul aspersion, *that Texas is an unhealthy country*, back into the teeth of those croaking skeptics who would have the world believe that they hold in their individual hands all the good that can possibly be given to man by a bountiful Creator.

The effects of these Pills upon the system, is thoroughly to cleanse the stomach and bowels, and at the same time to give them a healthy and invigorating tone; and certain relief can always be depended upon, by following the

DIRECTIONS.

In all violent and sudden attacks of any disease, such as *Bilious Fever, Congestive Fever, Yellow Fever, Cholera Morbus,* &c. &c., where a change is felt in a few hours from comparative health to such symptoms of disease as pains in the stomach, side, neck, and head, and a general feeling of lassitude and debility, nausea of the stomach, and a complete prostration of the powers of the mind and body, no time must be lost, as it is of the utmost importance to check the disease in its first attacks. Take from 4 to 7 Pills, according to the age and constitution, so as to procure powerful evacuations in order to carry off from the system that accumulation in the stomach which is the *cause* of the disease; and these evacuations must be kept up by using 3, 4 or 5 pills till the disease is broken of its power and regular stools are obtained; at the same time a light diet should be followed for a number of days so as to bring back the system to its wonted state of health.

FOR DIARRHŒA,

Take from 3 to 6 Pills for a dose which will remove that peculiar soreness from the stomach and bowels, and also all other disagreeable parts of this complaint. One or two Pills should be taken for a few nights after the disease is checked, in order to strengthen and invigorate the stomach and give back its original health and vigor.

IN FEVER AND AGUE, take from 3 to 6 Pills to cleanse the system, and then (if Quinine can be obtained,) follow with alternate doses of Pills and Quinine, so as to cleanse and strengthen at the same time, and this troublesome enemy to comfort will soon disappear.

In *general feelings of languor and debility*, especially in the Spring of the year—take 3 or 4 Pills to move the bowels, and then take one or two to work in the blood and to *assist nature* in performing her functions, without drawing too largely from her bountiful resources;—and as

GENERAL DIRECTIONS,

in all active and acute diseases, keep up large evacuations to cleanse the system of the *cause* of the disease; *always keeping in mind* that the *stomach* being the receptical of the nourishment requisite to support nature in all her operations,—it is of the utmost importance that all its impurities should be purged,—well knowing that a corrupt fountain cannot send forth pure waters.

In mild complaints, the object is first to clear the system, and afterwards, to strengthen and invigorate it, by frequent doses of the Pills, just assisting nature to shake off the evils to which she is liable.

Houston, 1838.

These Pills can always be obtained of the regular appointed Agents, at---Galveston, Harrisburg, Houston, Velasco, Quintonia, Brazoria, Columbia, Richmond, San Felipe, Washington, Bastrop, Matagorda, &c.

Broadside of "Texan Universal Pill," 1838.

Courtesy Archives Division, Texas State Library, Austin

> bility, diseases of the kidneys, and all diseases arising from a disordered liver or stomach, such as constipation, inward piles, fullness of blood to the head, acidity of the stomach, nauseas, heartburn, disgust for food, fullness or weight in the stomach, sour eructations, sinking or fluttering at the pit of the stomach, swimming of the head, hurried and difficult breathing, fluttering at the heart, choking or suffocating sensations when in a lying posture, dimness of vision, dots or webs before the sight, fever and dull pain in the head, deficiency of perspiration, yellowness of the skin and eyes, pain in the side, back, chest, limbs, etc., sudden flushes of heat, burning in the flesh, constant imaginings of evil, and great depression of spirit.

Quackery was present on the Texas frontier from the beginning. Even in the Austin Colony days, there were those who identified quacks and did their best to warn others. Some were unjustly accused. Whether this was the case with a Dr. J. C. Wright is not known. He felt that he had been accused falsely of being a quack, and he protested to Stephen F. Austin that the local judge did not respect his position as a licensed physician.

During the period of the Republic, the following editorial on quackery from *Telegraph and Texas Ranger,* 24 June 1837, warned:

> We may be styled goose, gosling, or *quack, quack, quack,* but we shall certainly prescribe a remedy for a species of vermin which infests our country, distinguished by the once august title of Doctor. These pseudo "M.D.s" or "Drs." are, we sincerely believe more dangerous than the hostile Indians; and not considerably less numerous . . . We had rather at any time see a company of armed Mexicans in battle array, than a squad of these grave gentry, parading with their "Pandora boxes" in the shape of pill bags — which are seldom opened without entailing on the community disease and death . . .

Quacks and quackery continued to enjoy prosperity. Apparently, warnings availed little. But by 1853, the newly-organized State Medical Association of Texas received a stirring denouncement of quackery in its first presidential address by Dr. George Cupples:

> The standing, social and individual, of medical practitioners as a class, is confessedly lower here than in any other country of Christendom. Charlatanism and Imposture, the offspring of ignorance, general and professional, reign rampant in the land: no legislative check restrains the indiscriminate and unregulated practice of

> physic by unqualified persons, the incredible and destructive abuse of nostrums and secret remedies; humbug is the order of the day.

In spite of such efforts, restrictions on claims of quack medicine were not forthcoming until the end of the nineteenth century when scientific medicine emerged. The lawful answer came in 1906 with the passage of the Pure Food and Drug Act. Then, a better-educated public became more aware that every disease did not have a quick cure or simple remedy.

Saddle Bag Medicine. Photo by Nicky Olson.
Courtesy History Collections, The Museum,
Texas Tech University, Lubbock, Texas

11

Leading the Way: *Social Change*

The British Medical Association was organized in 1832, four years before Texas became an independent republic.

The American Medical Association was organized in 1847, one year after Texas became a state of the United States.

The earliest evidence of an organization of physicians in Texas reports a meeting August 1, 1838, of the Medical and Surgical Society of Houston. The purpose of this group was to educate its own members, to oppose quackery, and to promote unity in order to become a constructive force in the area. This organization published a scale of charges, but there is no other documentation that this society continued in existence until the year 1857.

In 1848, Galveston doctors, including Dr. Ashbel Smith, petitioned the Legislature to charter the Medical and Surgical Society of Galveston. This effort was not successful. The name was then changed to the Medical and Surgical Society of the State of Texas, a change which still did not keep the bill from being defeated. A group of Austin doctors, however, made another attempt at organization soon after the half century mark.

An appeal was published in the *Texas State Gazette* of Austin and in the *Texas Monument* of La Grange on December 11, 1852, to

Painting by Robert Thom of the first meeting of the TMA in Austin, January 1853.

all regular authorized physicians of the state to meet in Austin on January 17, 1853, for the purpose of forming a state organization. The appeal was signed by ten Austin doctors, men who have been called the fathers of organized medicine in Texas.

Thirty-five Texas physicians answered this summons, arriving on the appointed date by stagecoach, horse, and rail. Among those present at the three-day session held in the Methodist Church were Dr. Ashbel Smith and Dr. James W. Throckmorton. Dr. Joseph Taylor of Harrison County, who probably rode three hundred miles astride a horse to attend the meeting, was elected the first president of the association. The first vice-president was Dr. W. A. Morris of Austin. Thus began the Texas Medical Association.

To provide a permanent record of their accomplishments, those who attended the meeting authorized the *Texas State Gazette* to print five hundred copies of the proceedings, the constitution, and the by-laws. These were published as *Proceedings*. In 1869, the *Proceedings* were published and also made available "to the more intelligent portion of the citizens." Each annual meeting thereafter published the

Proceedings until 1884, when the publication of *Transactions* replaced the *Proceedings*. The cost of publishing *Proceedings* was sometimes more than the treasury had on hand; on more than one occasion the costs were paid by "private sources," meaning several faithful members chipped in to pay the bill.

At the January 1853 meeting, a committee was appointed to petition the Legislature for a charter. Although the Legislature incorporated the organization on January 28, it was not until ten months later that the Fifth Legislature approved the original charter, which was signed by Governor J. W. Henderson on November 28, 1853. This charter, officially establishing the Medical Association of Texas, remained in effect until 1889, when a second charter changed the organization's name to the Texas State Medical Association.

The original by-laws set the second Monday of November as the annual session date, naming Austin as the permanent location for the meetings. According to plan, the Association met for the second time in November 1853 in Austin. At this first "annual" meeting, Dr. George Cupples became president, giving an outstanding address to the members. In other action at the meeting, the name of the organization, the Texas Medical Association, was changed to the Medical Association of Texas. Dues were raised to ten dollars, a surprising move since at this meeting only twelve had paid the original dues of five dollars. Thirty-six of the forty-eight members were delinquent.

Dr. George Cupples (1815–1895) has been called "cultured scholar, skillful surgeon, orator, scientist, and distinguished citizen." The son of a surgeon in the British Navy, he himself served as surgeon in the British Army. After coming to America, he enlisted to fight in the Mexican War, serving as surgeon of the Second Regiment, Texas Cavalry. During the Civil War, he was Senior Surgeon in the Seventh Texas Mounted Volunteers.

Well-educated in both England and France, Dr. Cupples had graduated from the University of Edinburgh. He was referred to as the "Hippocrates of Early Texas," a fitting title for a scholarly man.

He was among the small group who in January 1853 met to form the Medical Association of Texas. He became the second president of the Association, serving two different times in this capacity. He is still remembered for his stirring presidential address, which he gave on 15 November 1853. Among his many recommendations, he urged the Association to persuade the Legislature to require compul-

Dr. George W. Cupples, Second President of the Texas Medical Association.
Encyclopedia of the New West

sory vaccination. He was later appointed by Governor Hogg to represent Texas at the Pan-American Medical Congress in Washington in 1893.

As a surgeon, Dr. Cupples was one of the most outstanding of his day. He was a pioneer in introducing the use of anesthetics in Texas, first ether and then chloroform. Among his many accomplishments, he is cited as the first to perform extirpation of the tongue for cancer by Nunnally's method. Dr. Cupples is also given credit for first successfully performing amputation at the hip joint and the knee joint.

A. W. Houston testified to his character:

> He lived here more than half a century; and, knowing him intimately as I did for half that time, I dare assert that he never disobeyed a call of duty or of friendship, and that he lived a blameless life worthy of the affectionate memory of all who knew him. That he accumulated little of this world's goods, with his unusual attainments and ability to earn wealth, proves that he was to a great degree an unselfish humanitarian. His learning made him great and his heart made him noble.

The Society did not meet again for sixteen years, though the exact reasons are not completely understood even today. There may have been dissension among the membership caused by two members who were expelled: Dr. S. W. Barker and Dr. E. McDonnell.

A more likely reason, however, is that conditions of life in the years immediately prior to the Civil War were not conducive to such gatherings. During this period transportation was difficult and slow, even sometimes dangerous in areas where Indian attack was a possibility. The number of epidemics in the 1850s also left physicians with little energy for organizational affairs.

The physicians of varied background and education who came to the first meetings had different ideas on medicine and the role of organization, differences which often resulted in bitter arguments and controversies. Many of these issues took half a century to resolve. These men also carried on their medical practice in an era of growing hostility between the North and the South, which affected every aspect of their lives. They were likely involved in disputes over the slavery issue as well as the issue of secession.

Since this period was followed first by the Civil War and then by the Reconstruction era, it is not surprising that further meetings were postponed for a long time. Whatever the actual reasons, the association finally reformed in 1869.

Austin doctors had been prominent in the earlier organization, but Houston and Washington County doctors now took the lead. The credit for reorganizing goes to physicians of the Washington County Medical Society, who issued a circular calling for a meeting to discuss the formation of the State Medical Association. Dr. Thomas Morris of Brenham put together the circular.

The meeting took place at a hotel, the Hutchins House, on June 15, 1869 in Houston. Travel to attend this meeting was not much easier than journeying to the meetings held in Austin in the previous decade. The doctors came by stage, rail, and boat. The trip from a distance as far as Waco involved an overnight stop.

At this three-day meeting, Dr. T. J. Heard of Galveston was elected President. Most of the time was spent on creating a new organization called the Texas State Medical Association, since the physicians apparently were unaware of the earlier organization. Even though more physicians attended the meeting, only twenty-eight signed the constitution and by-laws.

One of the talks at this meeting was by Dr. Ashbel Smith on

treatment of malaria with the leaves and bark of the willow tree as a substitute for quinine. There was also discussion on the various specialties, but action was postponed until the stand of the American Medical Association was known. It was not until the year 1871 that the custom of presenting formal papers at the yearly meetings was begun.

After the reorganization in 1869, despite persistent petitions to successive legislatures, years passed before a new charter was issued making the Texas State Medical Association legal. The proposed charter was similar to the original charter of 1853, which remained in effect until 1889.

Many possible projects of the Association were hampered by the lack of a legal charter. The publication of a medical journal which was advocated at the third annual meeting and the organization of a life insurance department were among the many-pronged projects held in abeyance. These programs had little hope for success without official recognition and the ability of the Association to act as a corporate body.

For many years, the annual meetings of the Texas Medical Association were not large. In 1870, only twenty-five members were present. In 1871, twenty-six came, and by 1874, one hundred members attended. Out of a member association of 449, 350 physicians attended the second meeting held in Dallas in 1886, even though less than one hundred doctors attended the 1886 opening session, and only twenty-seven were present to vote on important matters later in the meeting. By the year 1895, one hundred and fifty physicians registered for the meeting.

As Texas grew, the medical population increased, as well as the number of physicians who supported the state organization with their membership. Although many of these did not attend the annual meetings, the number of members grew in 1877 to 263 members. At the turn of the century, there were 297 members of the Texas Medical Association, a figure slightly down from some earlier years. Indicative of the times, a number of names were dropped from the membership list because of non-payment of dues.

Diverse opinions were often expressed at meetings of the Association. When tempers clashed, there were heated arguments, often resulting in drastic actions. In one particular meeting, two members were expelled and another was suspended. In retaliation, one member even made heated charges against a former president. Later the charges were dropped. In addition, at this cathartic meeting, expulsion was recommended for three more members. In 1886, one member was expelled for the separate sins of plagiarism and the act of seducing a young lady "under the most grave and heinous circumstances."

The Association should be credited with making initial efforts in many areas:

At the Association meeting in Dallas in 1874, a medical library was established. With the increase of meeting attendance and the number of scientific papers being read, the sessions were increased to four days. Printed programs were issued. In an effort to improve public relations, those in charge invited the news media to attend meetings.

In 1869, a standing committee on Climatology and Epidemics was established. The name of this standing committee was changed in 1877 to the Committee on State Medicine and Public Hygiene.

Since its inception, the Association had spoken out against quackery, but further action was needed. As the result of committee study, a letter addressed to the people of Texas was published in the *Galveston Daily News* of April 27, 1888 deploring quackery and pleading for better laws to protect the public from this menace.

At the first "annual" meeting in 1853, the Medical Association of Texas had adopted the 1848 Code of Ethics of the American Medical Association, based on *Medical Ethics* by Thomas Percival, published in 1803. A similar step was taken in 1869. Toward the end of the century, the national organization, the American Medical Association, created nationwide debate in medical circles proposing changes in its 1848 Code of Ethics. The Texas State Medical Association took a decisive step voting to retain this Code.

In 1853, the Association had elected twelve delegates to the American Medical Association. In 1873, the Texas Medical Association elected six delegates to the annual meeting, but only two attended, Dr. J. F. Matchett and Dr. D. R. Wallace. Prior to this time, various Texans had attended these national meetings as unofficial delegates from some of the county organizations. By 1875, seven delegates attended giving Texas official representation at the AMA.

The inability of the Association to act as a corporate body in securing a charter as well as lack of capital made the possibility of publishing a medical journal improbable. After two years, the Association passed a resolution to cooperate with "any professional brother" who would supply such a journal, more specifically, one who could financially underwrite such an undertaking.

Dream became reality in 1881, when the Association adopted the *Texas Medical and Surgical Record*, published at Galveston, as the official organ of the Texas State Medical Association. Unfortunately, all the members of the Association and the editors did not see eye-to-eye on the diagnosis and treatment of one medical case. Heated arguments continued until the journal's signed agreement with the Association dissolved at the end of two years. The *Texas Medical and Surgical Record* soon folded.

On April 23, 1889, the Legislature finally granted a second charter. The most apparent changes from the old charter related to the location and time of the annual meetings as well as the name of the organization. The charter provided that a majority vote determined the location of the meetings. These were also changed to the spring instead of November, hoping to achieve more participation. The charter designated the name of the organization as the Texas State Medical Association. Curiously, this title was forfeited ten years later for nonpayment of a state franchise tax of ten dollars.

The new charter also called for the establishment of a medical department at The University of Texas. In addition, it provided for a Board of Trustees to govern the Association.

One year the Treasurer of the Texas State Medical Association had to pay a deficit of $4.35 to keep the Association in the black. Even though the main expense of the organization was the publication of *Proceedings*, financial stability was difficult. Upon occasion, individual members advanced the Association ten dollars to insure publication.

Indicative of poor economic conditions, only half of the membership paid dues in 1880. Increasing prosperity, however, in the early 1880s changed the situation. By 1884, nearly every member paid the yearly fee.

The difficulties involved in gaining the 1889 charter diminished the outlook for the Association and resulted in growing internal discord. Membership and participation in the affairs of the association were lower. At the same time, interest in the county societies dwindled. In 1894, out of twenty-nine county medical societies in Texas, only thirteen were active.

As the twentieth century approached, the Texas State Medical Association continued to be in a period of decline. Even Dr. F. E. Daniel, editor-publisher of the *Texas Medical Journal*, aired some of

Name Changes of the TMA

The Association went through periodic name changes, but almost one hundred years after the first meeting, the original name of the organization was restored. The changes were as follows:

Texas Medical Asosciation	*January 1853*
Medical Association of Texas	*November 1853*
Texas State Medical Association	*June 1869*
State Medical Association of Texas	*1901*
Texas Medical Association	*1951*

the problems in his editorial, "Shall We Abolish the State Medical Association?" Fortunately, critics misjudged the situation.

Even in periods of decline, there were always a loyal few who believed in the Association and its future. Through their faithful efforts, the organization was kept alive until conditions were conducive to genuine growth. The groundwork laid by almost half a century of organized medicine was not in vain.

In the first years of the new century, many changes occurred. The Association membership roll dramatically increased. More money was available for publications, which brought the latest medical thinking to those even in remote situations. The Legislature granted another charter to the Association on May 25, 1901. A name change was required bringing about the rebirth of the name, the State Medical Association of Texas. Under this charter, the county societies became the basic unit of both the state and the national organization, a plan sponsored by the American Medical Association. The new plan, which ended much controversy over the matter, was put into effect in 1903, a year of historic importance in the history of organized medicine in Texas.

According to the By-Laws and Constitution adopted in 1853 by the Texas Medical Association, the main organization was to have subordinate societies in each county. Moved to action by this scheme, two counties formed societies shortly thereafter. The first of these was the Bexar County Medical Society, soon followed in the fall of 1853 by the Travis County Medical Society. Several years elapsed before physicians in other counties formed similar groups.

A group of doctors from Tyler tried to organize an East Texas Medical Society in 1856, but if they were successful, they did not leave lasting records. Six months later this group published a fee schedule in the *Tyler Standard*, as well as a notice that they had agreed not to make annual contract arrangements with families to practice medicine.

Following the Civil War, many counties formed medical organizations. Not all were affiliated with the state organization. Both Galveston and Waco formed societies in 1866.

The Waco Medical Association, organized by ten physicians, insisted upon unanimous approval of new members, even though the adopted constitution did not require a diploma for membership. The provisions stated: "Any person not being a graduate of a Medical College, but who has been in the regular practice of medicine for five years, may become a member of this Association, if elected by unanimous vote by ballot."

In Houston, the Harris County Medical Association was formed in 1868. The Medical Association begun in Houston in 1857 and continuing in existence for two years became inactive during the Civil War. In the summer of 1887, Drs. Samuel Clark Red, R. W. Knox, and J. T. Scott organized the Harris County Medical Society.

Dallas formed a society in 1869 the same year the Texas Medical Association was reorganized. Other counties soon followed suit, and by 1889, there were twenty-four auxiliary societies, a gradually increasing number which marked the growth of organized medicine in Texas.

Following the trend to form medical societies, Negro doctors met and formed the Lone Star Medical Association in 1886.

The first native black Texan to practice medicine was Dr. Monroe Alpheus Majors, who obtained his medical degree from the Medical Branch of Central Tennessee College (now Meharry) in 1866. Another black physician was Dr. Quinton Belvedere Neale who arrived in Austin in 1883. He has been called "Austin's first bona fide Negro physician."

Under the government of Spain, licensing of physicians and apothecaries was attempted as early as 1795. The city council of San Fernando de Bexar was charged with the licensing of physicians and with other measures to insure the public health.

Under Mexican rule and in Austin's colony in 1828, physicians had to show their diplomas before they could practice, a serious attempt at licensing physicians.

During the days of the Republic of Texas, Dr. Anson Jones had done his best to secure legislation for medical licensing in the First

Congress of the Republic. Even though he did not succeed, his efforts were not in vain. The Second Congress of the Republic of Texas passed a bill on December 14, 1837, creating a Board of Medical Censors and outlining requirements for licensing of physicians, which included an examination of the candidates.

The three leading doctors responsible for the passage of this bill were Doctors Anderson, Ewing, and Ashbel Smith. Dr. Philip Anderson, a learned man, had been Chief Surgeon of the Texas Navy; Dr. Alexander Ewing had served as Chief Surgeon of the Texas Army; and Dr. Ashbel Smith was a statesman of rare talents. As educated doctors, all of these men realized the necessity of some type of law regulating the practice of medicine. They used their influence to encourage the enactment of the law, which was later repealed by the Second Legislature of the State of Texas in 1847.

The Board was composed of one physician from each senatorial district, making a total of eleven medical censors, and each board member had earned a degree. Despite the fact that Dr. Ashbel Smith was head of the Board, it was probably not very effective. It did not meet in 1839, and the next year, one member of the Board declared that "it operates a serious inconvenience without the smallest advantage."

For a fee of twenty dollars, the Board issued licenses to those who passed its examination. Without such a license, the physician could not collect unpaid fees in court. There is no evidence, however, that the Board prosecuted violators of the licensing laws.

When annexation came in 1845, and Texas entered the Union, the new state did not enact laws regulating medical practice for about a quarter of a century, even though some were considered. Physicians looked to compulsory state licensing to limit the number of medical practitioners. In some states the irregulars tried to establish two licensing boards, fighting legislative attempts to require licensing.

In 1873, however, the Texas Legislature passed a law which provided for some regulation. The law called for a board of examiners in each county and demanded that practitioners either have a degree from a recognized medical school or a certificate from a board of examiners.

The new Texas Constitution of 1875 also provided for the Legislature to pass laws stating the minimum qualifications for medical practitioners. The next year the Legislature repealed the law of 1873 and enacted a new law. This law remained in effect until 1901, when the Legislature divided the medical profession into three branches, each having its separate board of examiners. The three boards established by this act were the Board of Medical Examiners, the Board of Eclectic Examiners, and the Board of Homeopathic Medical Examiners.

The existence of these three boards created much confusion. A doctor who failed to pass one board could then attempt to pass another. In an attempt to simplify the situation in 1907, the Legislature passed the Texas Medical Practice Act, the amended law under which physicians practice today.

In 1891, a National Confederation of State Medical Examining and Licensing Boards was established. Even at this time, students were allowed to study one year with a preceptor to replace one year of formal education. The Conference in 1891, however, forced many schools to adopt the three-year graded course. This was an important first step which paved the way for further developments in the twentieth century: a national board of examination and effective state licensing.

Since the days of Spanish rule, government has attempted to deal with epidemics and other public health problems. Royal orders concerned care of those in need of medical help in the Province of Texas as far back as 1777.

In 1831, the First Board of Health in Texas was formed at San Felipe de Austin. The next year, the second Board of Health was formed in San Antonio, soon followed by boards in Goliad and Nacogdoches. These boards were organized to deal with panic caused by epidemics of smallpox and cholera. The health board ceased functioning when the epidemic passed.

In 1840, the Republic of Texas granted authority for the city of Austin to establish a hospital and to take other steps for the health of the community. These measures were specified in the Act of Incorporation of the municipality, the first such Act in Texas which included provisions for public health.

Although physicians had appealed to the legislature since 1849 to enact a law which would establish a state board of health, their efforts were not successful. The governor had limited authority. He could declare quarantine in coastal areas, but he could only appoint health officers in areas where local authorities were not able to appoint them.

Individual communities took steps to protect their citizens

from dreaded diseases. The first quarantine regulations were passed March 31, 1850 in Galveston after several epidemics of yellow fever. Galveston's efforts were not as effective, however, as those of Matagorda Bay, a little town which also established a quarantine in 1854. Enforced by a quarantine boat operating in Dog Island channel in Matagorda Bay, no communication was allowed with Port Lavaca, Indianola, or Galveston.

Houston laid a quarantine on Galveston each time yellow fever broke out. Galveston, on the other hand, would down play its own epidemics. The *Galveston News* reported in 1853, that the yellow fever epidemic was much worse in Houston, Indianola, and Port Lavaca, even though Galveston lost four physicians and six of eight Catholic priests.

After this period, there was no quarantine until 1870 when the Galveston local board of health placed a quarantine on the city of New Orleans. Houston in turn placed a quarantine on Galveston, as well as New Orleans, in 1873. The same year Navasota did not allow trains to pass through town. In 1878, Galveston again declared quarantine against New Orleans, and Houston followed suit. In 1888, State Health Officer Dr. Rutherford described the situation thus:

> Like all actions of this sort it spread like wildfire, and passed up the Central Railroad in the shape of an alarm, as the fever had done in 1867. Brenham quarantined against Houston, Hempstead against Brenham, Bryan quarantined against Millican, and so on through the catalogue, each individual municipality acting under its own jurisdiction, countenanced by the only law then extant, the law of 1859, which was simply a law of permission, and allowed communities to protect themselves from one another and from plagues that existed outside. This nature of affairs, each little municipality acting in its own individual capacity, brought about a convention of health officers, which took place in the city of Houston on September 19, 1878.

The city of Austin talked of some form of quarantine in the early 1870s when yellow fever cases were reported. The newspapers issued the following comment: "An old and experienced physician, J. M. Litten, of our city says that after exhaustive investigation he is able to assert that yellow fever has never generated at an altitude above 400 feet above the level of the sea. Let the panic stricken from the wasted areas come here."

Such comments aroused much speculation about the effectiveness of isolating sick patients or using some form of quarantine. Those who were able traveled to escape epidemics. Many who lived on the coast traveled inland. In 1867, many families moved to Austin during the summer and fall months, nor did they return to their homes until past November.

One argument used by those who opposed quarantine referred to the necessity of both a "terrine" [*sic*] and an "aerial" cause for illness. Speaking of the "terrine cause," the following comment was made in the Report on Climatology of the *Transactions of the Texas State Medical Association, April 1877*:

> This cause, then so absolutely essential to the out-break of an epidemic, being indigenous, and not exotic or imported, shows, beyond a doubt, the inutility of a quarantine to prevent the occurrence of epidemics and the value of sanitary police.

The Governor was given authority by the Legislature in 1870 to establish quarantine stations, the beginning of the quarantine system for the state of Texas.

The yellow fever epidemic of 1878 showed the necessity of further action on the part of the state. The State Constitution of 1875 provided for the establishment of a state health board, but this was not done. In 1879, the earlier quarantine law was amended. The new law made the governor the head of a state department of health with authority to appoint a state health officer, known as the State Medical Officer. The Legislature took this action in April, no doubt anticipating the summer seasonal outbreak of epidemics. Dr. Robert Rutherford was appointed state health officer, followed two years later by Dr. R. M. Swearingen, a man who achieved recognition even on the national level as an outstanding contributor to public health.

The 1879 law provided the basis for the first state-wide system of quarantine. Certain defects of the law became apparent, however, following the outbreak of yellow fever in 1883. At that time the law was amended giving the governor and state health officer control of all subordinate officers. During the winter of 1889–1890 when smallpox was rampant in many areas of the state, other defects of the law were evident leading to further revisions in April 1891. The department then became the Texas Quarantine Department. The powers, duties, and responsibilities of all state health officers were outlined, including details of financial responsibilities. City physicians were subordinate to the state health officer, as were county physicians.

The fight against yellow fever. Signalling a night train to stop, Health Officers in Dallas, Texas, quarantine the train. Sketched by P. T. Ryan, 1873.

The Kubler Collection, Courtesy of the Cooper-Hewitt Museum, The Smithsonian Institution's National Museum of Design.

When Dr. Walter F. Blunt of Lockhart became State Health Officer, some of the harsher measures he advocated went so far as to arrest and detain persons exposed to disease. Clothing had to be boiled or soaked in acid or bichloride of mercury solution. Physicians had to wash their face and hands in bichloride as well as brush their clothing and shoes in a whisk broom dipped in bichloride. Physicians were also encouraged to wear long rubber cloaks while visiting the sick.

In the early 1890s, there were six quarantine officers on duty during the yellow fever season from 1 May, to 1 November, of each year. They covered the following ports of entry: Aransas Pass, Brazos de Santiago, Galveston, Pass Cavallo, Sabine Pass, and Velasco. There were temporary quarantine officers stationed at railway entries into the state. Other quarantine inspectors were on duty along the Mexican border.

With increased personnel, quarantines were used more frequently towards the end of the century. In 1897, train traffic was stopped in east Texas because of the quarantines on water supplies. In addition, visitors were prevented from entering some communities.

Quarantine regulations led to the building of quarantine stations. The earliest regulations in the 1850s had provided for a station on the east end of Galveston Island. The Mayor received permission from Washington to use the federal lightship "as a quarantine lighter." This was anchored offshore for a five-day detention of incoming freight.

A station built by the city of Galveston in 1870 was destroyed in the hurricane in 1875. Later there seemed to be a need for larger facilities. In 1892, the state health officer appealed to the city of Galveston for ten acres near the shoals of Pelican Island to be used for a quarantine station. The city then donated the area to the state. Quarantine buildings were built with various isolated accommodations.

Quarantine stations were often vulnerable to disasters. The quarantine station built at Corpus Christi known as Shell Banks Hospital was destroyed by fire.

R. M. Swearingen, State Health Officer, testified to the effectiveness of the Galveston quarantine station and others as protection against yellow fever and cholera. Protection against smallpox was another matter, however, due to the long period of incubation of smallpox as well as the prevalence of the disease in Mexico. The difficulty of the situation made Dr. Swearingen declare in 1894: "An army of men could not guard against invasion of smallpox along the Mexican frontier under existing conditions."

In 1903, the Texas Quarantine Department became the Department of Public Health and Vital Statistics, and in 1909, the six-member Texas State Board of Health was created, a result of many previous ventures in public health. Ineffective as many of these early attempts were, they served as groundwork for more enlightened policies, including the development of the first sanitary code.

12

Moving Ahead:
Medicine Progresses

Nature knows no pause in progress and development, and attaches her curse on all inaction.

Goethe
(1749–1832)

The earliest nineteenth century women in medicine were midwives. Surprisingly, even while Texas was under the Spanish rule, Governor Cordero took steps for the licensing of midwives in 1809. Accordingly,

> . . .all women desirous of practicing midwifery must first register with the city council, and pass an examination to obtain a license. This obstetrical law was adopted to reduce infant mortality which was attributed in part to the lack of knowledge and experience of many women who posed as midwives. Those who secured the coveted license by presenting evidence of their skill and ability were to indicate their rating on a sign affixed to the doors of their homes.

Women have long performed medical nursing services, but not as professionals until the establishment of nursing schools and hospitals later in the century. During epidemics, both men and women served as nurses to the ill. An organization of volunteers known as the Howards nursed the victims of various epidemics. The majority of these workers had suffered previously from the disease. In Galveston as well as in other cities, many brave ladies, often the wives of leading citizens, nursed the ill in their own homes.

Kezia de Pelchin from Arkansas, was touched by the appeals for help with yellow fever from epidemic-stricken communities and answered the call for help with yellow fever from Houston in 1878. Skilled in performing many charitable works in Little Rock, she visited with several local doctors to learn how best to nurse people ill with yellow fever. During the months following, she nursed the sick until the epidemic subsided. By the end of 1883, she functioned as head nurse, often the only nurse, of the city hospital. For five years, she did what she could for the suffering inmates, campaigning for better facilities, supplies, conditions, and equipment.

While some formal education to train young women as nurses began in the United States in 1873, the first such educational program in Texas was established in 1890 and called the Training School for Nurses. The women of Galveston helped organize this school which was associated with the John Sealy Hospital. When the school was taken over by The University of Texas in 1897, it became the John Sealy School of Nursing.

The two-year program had entrance requirements of good moral character, age nineteen to thirty-five, and a physician's certificate affirming good health. The probationary period of schooling additionally required a student nurse to pass an examination in reading, writing, arithmetic, and English. Eighteen entered the John Sealy Hospital School of Nursing that first year; six graduated two years later.

Another school, St. Mary's School of Nursing, was founded in Galveston in 1897. The next year, a hospital school of nursing began in El Paso at the Hotel Dieu Hospital, frequently called "Sisters Hospital."

Well-trained nurses then increasingly joined the ranks of health-care professionals.

Women were long denied admission to established colleges to study medicine. To achieve adequate training, women were obliged to open their own schools and hospitals. As the issue of women's rights gathered strength, generous donations were given in some schools to admit women. Eastern colleges in Philadelphia, New York, Chicago, and Baltimore were the first to open their doors.

The first woman in the United States to receive a medical degree was Elizabeth Blackwell, who graduated from Geneva Medical School in New York State. She had also "read" medicine with Dr. Samuel Dickson of Charleston Medical School, but she was forced to go to Europe for further study because hospitals excluded her from practice. She later opened a private dispensary for women and children.

Another outstanding woman doctor of the last century was Dr. Mary Edwards Walker, the only woman to receive the Congressional Medal of Honor during the Civil War, a medal which was later revoked in 1917. She was an assistant surgeon of the Union Army, who had received the honor for bravery in rescuing the wounded. Her daring in wearing pantsuits also added to her fame.

Women interested in a medical education gradually overcame long-held prejudices, but they found only more ridicule as they entered practice. Many were barred from using the hospitals. To escape such obstacles, some who were trained in the North came southward after the Civil War, while others sought the new western frontier.

Dr. Sofie Herzog was one such woman. A surgeon's daughter who did not meet the usual drawing room, hoopskirt image, Vienna-born Sofie was educated in Europe. She came to New York in 1886, practicing there for awhile before seeking a more adventurous life in Texas, a goal she attained by practicing medicine in Brazoria for many years.

Dr. Sofie's reputation as the local surgeon for the Gulf Coast Lines spread far and wide. To reach her patients, more often than not to extract a bullet, Sofie rode the train. She rode the engine, the caboose, the boxcars, and the handcars. According to legend, this gritty little woman wore a necklace of twenty-four lead bullets, tokens of operations she had completed. To be sure, Sofie found a life of adventure and service. Since she also married and had fifteen children along with her successful medical career, her achievements seem even more admirable.

The first woman to practice in Harris County was Dr. Margaret Ellen Holland, born in Newburyport, Massachusetts, in 1840. Orphaned as a child, Margaret was subsequently adopted by a prosperous farmer-landowner.

After graduating from the Woman's Medical College in Chicago in 1871, she journeyed to Houston with Major and Mrs. R. B. Baer. As a physician, Margaret assumed the constant care of the invalid Mrs. Baer until Major Baer's death.

Though Dr. Holland never married, she spent her life in service to others. She reared and educated three of her brother's children and Major Baer's niece. In addition to these obligations, she assumed financial responsibility for the education of many others.

Dr. Josephine Kingsley was the first woman physician in San Antonio. She graduated from the University of Michigan in 1873 in the first class to admit women to the medical department. She came to San Antonio in 1878, practicing with her brother, Dr. B. F. Kingsley.

Dr. Ella Ware was the first woman graduate of The University of Texas Medical School at Galveston in 1899. Her people were pioneers at Stockdale, the town where she later returned to practice. She was held in high regard by the community, and many baby girls were named after her.

Dr. Mary Jane (Polly) Whittet practiced in the Somerset-Anchorage area before 1900, probably coming to that community with her husband and children in 1887. She helped organize the Atascosa County Medical Society.

A native Texan, Minnie C. Archer was born in Houston in 1872. Graduating from the Philadelphia Woman's Medical College, she specialized in diseases of the eye, ear, nose, and throat in Houston. She had a reputation for her impeccable mode of dress. She presented a stirring sight driving around town in one of the first electric coupes brought to Texas.

La Porte, Texas, claims Dr. Juliet E. Marchant as its first female physician. In fact, she was one of the first physicians there. She came on one of the first excursion trains in 1893, liked what she saw, and stayed the rest of her life. A graduate of the University of Michigan in 1877, she practiced in partnership with another female physician for several years in Rome, New York, before settling in La Porte, where she maintained a residence and owned a farm in the Lenox community.

Dr. Marchant received a modest income from her patients around the countryside, at the same time doing a great deal of charity work. She was undaunted by the difficulties of transportation. Hurrying to a patient, eschewing a horse and buggy that could mire in the mud, she was seen many times afoot, black bag in hand. Dr. Marchant's life of service ended at the age of eighty-four.

Dr. Charlotte Schaeffer, another native Texan, was born in San Antonio in 1874. A graduate of the Texas Medical Branch in Galveston in 1900, she had an illustrious career after the turn of the century. After she completed postgraduate work at the University of Chicago and Johns Hopkins, she became demonstrator of histology at the Medical Branch, as well as resident pathologist at John Sealy Hospital. Later, she was elected associate professor in biology and histology at the Medical Branch, before she was made full professor of embryology and full professor of histology.

Dr. Daisy Allen of Content, Texas, claimed to be the "first woman doctor in Texas." In the days of poor communication, it is quite possible that she knew nothing about her female counterparts in other parts of the state. She graduated from the Medical Branch of Fort Worth University in 1897, before moving with her husband, Dr. J. W. Allen, to Content. They lived and practiced there in the early 1900s. She may have been the first woman to graduate from a medical school in Texas.

Dr. Mary C. Harper of San Antonio, Texas, was the first pediatrician in Texas. Through her efforts, pediatrics became a specialty. Finding the milk situation deplorable in San Antonio, she took steps which resulted in certified milk. She graduated from the Medical Branch in Galveston in 1910, at the age of forty-two. She died in 1952.

Dr. Florence Collins of Austin was admitted to the Texas Medical Association as its first woman physician. She practiced in Austin where she married, during the last decade of the century, a Dr. Matthews, a member of the School Board.

Before there were hospitals, some towns had structures housing charity cases suffering from varying disorders and diseases. These early "hospitals" or almshouses provided beds for the sick but had few other facilities.

Many of these institutions operated under a contract system, which was often a source of problems and abuse. Those in charge awarded the contract to the lowest bid by a doctor, who then had sole control and management of the hospital. Unfair to the patient, this system gave opportunity to the lowest bidder to sponge on the contract to realize a profit.

Before 1891, few towns in Texas had hospitals. Austin, Galveston, Houston, San Antonio, Fort Worth, and Dallas were among the towns which did, but many of these were poorly equipped. Often called sanitariums, by 1900 a total of nineteen hospitals in Texas were registered by the American Medical Association.

Railroad companies sponsored hospitals in many cities; many

of these were the first and the best-staffed hospitals in the area. Such hospitals developed in the 1890s or soon thereafter in the following cities: Houston, Galveston, San Antonio, Corpus Christi, Temple, Fort Worth, Dallas, Marlin, Tyler, Marshall, Palestine, Longview, Texarkana, and El Paso.

Other than the Alamo, which housed what is considered the first hospital in Texas, the City Council of San Antonio recommended in 1853 the establishment of a hospital and poorhouse for the "indigent sick and poor persons." An elected Board of Commissioners was given the task of screening the applicants.

The Catholic Church built the first civilian hospital in San Antonio in 1869, a predecessor of the Santa Rosa Hospital, established in 1874. This institution was moved in 1884 to a larger location on West Houston Street.

By 1837, there was a type of "hospital" in Houston. In the 1870s Dr. Joshua Larendon and Dr. D. F. Stuart were instrumental in the establishment of the first railroad hospital in Houston, called the Houston Infirmary.

This hospital was in existence for forty years. Various city doctors were hired on a contractual basis to operate the hospital, paying all the expenses of the institution themselves. They received money on a per diem basis for charity cases, which included patients who were insane, aged, homeless, mentally retarded, and girls with fatherless babies.

Dr. Charles Owens was the first physician to take charge of the hospital under the contract system. He continued as head of the institution until his death in 1874. At that time, a new contract was made with Dr. T. J. Boyles and Dr. D. F. Stuart to give food, shelter, and medical service to the indigent sick for fifty cents per day per patient. By 1883, that particular group of frame buildings owned by the County Commissioners on Washington Avenue was known as "Charity Hospital," "County Hospital," the "Poor House," or the "Stuart & Boyles Infirmary." The location of the hospital was subsequently changed to the old Brashear home near the railroad.

In the years that Stuart and Boyles operated this institution, they were under constant criticism for inadequacies. Some of the patients did not have sufficient clothing or bedding; indeed, one report claimed patients were sleeping on the floor. In addition, the hospital required patients to wait upon each other in order to save labor costs. In defense of the doctors in charge, they made every ef-

St. Joseph's Infirmary in Houston about 1887.
Courtesy Houston Public Library, Houston, Texas

fort to maintain and develop high standards, while providing the best medical care within their means. They arranged a program to train interns, and they also actively opposed the increasing number of medical quacks who were then practicing in Houston.

When the contract expired in September 1889, a new contract was awarded to St. Joseph's Infirmary for two years. The rate was set at fifty cents a day for each patient. The physicians in charge were Drs. J. J. Burroughs and A. M. Autrey. St. Joseph's Infirmary, considered among the first Texas hospitals still in existence, had opened in Houston in 1867 as a private, inpatient institution.

A crude hospital had been established in Galveston during the days of the Republic, supported in part by a small tax levied on all passengers arriving from outside ports. Before this tax was declared illegal in 1843, the institution was referred to as "that shell of misery, that great coffin of the unburied dead."

Even older than St. Joseph's in Houston was Charity Hospital or St. Mary's Infirmary in Galveston. This hospital, a two-story frame structure, was begun October 1866 and opened in April 1867

St. Mary's Infirmary in Galveston, 1880. This hospital, which was established as Charity Hospital in 1866, is the oldest hospital in Texas still functioning. The building above was built in 1875.

Courtesy Rosenberg Library, Galveston, Texas

by the Sisters of Charity of the Incarnate Word. In 1875, a three-story brick building, known as St. Mary's Infirmary, was constructed. The hospital is the oldest in Texas still functioning.

A separate facility was established by Dr. Greensville Dowell. He leased the Island City Hospital in 1866 for use in training students of Galveston Medical College. This Island City Hospital became the City Hospital.

John Sealy Hospital, completed in 1889, occupied the same site. That same year this hospital building was donated to the city of Galveston. The next year the city ceded the hospital to The University of Texas in anticipation of the opening of the University's Medical Department.

Dr. James E. Thompson, Professor of Surgery at the Medical Branch of The University of Texas later described his arrival on the scene:

> My first visit to the John Sealy Hospital was a bitter disap-

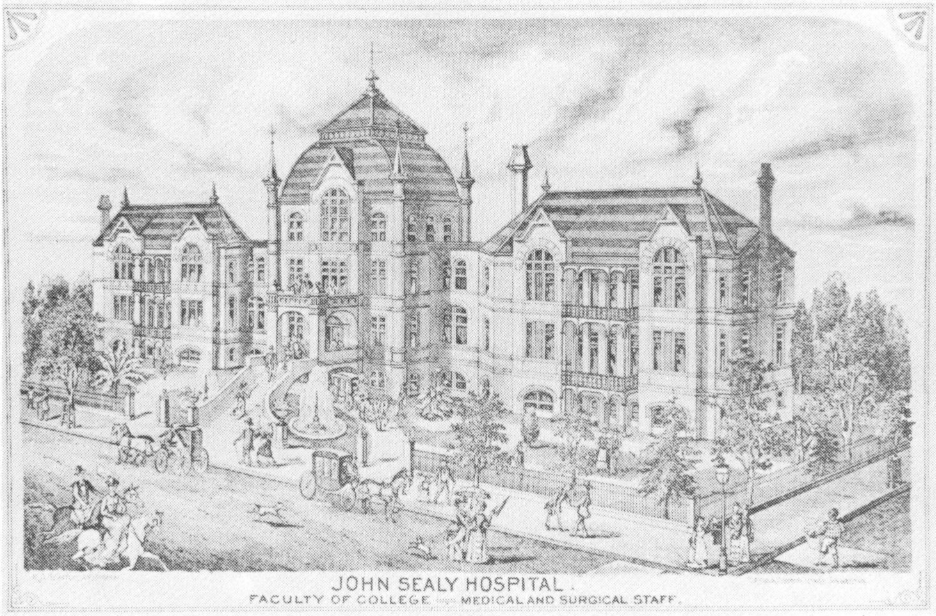

John Sealy Hospital, ca. 1890.

Courtesy Moody Medical Library,
University of Texas Medical Branch, Galveston

> pointment, because I found that clinical material was very scanty and that the available cases were of little value for teaching purposes. Knowing, however, that personal supervision and attention had never yet failed to build up a clinic, I did not despair.

In 1840, an act of Congress of the Republic of Texas appropriated ten acres of land for a hospital in Austin. This project was probably abandoned.

In 1861, the Austin State Hospital opened, which has also been called "the oldest known functioning hospital in the state."

Often the first hospital in an area was the military post hospital. In Austin, the Military Post Hospital began in 1867, under a Dr. Kirk. No records exist until November 28, 1868 when Brevet Major J.N.D. Middleton was appointed Post Surgeon. He left detailed records of the structure of the hospital and its operation. The hospital ward accommodated twelve beds with "an average occupancy of six." Among the disorders the patients had at this time

John Sealy Hospital Ambulance around 1890.

Courtesy Moody Medical Library,
The University of Texas Medical Branch, Galveston

were: "chronic rheumatism, contusions, convalescent typhoid, fractured femur, fractured rib, primary syphilis, and insanity."

Austin's first City–County Hospital opened in 1884 with twenty beds for the ill. Built with $10,000 in funds from the city and county, the large stone structure with typical bays and pinnacles was a fine example of Queen Anne architectural style. The cost to the taxpayers for operation of the facility was close to $4000 in its second year of operation.

Dr. Berthold E. Hadra opened the first private hospital in Austin in 1873. Dr. Hadra's infirmary was located at the Wahrman House near the Capitol. In 1885, he opened a Hospital for Women's Diseases, the Ladies Infirmary. The Austin Sanitarium took over the management two years later, even though Dr. Hadra was still in charge. The hospital then was open to all but contagious diseases.

Another private hospital in Austin in the 1870s was Dr. Sledge's Female Infirmary on Capitol Hill. This infirmary was also called Alhambra House. According to the newspaper of that time, Mrs. Sledge assisted the doctor in their infirmary.

The Austin Sanitarium was organized in 1877, and Dr. R. M. Swearingen was involved in this group effort.

Hospitals were sometimes organized for particular therapies. In 1893 Dr. J. J. Tobin and Dr. T. S. Petty organized the Hagey Institute of Austin. They gave the Bichloride of Gold Cure for those suffering from "the liquor, opium, and tobacco habit."

The Eye and Ear and Throat Charity Hospital was incorporated in 1895.

Among early hospitals in Dallas were the first Parkland Hospital, opened in 1894, and St. Paul's Sanitarium in 1895. In 1898,an impressive building, designed by the architect H. A. Overbeck was built for St. Paul's.

Also in Dallas, Dr. Henry Keirn Leake opened a private sanitarium, the Leake Sanitarium, in 1892.

Some doctors converted their homes into hospitals. Such was the case in Marshall where Dr. John Hunter Pope's home, Valleloma, became a private hospital. The institution later became known as the Kahn Memorial Hospital.

The first General Hospital in Fort Worth was St. Joseph's Hospital begun in 1885 in a frame building. By 1896, this building was replaced with a three-story brick structure. At that time the hospital was called an infirmary.

Plans for All Saints Hospital began in 1896 at a meeting of women from Trinity Episcopal Church. A charter was not issued for four years, however.

The first private hospital in Fort Worth, Florence Sanitarium, was named for Dr. Carroll M. Peak's wife, Florence. Dr. E. J. Beall established this institution.

The Spohn Sanitarium, built in Corpus Christi in 1900, was named in honor of Dr. Arthur E. Spohn of that city. Dr. Spohn had been director of the United States Marine Hospital at Corpus Christi for fifteen years.

In Bell County, the Santa Fe Railway Hospital was built in the young town of Temple. In 1892, Dr. A. C. Scott arrived in town to be chief surgeon. Two years later he entered a partnership with Dr. R. R. White of Cameron, which later resulted in the formation of the famous Scott and White institution.

Toward the end of the nineteenth century, many cities had hospitals, but there was little treatment for contagious diseases such as smallpox, scarlet fever, and diphtheria. To avoid the danger of spreading infection at a hospital, doctors prescribed quarantine and isolation.

Obviously that meant housing infectious patients in a separate location away from the main hospital building. Many small Texas towns had pesthouses. In places with greater populations, like Austin, the city established pestcamps or tent cities on the outskirts of town to house victims of many diseases. Physicians who took medicine in their wagons to the pestcamps and attended these patients received extra pay from the city.

People continued to fear contagious diseases for other than the obvious reasons: whole families could be taken from their homes and put in a pesthouse or in the pestcamps; failure to report a case of an epidemic disease could result in a city-ordinance fine of $100.00.

In 1856, the State Legislature planned the State Eleemosynary System. They allocated $10,000 for a Blind Asylum, which opened in 1857; $10,000 for a Deaf and Dumb Asylum, which opened in 1857, and $50,000 for a State Lunatic Asylum. From 1881–1883, Dr. Rip Ford was superintendent of the Deaf and Dumb Institute.

Dr. J. O. Perry, who arrived in Texas in 1856, became the first superintendent of the State Lunatic Asylum. He was involved in planning the initial physical plant of the institution.

The *Tri-Weekly Statesman* of Austin reported on 25 November 1871: "within the state of Texas there are 2,000 persons bereft of reason; in the State Lunatic Asylum under the management of Dr. G. F. Weisselberg, there are less than fifty rooms for one hundred fifty-two patients."

In 1891, the superintendent, Dr. W. W. Reeves, was killed by a discharged patient. His successor, Dr. Frank S. White, refused to admit the murderer of Dr. Reeves to the institution. Only after the murderer went on a hunger strike in the county jail and threatened to kill the governor was the murderer readmitted to the asylum.

Demented patients were not the only dangers encountered by those in charge. During the administration of Dr. White, lightning hit one of the dormitories causing a destructive fire. All the patients survived, and Dr. White was later praised for having planned an emergency water supply.

In 1899, the Legislature passed a bill creating an asylum for epileptics in Abilene. This action was recommended by Dr. F. S. White in 1896.

The growth of public and private health-care institutions slowly approximated other advances in the field of medicine. Perhaps the biggest stride occurred when patients began to view a hospital as a place to get well instead of a place to die.

Since medicine is not a science in itself but rather an art which draws upon the sciences . . . scientific knowledge had to reach a critical mass before it could begin to shape medical practice. So wrote John Duffy in *The Healers: The Rise of the Medical Establishment.*

Technology reached new plateaus in the nineteenth century, making developments in medicine possible. Achievements in one field of science led to advances in other areas. The manufacture of chemicals or aniline dyes, which were used in staining bacteria to improve their visibility, is an example of that type of technological breakthrough. The Germans developed many new dyes in the 1850s. Such discoveries led to studies and observations not previously possible in the laboratory.

Not until the latter part of the century did the science of bacteriology reveal the mysteries of germs as well as knowledge about their growth and spread. The practical applications were revolutionary. By the turn of the century, persons suffering from diphtheria could be precisely diagnosed and treated with antitoxin, and the detection of carriers was also possible. Other diseases were diagnosed in the laboratory.

Physicians in centers of learning accepted the germ theory with surprising speed. Homeopathic physicians accepted the findings of bacteriology about the same time as their regular counterparts. By 1886, a number of favorable papers indicate that bacteriology was accepted by the American Institute of Homeopathy. Some doctors even went overboard with the new findings. They believed that someday a bacillus would be discovered for every disease and an appropriate antitoxin.

Texas was behind in accepting these advances. Many of the germ theories met with scorn and great resistance on the part of physicians when they were first put forth. Until bacteriology contributed to therapeutics, the average physician in Texas and elsewhere was not much impressed or convinced. Always there were questions and exceptions which fed the inclination of the skeptic. Only improvements in medical education remedied the situation.

For most of the century, doctors who came to Texas were trained elsewhere, since Texas was behind many other states in the

Germ Theory Fad

A Texas Medical Journal of 1899, reported on a doctor who staunchly resisted the new-fangled germ theory and had overwhelming proof for his belief.

The unnamed doctor, after the fact, was privy to a patient's do-it-yourself castration. The doctor related:

> He [the patient] proceeded to do the operation on a quick and non-expensive, non-aseptic plan. He applied cocaine solution to his scrotum until all sensibility of the parts was destroyed, and with a common tobacco pocket-knife opened the scrotal sack and took out his testicles, severed the cord, and put the organs away in a pickle bottle, and has them preserved in alcohol. There was much bleeding but no infection. The success of this operation without any regard "aseptic regime," certainly knocks out that fad.

establishment of medical schools. Changes took place, however, in the schools where many Texas doctors received their training.

Many medical schools came into existence in the second half of the nineteenth century. Following the Civil War, most of the students from the South were graduated from southern medical schools, but the South was behind the North in both medical training and hospital treatment.

Most medical schools of the day were commercial, self-supporting institutions. Some were in the business of operating drugstores and other money-making enterprises. As science developed, however, the legitimate schools were required to make substantial investments in laboratories and equipment. Money was also required to hire scientists as teachers, rather than utilize part-time practicing physicians as teachers. The custom to place the faculty on salary became a trend. With these needs for additional funds, many poorly-supported institutions closed. The surviving medical schools were forced to look for financial support from sources other than the tuition of their students. By the beginning of the twentieth century, there was a decrease in the number of medical schools over the nation.

This trend was slower developing in Texas where a number of medical schools sprang up around the turn of the century. In fact, over a period of years, Texas had thirteen medical schools compared to the handful in existence today.

The progress of science also affected the curricula of all types of schools. Before the Civil War, most college school terms lasted thirteen to sixteen weeks, and the curriculum was designed to be completed in two years. In the period following the war, most college terms were increased to eighteen weeks or even longer. As the quality of the general education of the lower schools improved, the quality of the medical schools improved also. One significant change in medical education in the last half of the century was the change to a three-year graded curriculum.

For many years, medical training was weak in the medical sciences and in actual clinical training. Students spent most of their time on practical case histories rather than in the laboratory. Some observers complained that a medical student could graduate without ever looking through a microscope. Gradually, a trend developed to add clinical and hospital training to the required courses of medical instruction.

A knowledge of anatomy had been attained in Europe over the past several centuries, but because of the scarcity of medical schools during colonial times, this knowledge was not widespread in America. In the nineteenth century, however, as more medical schools were established, an increasing number of doctors were better-educated in anatomy.

Some medical schools made an effort to be more selective in admissions. The trend developed to require a college degree for admission as well as written examinations for graduation.

As regular medicine grew stronger, the medical schools of the various sects lost support. Many schools supported by the eclectics and the homeopaths were forced to close as costs increased. Some homeopathic schools such as the Boston University School of Medicine became regular schools. Their teaching of homeopathic drug use was then deëmphasized.

Graduates of legitimate medical schools had to compete for public favor with graduates of the various diploma mills, which gave anyone a diploma with fifty dollars to spare. Some of these institutions operated under state charters. In Texas, the New York Medical College of San Antonio was an embarrassment to the state, but under the existing laws, little could be done to protect the public against its claims as a teaching institution. A six-year-old child was even listed on the faculty.

Prior to the Civil War, Soule University of Chappell Hill (later spelled Chapel Hill), in Washington County, made plans to establish a medical department and appointed a faculty. The charter for the medical school provided that its graduates receive a doctor of medicine degree, but this first paperwork attempt to provide medical education in Texas collapsed under financial strain during the difficult days just prior to the Civil War.

Unfortunately, the Civil War intervened before the medical department ever opened. The school was reorganized in 1866 and may not have functioned until 1869. In that year, the first and perhaps only class was graduated.

Galveston Medical College formulated plans of instruction in 1865. The faculty, the first on record, included such men of note as Dr. Greensville Dowell. As dean, he also held the chair in surgery. During his tenure, Dr. Dowell leased the Island City Hospital where the students became interns.

At first, the school was held in the second story of a frame building. There were fifteen students for the first session, and the cost to each was $150. Another $30 was required for graduation. Later the school moved to a two-story frame building which became known as Dowell's Medical College.

Operating with limited funds, the school had many difficulties which caused dissension. A petition was passed for Dr. Dowell's resignation, a move which failed resulting in the resignation of all the faculty. For a time Dr. Dowell alone remained, but when Soule University moved to Louisiana in 1873, the medical school disbanded. Another school reorganization occurred in 1873, and the medical school at Galveston became Texas Medical College.

An address by Dr. J. E. Thomson gives his first impressions of the medical school and Dr. Keiller:

> I saw a slender looking man bending over a large stone crock, filled with preservative fluid. I was told that he was Dr. Keiller, the professor of anatomy. As I approached, he raised his head, and I saw that he had blue eyes and a brown beard. He spoke to me in a Scottish accent, and my heart warmed to him; because, although I am English by birth and education, I am Scottish by descent. He showed me his equipment, and I gasped with dismay, for you will hardly believe me when I tell you that all he possessed were a few stone crocks, a skull, several papier mache models of the human body and special sense organs, and a set of his models of the viscera. There was no articulated skeleton, very few individual bones and not a single prepared dissection.
>
> In spite of the discouraging outlook he seemed remarkably cheerful. . . .

"Old Red," The Ashbel Smith Building of The University of Texas Medical School.

Courtesy Moody Medical Library,
The University of Texas Medical Branch, Galveston

In 1891, the Galveston school became the Medical Branch of The University of Texas. It was not until 1897 that a four-year curriculum was adopted, in keeping with the requirements of the Association of American Medical Colleges adopted in 1894. Not all schools followed this recommendation. The Medical Branch of The University of Texas, however, followed this trend and established the school as a leader in Texas medical education — a leader which out-ranked all other schools in the state by the turn of the century.

Another early medical school founded in 1893, was the Medical Department of Fort Worth University. This school, later called Fort Worth Medical College, was the third oldest medical school in Texas. Dr. Theodore Field was one of the organizers of this institution, and he served as Professor of Obstetrics "during the entire life of the Medical School."

In 1900, a medical school called the University of Dallas opened. Differences of opinion developed among the faculty and soon another school opened, the Dallas Medical College. In time these two schools merged.

The various medical schools gained strength by alliances with universities and larger schools. By 1909, under the Deanship of Dr. E. H. Cary, the University of Dallas formed an alliance with Baylor University.

Another group, The Texas College of Physicians and Surgeons, was organized in 1903, the third school in the Dallas area. This school developed an alliance with several universities: first, Trinity, then Southwestern University in Georgetown. At a later date, the school formed a brief alliance with Southern Methodist University.1

There was no known school existing in Weatherford known as the College of Physicians and Surgeons. There might have been a medical department in Weatherford College. With the avowed purpose of educating poor young men in medicine, they advertised that "the faculty, not being pressed financially, will accept in lieu of cash, cord wood, Johnson grass, chickens, eggs, or any other commodity the faculty can consume." The following liberal requirements were not calculated to discourage prospective students:

> . . . the candidate must be advanced as far as 'Baker' in the old blue-backed speller and know the multiplication table thoroughly. The candidate must be of good moral character, and at least have no present indictment pending, and in event of having served a term in the penitentiary, he must have had his citizenship restored by the governor.

Dr. J. B. Haynie (1800–1871), who became an outstanding medical man in Austin, arrived in Texas from Tennessee in 1837 while Texas was still a Republic. His political abilities were soon recognized and he became a member of Congress from 1840–1842. Dr. Haynie opened a drugstore in 1845 to supplement his income, as well as to help the public obtain medicines more readily.

Always interested in public affairs, he later became the second mayor of Austin in 1850, serving two terms until 1852. He filled the office four times in all. His public services were many. He served as Postmaster, and in 1861, he became Superintendent of the Blind Institute.

Toward the end of his career he realized a need to update his education. After thirty-four years of practice, in 1871, he applied to the Texas Medical College at Galveston. There he attended a series of lectures which led to the degree of Doctor of Medicine with vale-

An Ad For the "Comparatively Young"

A medical department will be opened at Galveston, in connection with The University of Texas, in the autumn of the present year. The buildings are fitted with all the necessary equipment for the teaching of medicine and surgery and the ancillary sciences. A three years' graded course of instruction will be given, each "annus academicus" to consist of eight months. There will be nine professors "to begin with," who will be paid on the average 3000 dollars each for the session. "Comparatively young men, possessed of elements of success and capabilities of making reputation for the institution, would, in the main, be preferred." If there are any "comparatively young men" who would not mind exchanging the barren pavements of London for what Johnson would have called "the potentiality of growing {well} beyond the dreams of avarice" in the Great West, they might think it worth while to apply to Dr. Thos. D. Wooten, of Austin, Texas, President of the Board of Regents of The University of Texas, who would, no doubt, give any information that might be required. It may be mentioned, as a matter not altogether irrelevant to the subject, that Galveston is a growing place, and is believed to have a great commercial future before it.

From *The British Medical Journal,* June 17, 1891

dictory honors. When he died later that same year, Dr. Haynie was mourned as one of Austin's outstanding citizens.

Herodotus wrote in the fifth century, B.C.,

> . . . The art of medicine among them is distributed thus: each physician is a physician of one disease and no more; and the whole country is full of physicians, for some profess themselves to be physicians of the eyes, others of the head, others of the teeth, others of the affections of the stomach and others of the more obscure ailments.

Roughly fourteen centuries later, specialization in medical practice developed with the growth of scientific medical knowledge. When those interested in a specialty could support themselves by limiting their practice to that pursuit, various specialties emerged. This trend developed during the 1870s and the 1880s. Several discoveries were responsible, particularly the discovery of anesthetics in the 1840s and the inventions of the ophthalmoscope in 1851 and the laryngoscope in 1855. These new instruments were contributing factors in making ophthalmology the first specialty to develop, followed soon after by surgery.

The American Physiological Society, formed in 1837 in Boston, was the first medical society limited to a medical specialty. This group was in existence for three years. Fourteen other societies were organized to develop other specialties by the end of the century.

Other contributing factors in the development of medical specialties were the curricula of the medical schools, which divided medical knowledge. Medical societies were formed out of these basic divisions. In Texas, the division of medicine into various specialties hastened with the development of the medical branch of The University of Texas in 1891.

General practitioners objected to the trend, even trying to keep specialists out of the AMA. They were not successful. This body passed a Code of Ethics in 1869, which recognized the various specialties but prevented them from advertising.

In Texas, medical specialties developed gradually toward the latter part of the century, although when the Texas Medical Association was reorganized in 1869, there was a short discussion of specialists. A resolution was introduced but not formally adopted at the 1871 meeting of the Texas Medical Association, which encouraged specialists in Medicine and Surgery. The resolution made clear that "we only recognize as a specialist one who abandons the general practice of Medicine and Surgery."

In general, there was much feeling against specialties by the general practitioner. Such feeling was expressed in 1883 by Dr. T. H. Nott at the regular meeting of the Texas Medical Association. He urged the following: "Let us put in a plea to keep our people out of the hands of the born specialist, . . . which shall forbid any person to practice a specialty in this state who has not done a general practice for at least ten years."

There was discussion at future meetings of the Texas Medical Association on the problem of specialists. One paper made a pithy reference to a specialist as "a sort of one-horse doctor." Other papers took a more far-sighted look. Fortunately, the doctors were more eager to fight the menace of quackery than the growth and development of specialization.

In the last quarter of the century, some physicians specialized in treating eyes, ears, noses, and throats. They were probably the first "specialists" of our state.

In Texas, one of the first physicians to limit his practice to ophthalmology was Dr. M. Josephthall of Waco, but ophthalmology at that time included treatment of ear, nose, and throat diseases also. In

1873, Dr. Josephthall became a partner of Dr. T. D. Manning. Both men served the state blind asylum in Austin as consultants.

Dr. T. J. Boyles of Houston did not limit is practice to ophthalmology, but he had received a degree in diseases of the eye from the Royal College of Surgeons in London in 1879.

In 1880, Dr. R. H. Chilton began practice in Dallas as the first eye, ear, nose, and throat doctor there.

When the Medical Branch of The University of Texas opened in 1891, Dr. Ronald C. Hodges was lecturer for two years on diseases of the eye, ear, nose and throat. The fact that oto-rhino-laryngology was made a separate department in 1892 illustrates the trend to further specialization. Apparently, the teaching of ophthalmology was first separated from otolaryngology in 1900 when Dr. John B. Haden and Dr. Henry C. Haden, two brothers, taught at the Medical Branch. One lectured on the eye, and the other lectured on ear, nose, and throat.

Dr. John H. Foster was possibly the first to limit his practice to ear, nose, and throat. Dr. Wallace Ralston and Dr. Vard Hulen were possibly the first to strictly limit their practice to ophthalmology.

Surgery made a dramatic rise in the nineteenth century, making more progress than any other branch of medicine. At the beginning of the century, surgery had not changed significantly since the days of the Pharoahs in Egypt, where the first known pictures of an operation have been found carved in stone. In Europe, as well as in colonial America, surgeons were barbers — an occupation of the lower classes. Doctors performed a great number of operations on the wounded during the Civil War, greatly enhancing the knowledge of surgery. By the end of the century, surgeons were leaders in the medical profession, partly due to the effective cures they were able to achieve through new discoveries.

The use of anesthesia first spurred progress in surgery. Dr. Crawford W. Long was the first to use laughing gas in 1842, but he did not report the event until 1848. Another milestone occurred in 1846, when ether was first used for surgery at Massachusetts General Hospital. Not long after, chloroform was used in Britain. During the latter half of the nineteenth century, chloroform, ether, and nitrous oxide were the available anesthetics, and word spread fast about the remarkable results achieved by these agents. Even though their use became widespread, the mortality rate for surgery remained high due to infection.

Champagne Recovery

The Post Surgery Report by Dr. Rudolph Menger, of an operation for "multiple colloid cystoma of the left ovary" in the 1880s.

. . . She was then removed to a clean bed, covered with woolen blankets, and four hot water bottles were put to her body. Reaction followed very slowly, and at several times during the first day she was in a collapsed state, but by the use of hypodermic injection of ether, etc., and drinking champagne, she slowly and radically survived the shock.

Better ways to control infection after surgery grew from the work of Joseph Lister, the British surgeon. Louis Pasteur had proved the presence of germs; Lister concluded that germs were the cause of infection in wounds. If the germs were destroyed, he believed that wounds would heal without putrefaction.

Using carbolic acid as an antiseptic, Lister developed a procedure for surgery. Although on the right track, he and his followers did not realize that their clothes, hands, and fingernails, as well as everything they touched had to be scrupulously clean and sterile. Because sufficient sterilization was not achieved, their record was not much better than those who did not believe in antiseptic surgery.

Improved methods of cleanliness, however, as well as steam and dry heat sterilization were gradually employed the latter part of the century, greatly enhancing the recovery rate of surgical patients.

Generally though, for most of the century, doctors were urged not to tamper with the internal body. In the words of Dr. J. A. Abney, who was graduated in 1871 from Galveston Medical College: "Our ablest surgeons taught that the internal cavities were forbidden territory and we were advised never to enter it, only as a dernier resort."

In the 1880s, however, surgeons began regularly operating on the abdomen, the head, and the chest. As the demand increased for surgical operations, doctors who could perform these procedures began to limit their practice. Surgery soon became a specialty, a fact marked by the establishment of the American Surgical Association in 1880. The discovery of the X-ray in 1895 facilitated more precision surgery.

Usually only doctors who had studied anatomy attempted surgery because, without sufficient knowledge, even the most presumptious of the unorthodox physicians were afraid to take such risks. There were only a few eclectic surgeons, and even the various types of quacks were reluctant to perform surgical procedures.

Homeopathic as well as regular doctors practiced surgery, however. One of the earliest antiseptic operations, an ovariotomy, was done by a homeopathic surgeon, William Tod Helmuth in 1876. Within the decade the American Institute of Homeopathy had reported favorably on antiseptic surgery to its members.

Although ether was considered safer than chloroform, according to a poll made by the Texas Medical Association, chloroform was the popular choice of Texas surgeons prior to 1876. Operations were short, usually lasting less than ten minutes, perhaps explaining the popularity of chloroform over ether. Controversy developed over which was the better method. Some Texas doctors did not understand either procedure, preferring to reduce pain through whiskey or spirits instead.

Post-operative infections continued high throughout the century. There was much misunderstanding about how bacteriology affected cleanliness in all that a physician did. Even as late as 1902, one physician recommended that "a knife, probe, needle, or other picke-case instrument can be readily cleaned and disinfected, both before and after using, by thrusting it several times through a wet, well-soaped towel or rag, or into a cake of wet soap."

Dr. George Cupples as chairman of the Special Committee on Surgery presented the Texas Medical Association a report in 1886. His committee mailed more than six thousand questionnaires, 700 letters, and 1500 postcards. They asked for specifics on every operation which had been performed during a designated period.

One hundred thirty-eight Texas surgeons responded. Some surgeries were done in the pre-Listerian time period. Some were done under extraordinarily difficult circumstances, such as: ". . . deprived even of necessary instruments, . . . compelled to amputate a limb in a Negro cabin with a Bowie knife and carpenter's saw."

The widely acclaimed report covered 4293 operations, most of which were not performed in hospitals. Chloroform was the chosen anesthetic thirty-five to one. Carbolic acid was practically the only antiseptic used; iodoform and mercurichloride were occasionally mentioned.

The courage of doctors in performing surgery is evident in the face of the following mortality statistics: trephining, 15%; splenctomy, 100%; herniotomy, 26%; abdominal hysterectomy, 92%;

and transfusion, 75%. The total number of all major operations (2080) had a 16% mortality rate.

Dr. L. L. Shopshire of San Antonio recounted an amusing story of a surgical case he was *deprived* of doing. As he was taking a small boy, accompanied by his mother, toward Santa Rosa Hospital for a hydrocele operation, they passed Dr. Ferdinand Herff's house.

They stopped and asked Dr. Herff to come out to see the boy. He did, and after examining the boy, Dr. Herff removed a small folding knife from his pocket and rapidly made an appropriate incision. Dr. Herff announced: "That's all there is to it." The relieved mother inquired how much she owed, and Dr. Herff replied, "One dollar." As an example of second opinion consultation, there is no evidence there was any fee-spliting involved.

Some noteworthy firsts were performed by Texas doctors. In May 1850, Dr. George Cupples and Dr. J. B. Wright of San Antonio amputated a gangrenous leg, which was "the first time that chloroform has been used in Western Texas," according to Dr. Cupples's journal. Two years earlier, Dr. Cupples had been the first surgeon to use ether in Texas.

Dr. George T. Veal of Dallas, a charter member of the Dallas County Medical Society, was the first surgeon to use plaster of paris bandages on a broken limb.

In 1891, Dr. Spohn of Corpus Christi performed the first successful Porro cesarean section in the United States.

Another important milestone in the history of surgery was the description of the operation for appendicitis by Reginald Fitz in 1886. Dr. Henry Keirn Leake of Dallas and Dr. Bacon Saunders of Fort Worth were among the first doctors to perform this operation in Texas.

Dr. Saunders, who graduated in 1877, from Louisville Medical College and received surgical training in New York, first established medical practice with his physician-father in Bonham. Soon thereafter, Dr. Saunders was called to the bedside of a patient twenty miles out of town. After careful examination, it was clear that the man had acute appendicitis and the only way to save his life was to operate.

Also clear to Dr. Saunders was the fact that he had never done an appendectomy; he had never seen an appendectomy done. In point of fact, he had never seen a case of appendicitis before. But he had read of such a case in a recent medical journal.

Dr. Saunders apprised his patient of the situation, who consented to surgery nevertheless. He returned to his seriously ill patient the next day with the senior Dr. Saunders. After taking antiseptic measures, they put the patient on the kitchen table and administered chloroform. The operation was successful.

Dr. John F. Y. Paine, a professor of obstetrics and gynecology at The University of Texas Medical Branch in Galveston, was responsible for the fact that in teaching and practice, obstetrics and gynecology were considered a single specialty. Dr. Paine, who served as professor from 1892–1910, was the first physician in Texas to limit his practice to this specialty.

Dr. Berthod Ernest Hadra, having been educated at the Universities of Breslau and Berlin in his native Prussia, settled in San Antonio in 1870 at the age of twenty-seven. He moved to Austin in 1872, where he opened the first private hospital in 1873 at the Wahrmann house near the Capitol, the Austin Infirmary.

During this period, Dr. Hadra reported several cases of trichinosis to the Travis County Medical Society, which indicates that he was using a microscope in his practice. Due to this report, the Society recommended that all pork be thoroughly cooked before eating to avoid the disease, a scientific recommendation which was a step forward at the time.

Dr. Hadra gave advice to other young physicians in his book, *The Public and the Doctor.* He was known not only for his commonsense admonitions, but even more for his descriptions of surgical procedures in the field of gynecology and obstetrics. In 1888 his paper, "Lesions of the Vagina and Pelvic Floor," gained considerable attention as a turning point in American gynecology. He also wrote papers on nine Kraske operations for cancer of the rectum. Another paper described wiring vertebrae as treatment for tuberculosis of the spine.

Dr. Hadra's activities were numerous. Moving to Galveston in 1877, he soon became Professor of Surgery at the Texas Medical College. Never staying long in one place, Dr. Hadra returned to Austin in 1885, where he opened the Hospital for Women's Diseases. (See under Hospital) He served not only as president of the Medical Association of Texas, (1899–1900), but also as regent of The University of Texas.

Following his own advice for "honorable endeavor and patient, manly conduct," he achieved a position of esteem in Texas as one of the most outstanding surgeons of his day. In spite of his achievements, he never achieved financial success, which probably accounts for his many moves. He moved to Waco in the 1890s and to Dallas soon after the turn of the century. There he was professor of surgery at the Medical Department of the University of Dallas.

Dr. Ashbel Smith has been called "father of internal medicine in Texas." His clinical and detailed records on yellow fever have been noted, even though he was not acting as a specialist at the time.

Internal medicine as a specialty made strides when Dr. H. A. West became the first professor of medicine at The University of Texas Medical Branch. He achieved national recognition for being able to distinguish between dengue fever and yellow fever when both occurred simultaneously in Galveston in 1897.

Dr. James W. MacLaughlin replaced Dr. West in 1898. After hearing about discoveries in Germany, Dr. MacLaughlin used the stomach tube as a diagnostic aid in gastrointestinal diseases.

Dr. William Penny has been called the first pathologist in Texas. He was head of the Department of Physiology and Pathology at Texas Medical College, which was established in 1873. Studies in pathology at the time may have been simple or even non-existent. As late as 1889, Dr. Ferdinand Herff declared that there were no pathology laboratories in Texas. Interest was growing, however, because when the State Medical Association of Texas met in 1893, a Section on Microscopy and Pathology was created. Dr. Allen J. Smith became chairman.

The specialty boards organized in the twentieth century brought about stricter specialization and the arrival of a new era.

The microscope which had been used for some time was refined during the nineteenth century. The development of the achromatic lens in the 1830s was followed by the water immersion lenses of the 1860s and 1870s. Oil immersion lenses were then developed.

Dr. Isaac Lycurgus Van Zandt, who came to Fort Worth in 1868, is credited with bringing the first microscope to that city, one of the first in the state. He was the third physician in the small settlement of Fort Worth. Some of the leading citizens gathered in his office one evening in 1873. Dr. Van Zandt had recently attended lectures at Bellevue Hospital in New York where he obtained and brought back a remarkable new instrument.

Demonstrating, he placed the webbed foot of a live frog under the microscope lens. Then he directed his visitors to look. They were amazed to see before their eyes the movement of the frog's blood corpuscles.

The following year in 1874, Dr. B. E. Hadra, using a microscope, identified worms in uncooked pork which resulted in six cases of trichiniasis. The microscope was probably used by a number of doctors at this time, but Dr. Hadra was one of the few doctors who wrote about the use of the microscope in Texas.

Francis Rynd of Great Britain was the first to use hypodermic injections in 1845. Fordyce Barker introduced the hypodermic syringe to the United States in 1856, just before the Civil War. By 1875, the hypodermic syringe was used regularly by physicians. It was popularly used to give nourishing substances, such as cod liver oil.

The clinic thermometer was used during the Civil War period as the newest diagnostic instrument, but its use was not widespread. It has been said:

> Thermometers were not commonly used in urban areas until the 1880s, primarily because they were impractical and unwieldly. The best thermometer available in 1870 was nine or ten inches long, not self-registering, and had no magnification of the mercury column. It was cumbersome to use and difficult to read in a darkened sick room.

Dr. Robert S. Hyer, professor of Physics and later President of Southwestern University of Georgetown, was quite interested in the discovery of the X-ray by Wilhelm Conrad Roentgen, which was announced in Germany in 1895. Dr. Hyer made a trip to the continent to see the discovery himself. Apparently, anticipating its diagnostic value, he returned to Texas with an X-ray tube.

Not long after his return, Dr. Hyer volunteered to use his new apparatus on the victim of a local shooting. He was able to see that the bullet had cut the spinal column in two. With this knowledge, doctors were able to remove the bullet. This may have been the first use of the X-ray in Texas as a diagnostic tool.

A year following the discovery of the X-ray, an Austin photographer, George Townsend, experimented with the X-ray in Austin, another early diagnostic use of the X-ray in Texas. After a report that blindness could be cured by X-ray, Townsend collaborated with Dr. Rector of the State Blind School. Townsend was requested by doctors in Austin to take X-ray pictures for various diagnostic purposes. In one case he used X-ray pictures to help locate a needle which had lodged in the foot of Dr. Morris's wife.

The Shocking "Shocking Machine"

Kept for many years in Doctor Kelley's library after his death in 1888 was a battery-operated "shocking machine." The battery was the zinc sal ammoniac "wet" cell which preceded the dry cell of our day. A two winding coil provided with a movable core was fitted with electrodes for the patient. The complete outfit delivered a wallop about like that from the ignition coil of the Model T Ford. Doctor Kelley probably first heard about the use of electric shock treatment in the diagnosis and treatment of nervous diseases at Transylvania University. Professors there could draw on European experience where Faradic and Galvanic electricity were introduced, prior to the use of static electricity.

From Dr. William Dennis Kelley: Texas Physician and Surgeon 1825–1888, *by William Wallace McCullough, Jr.*

Out of necessity, doctors of the last century devised tools as well as new ways to meet their medical needs. The following is a partial list of some accomplishments.

Dr. A. E. Spohn, born in 1845, invented a tourniquet for bloodless operations in the field, a procedure used by surgeons in many armies of the world.

Dr. Samuel Raymond Burroughs, born in 1842, devised an instrument for irrigating the thoracic cavity in empyema without admission of air to the chest.

Dr. Q. C. Smith, also born in 1842, was the inventor of the "Q. C. Smith embryotomy shears." He devised a number of improvements for surgical instruments and apparatus.

Dr. James Addison Abney, born in 1846, twice devised emergency instruments with which he successfully extracted foreign bodies. In one case he used two hairpins fastened to twigs to extract a grain of corn from the trachea. In another case in the early 1870s he effected the removal of a twenty-five cent piece from a patient's esophagus.

Dr. Belitha Powell, born in 1832, devised a bone saw during the Civil War which he made in a blacksmith shop. He was also known for making other ingenious surgical instruments for his own use while he practiced in Houston.

The Hodgen splint, devised in 1863, was a surgical technique developed during the Civil War. The limb was kept in traction, facilitating the dressing of the wound. Another development from the

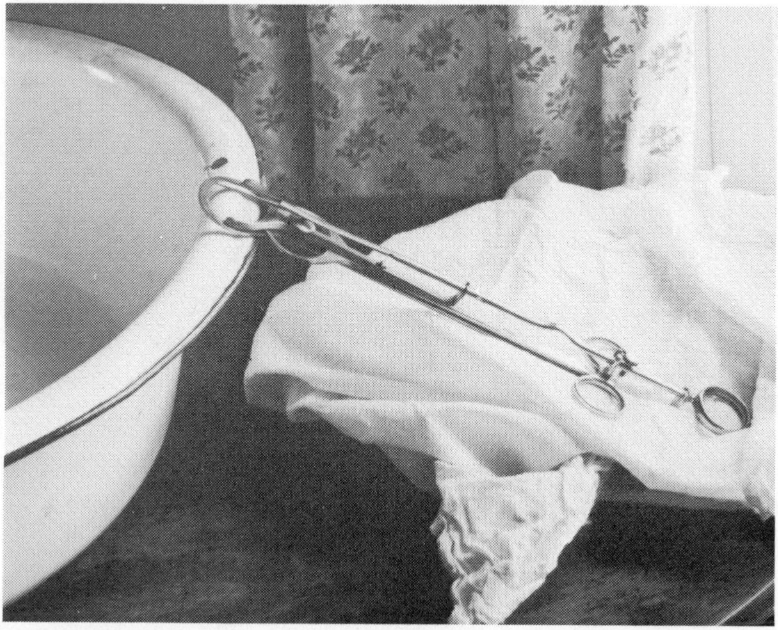

The MacKenzie Tonsillotome for tonsillotomy, or partial removal of the tonsils, used in the 1890s. Photo by Nicky Olson.

Courtesy History Collections, The Museum,
Texas Tech University, Lubbock, Texas

war period was Dr. J. B. Bean's interdental splint, devised for a fracture of maxillary bones.

These many accomplishments were often the result of tedious hours spent quietly following medical duties. Dr. Morris said in an 1875 address to the Texas Medical Association:

> The hero of the pestilence finds his reward in the consciousness of a noble discharge of duty, and in the heartfelt tribute of his patients — the rich and the poor — by whose bedside, in the lone vigils of the night, the silent victory has been fought and won.

Nineteenth century Texas doctors achieved an untold number of those silent victories despite poor odds for success. That same noble spirit will quietly conquer other medical frontiers in the years to come. We applaud the progressive march of medical science and the dedication of men and women who continue to practice the art of medicine.

Photographic copy of a sketch of the first Santa Rosa Hospital on Military Plaza in San Antonio in 1869.

University of Texas Health Science Center, San Antonio

Ambulance at entrance to Physicians and Surgeons Hospital of San Antonio, 1903. A descriptive brochure supplies this legend: "The Institution has provided a modern, thoroughly up-to-date hospital ambulance, with rubber tires, pneumatic swinging bed, and roller bearing axles. This van is always ready to meet trains or go anywhere for patients. The cost of this service is $5.00." The hospital later became the Baptist Hospital.

Photocopy from Archives, University of Texas Health Service Center, San Antonio

San Antonio Infirmary, 1885, with improvised skylight for the operating room. In front, the horse and buggy of Dr. G. Graham Watts.
Courtesy Archives, University of Texas Health Science Center, San Antonio

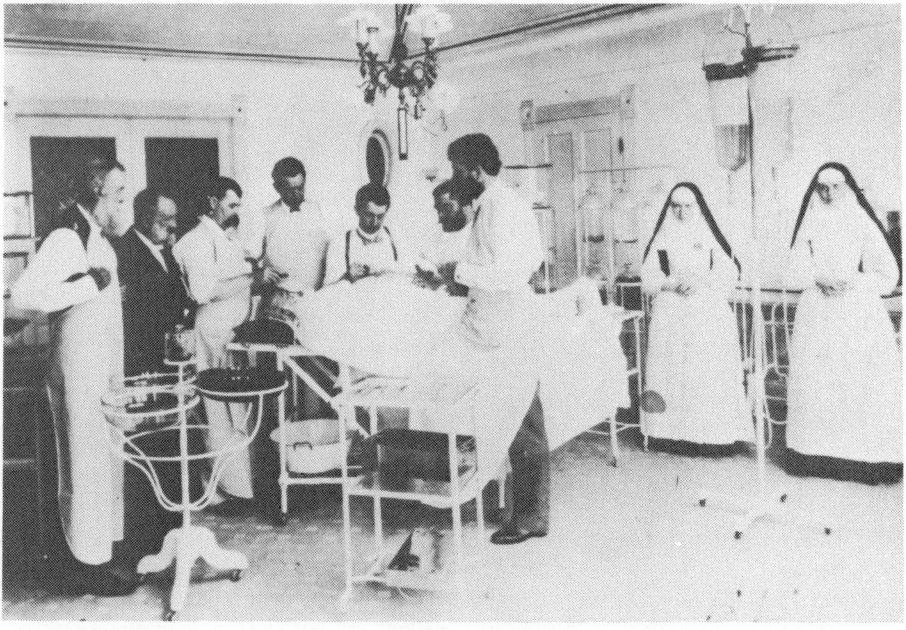

Operating room at Santa Rosa Hospital, 1895.
Courtesy Archives, University Texas Health Science Center, San Antonio

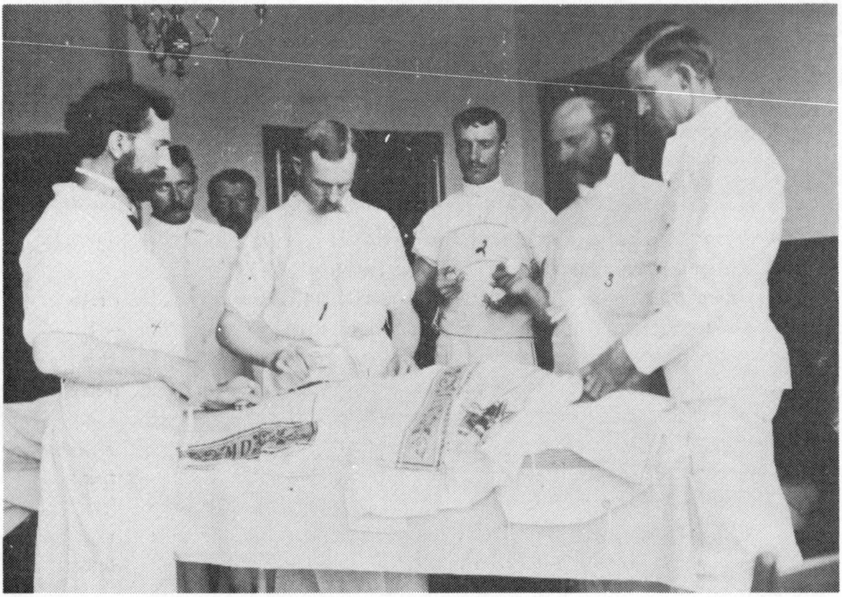

Operating room in a San Antonio hospital. Doctors pictured, left to right, Doctors Moss, Kendall, Starck and Paschal.

Appendix

Acknowledging Medical Contributors

Legend and Fact Concerning Texas Place Names

Physicians played a part in the development of place names for our state. Their influence was felt not only in naming counties but in naming towns, communities, creeks, and other landmarks in Texas. Some of these were named in honor of outstanding individual doctors. Other names were adopted on the suggestion of doctors, who were sometimes town founders or community leaders.

Counties Named for Doctors

Archer County: This county, named in honor of Branch Tanner Archer, was authorized by the legislature on 22 January 1858. Dr. Archer, sometimes called the Father of the Texas Revolution, loudly protested Mexican policies toward Texas. He then served as commissioner to go to the United States to seek aid for the Texan cause. During the period of the Republic of Texas, he served as Secretary of War, member of the House of Representatives, and Speaker of the House.

Baylor County: The naming of Baylor County for Dr. Henry W. Baylor commemorates his service to the state of Texas. He was born in Kentucky in 1818, attended Transylvania University. Visiting in Texas in 1839, he engaged in military battles against Indians. He settled in LaGrange, Texas, where he practiced medicine. During the Mexican War, he served as a surgeon in the Texas Rangers.

Hill County: This county honors Dr. George W. Hill, a physician-statesman originally from Warren County, Tennessee. After graduating from Transylvania University with a medical degree, Dr. Hill settled in Robertson County to practice medicine. Moving to Navarro County, he served in the Texas Congress from 1839 through 1842. President Sam Houston appointed Dr. Hill Secretary of War in 1843, and reappointed by President Jones in 1844. Thereafter, Dr. Hill served in the Texas Legislature. During the period of service to the state, Dr. Hill maintained his medical practice.

Irion County: Honoring Dr. Robert Anderson Irion, this county was created in 1889. Dr. Irion, from Tennessee, graduated from Transylvania University with a medical degree. "Texas fever" prompted his move to Nacogdoches where he became a surveyor and trader. He became a

Senator in the First Congress of the Republic of Texas. President Sam Houston appointed Dr. Irion secretary of state. He was also a charter member of the Philosophical Society of Texas.

Jones County:The memory of Dr. Anson Jones and his service to Texas is honored in the naming of this county. Active in many political offices, Dr. Jones served as last president of the Republic of Texas. He was called the "Architect of Annexation."

Kerr County: This county was named in 1856 for Dr. James Kerr, an *empresario*, who came to Texas in 1825. As surveyor of De Witt colony, he planned the town of Gonzales, naming it in honor of the first governor of Coahuila and Texas at that time. With many political interests, Dr. Kerr initiated the first law in Texas to prevent duelling.

Motley County: Misspelled but named for Dr. Junius William Mottley, this county honored one of seven doctors who signed the Texas Declaration of Independence. Dr. Mottley arrived in Texas in 1835, and became surgeon of the post at Goliad. He also served as aide-de-camp to General Thomas J. Rusk. He was one of nine fatalities in the Battle of San Jacinto.

Shackelford County: The memory of Dr. John (Jack) Shackelford, brave leader of the Red Rovers, and author of an eyewitness account of the Goliad massacre, was honored by the naming of Shackelford County.

Starr County: This county was named for Dr. James Harper Starr who was born in Connecticut in 1809. After completing his studies, he was in the first class of the Reformed Medical Society of the United States of America. After practicing medicine in Georgia, he came to Texas and settled in Nacogdoches in 1837. He became Secretary of the Republic of Texas. A conscientious man, he efficiently carried out his office until August of 1840, resigning for financial reasons. Dr. Starr later became a successful land agent and banker. He has been called "Financier of the Republic."

Throckmorton County: This county was named for Dr. William Edward Throckmorton who was born in Virginia in 1795. He received his medical education, then moved to Tenneesee, Illinois, and Arkansas. Widowed with five children, he later remarried and moved to Texas. He was among a small group of pioneers who settled on the east fork of the Trinity River near the present town of McKinney. One of his children, James Webb Throckmorton, became Senator and later governor of the state of Texas. Throckmorton County was created in January 1858.

Zavala County: This county was named for Dr. Lorenzo de Zavala, another doctor who signed the Texas Declaration of Independence. Born in Mexico, this self-proclaimed Texan helped write the Constitution for the Republic of Texas. He then became Vice-President of the *ad interim* government of the Republic of Texas.

Towns named for — and by — Doctors

Anson: This town was named for the county and Dr. Anson Jones.

Archer City: This town was named for the county and Dr. Branch Archer.

Brenham: In 1844, this town in Washington County was named in honor of surgeon Dr. Richard Fox Brenham, sometimes called "the Mier Martyr," after he was killed on the Mier Expedition trying to escape his Mexican captors in 1843, at the Hacienda de Salado beyond Saltillo. Brenham bravely volunteered to lead an escape in hopes of helping his comrades.

Buckeye: Two Ohio natives were responsible for naming this town in Matagorda County. One of these men, Dr. A. A. Plotner, was an important landowner. The post office opened in 1907.

Cheapside: A Dr. J. Henry suggested the name for this community in Gonzales County in memory of the famous street in London. Some of the residents of the community were from England, and Dr. Henry had studied there. The community had a population of thirty-one in 1882.

Duffau: This town in Erath County may have been named for Dr. Francis Dauffau, who was a friend of Sam Houston and came to Texas two days too late to fight for Texas Independence. The town name may also be traced to a surveyor of that name or to an Indian Chief, Old Duffo, who was buried in the area.

Hico: This town in Hamilton County was named by Dr. J. R. Alford, the founder of the town, for his hometown in Kentucky. There is another theory, not so well accepted, that Dr. Alford named the town for the Hico Indians, "alternately spelled 'Waco' or 'Hueco' from the Spanish meaning 'a notching' or 'a hole,' probably for a gap in the hills." The first post office opened in 1860.

Homer: This town in Angelina County was named by a Dr. Manning, either for his love of the Greek poet or because he once lived in Homer, Louisiana.

Independence: Dr. Asa Hoxey was responsible for changing the name of Cole's Settlement in Washington County to "Independence," in honor of this historic event in Texas history. His suggestion was made in 1836, soon after the event had been declared at Old Washington twelve miles east of the community.

Kerrville: This settlement, originally called Brownsborough, was renamed honoring Dr. James Kerr.

Leo: A Dr. Stamper of Era, suggested this name for a community in Cooke County, which was settled in 1894. The good doctor thought that the Latin word for "lion" would be appropriate for a community set in rough and wild terrain.

McGregor: This town was named for Dr. Gregor McGregor.

Neblett's Bluff, {Louisiana:} This town in Calcasieu Parish was named for Dr. Robert Caldwell Neblett who practiced in this area before he came to Texas in 1840.

North Zulch: A community in Madison County was named for Dr. Julius Zulch, a beloved physician. Later, the citizens moved one mile to the north to take advantage of the railroad, and the community became North Zulch.

Snap: This community in Panola County was named for Dr. Snap Cariker, an early physician. A post office was there from 1899 to 1906.

Styx: The community of Styx, in Kaufman County, was named by a Dr. Gordon for the underworld river Styx of Greek mythology.

Sutherland Springs: This town was named for its founder; Dr. John Sutherland.

Texana: This town Texana, in Jackson County, was originally named Santa Anna, in 1832. While Texas was striving for her independence in 1835, the town name was changed by a Dr. F. F. Wells and Pamela Porter to Texana.

Venus: This community in Johnson County was first named Gossip. The name was changed to Venus, for one of several reasons. Some say that a Dr. Fontaine, who was one of the founders, thought the town was as pretty as a statue of Venus he particularly admired. Others say J. C. Smith wished to honor Venus Housby, the daughter of a local physician. The name change took place in 1888. At any rate, a name such as Venus is an improvement over Gossip.

Landmarks

Meridian Creek: Dr. J. M. Steiner named this creek after learning that its source lies at the ninety-eighth meridian. He also donated land for a town which was laid out in 1854. In turn, the town and state park took their names from the Creek. The town of Meridian lies in Bosque County.

Doctors Creek: This creek in Delta County may have been named for a doctor's horse and buggy which bogged down while crossing the stream. Another explanation attributes the name to Indians who gathered healing herbs on the creek banks and made their brews in the dry creek bed.

Other Namesakes

The Texas Navy ship *Archer* was named for Dr. Branch Archer. This ship was one of four turned over to the United States following the annexation of Texas by the United States.

In 1839, the sidewheeler *Zavala*, named for Dr. Lorenzo de Zavala, was commissioned in the Texas Navy. Originally christened the *Charleston*, the vessel deteriorated because of lack of funds. In rotting condition, it was run aground in Galveston Bay to prevent sinking, a sad ending for a proud beginning.

The Lorenzo de Zavala State Archives and Library Building in Austin was named in honor of that patriot.

The Labadie Wharf in Galveston, was named for Dr. Labadie.

Town Founders

The town of Chanute, Kansas, was founded by Dr. R. O. Prideaux.
Dr. Joseph H. Barnard was founder of the town of Richmond, Texas.
Dr. John Sutherland founded Sutherland Springs, Texas.

Fathers of Organized Medicine in Texas

Dr. J. T. Alexander
Dr. S. W. Barker
Dr. W. K. Brown
Dr. J. P. Duval
Dr. S. K. Jennings, Jr.
Dr. R. N. Lane
Dr. J. M. Litten
Dr. Arthur J. Lott
Dr. W. A. Morris
Dr. Edward McDonnell

These ten doctors signed the following summons on December 9, 1852:

> We the undersigned, Physicians of the City of Austin and vicinity, being desirous of promoting the advancement and improvement, as well as elevating the standard of our profession within this State, propose as an object conducive to that end a State Medical Convention, to meet at the City of Austin on the 17th day of January next; for the purpose of organizing a state medical society, and generally to do and take such action as will be most conducive to these objects.
>
> . . . And we furthermore express the wish and hope that all the members of our profession throughout the State who can, will meet with us at the time and place specified, and aid us in the proposed organization.

Nineteenth Century Presidents of the TMA

1853: Joseph Taylor of Harrison County
1853, 1878: George Cupples of San Antonio
1869: T. J. Heard of Galveston
1870: R. H. Jones of Brenham
1871: D. R. Wallace of Waco
1872: R. T. Flewellyn of Washington County
1873: D. F. Stuart of Houston
1874: A. G. Clopton of Jefferson
1875: H. W. Brown of Waco
1876: R. H. Harrison of Columbus
1877: W. D. Kelley of Galveston
1878: Cupples (see above) San Antonio
1879: John H. Pope of Marshall
1880: A. R. Kilpatrick of Navasota
1881: Ashbel Smith of Cedar Bayou, Harris County
1882: S. F. Starley of Corsicana and Tyler
1883: A. P. Brown of Jefferson
1884: H. C. Ghent of Belton
1885: E. P. Becton of Sulphur Springs
1886: T. H. Nott of Goliad
1887: Sam R. Burroughs of Buffalo
1888: J.F.Y. Paine of Galveston
1889: R. M. Swearingen of Chapel Hill
1890: W. P. Burts of Fort Worth
1891: W. H. Wilkes of Waco
1892: J. D. Osborn of Cleburne

1893: J. H. Sears of Waco
1894: J. W. McLaughlin of Austin
1895: P. C. Coleman of Colorado City
1896: J. C. Loggins of Ennis
1897: Bacon Saunders of Fort Worth
1898: J. T. Wilson of Sherman
1899: A. B. Gardner of Bellville
1900: B. E. Hadra of San Antonio

Location of Annual Meetings for the TMA:

Year	City	Meeting Place
1853	Austin	Methodist Church
1869	Houston	Hutchins House
1870	Houston	
1871	Houston	
1872	Houston	
1873	Waco	Roll call was in the office of Dr. D. P. Wallace and Dr. J. H. Sears. Other meetings were at the Masonic Hall.
1874	Dallas	Odd Fellows Hall. Some sessions were held in Fields Opera House, the Christian Church, and the Hall of the Knights of Pythias.
1875	Austin	Chamber of the House of Representatives
1876	Marshall	Opera House
1877	Galveston	Artillery Hall
1878	San Antonio	Wolfram's Garden
1879	Sherman	
1880	Brenham	Opera House and Armory Hall
1881	Waco	
1882	Fort Worth	District Courtroom
1883	Tyler	Opera House
1884	Belton	Opera House
Arts.		
1885	Houston	City Council Chamber
1886	Dallas	Merchants' Exchange Bldg.
1887	Austin	Chamber of the House of Representatives
1888	Galveston	Harmony Hall
1889	San Antonio	Casino Hall
1890	Fort Worth	Opera House
1891	Waco	City Hall
1892	Tyler	Opera House
1893	Galveston	Harmony Hall
1894	Austin	Senate Chamber
1895	Dallas	City Hall
1896	Fort Worth	Tarrant County Courtroom
1897	Paris	City Hall
1898	Houston	Turner Hall
1899	San Antonio	Turner Hall
1900	Waco	Waco Auditorium

Bibliography

Aikman, Lonnelle. *Nature's Healing Arts.* Washington, D.C.: National Geographic Society, 1977.

Anderson, John Q. *Texas Folk Medicine.* Austin: Encino Press, 1970.

Atkinson, Mary Jourdan. *The Texas Indians.* San Antonio: The Naylor Company, 1935.

Baird, Violet, ed. *Texas Medical History in the Library of The University of Texas Southwestern Medical School.* Dallas: The Friends of the Medical Library of The University of Texas Southwestern Medical School, 1972.

Barker, Eugene C. *The Life of Stephen F. Austin.* Austin: University of Texas Press, 1926.

Boatright, Mody C., ed. *The Healer of Los Olmos and other Mexican Lore.* Publication of the Texas Folklore Society. 24, 1951.

Bobo, Zack, Jr. *Ramblings of a Country Doctor.* Dallas: Southwest Offset, Incorporated, 1977.

Bracken, Dorothy Kendall, and Maurine Whorton Redway. *Early Texas Homes.* Dallas: Southern Methodist University Press, 1956.

Branda, Eldon Stephen, ed. *The Handbook of Texas: A Supplement.* Austin: The Texas State Historical Association, 1976.

Bricklin, Mark. *Natural Healing.* Emmaus, Pennsylvania: Rodale Press, Incorporated, 1976.

Brooks, Stewart. *Civil War Medicine.* Springfield, Illinois: Charles C. Thomas, Publisher, 1966.

Brown, John Henry. *A History of Dallas County, Texas: From 1837 to 1887.* Dallas: The Aldredge Book Store, 1966.

———. *History of Texas: 1682–1892.* (2 vol.) St. Louis: L. E. Daniel, Publisher, 1892.

Burrow, James G. *AMA: Voice of American Medicine.* Baltimore: The Johns Hopkins Press, 1963.

Carter, Hodding. *Doomed Road of the Empire.* McGraw-Hill, 1963.

Chapman, John S. *The University of Texas Southwestern Medical School.* Dallas: Southern Methodist University, 1976.

Clack, Tommie and Katharyn Duff. *Pioneer Days . . . Two Views.* Abilene: Reporter Publishing Company, 1979.

Cline, Isaac M. *Storms, Floods, and Sunshine.* New Orleans: Pelican Publishing Company, 1945.

Coe, Urling C., M.D. *Frontier Doctor.* New York: The Macmillan Company, 1940.

Coleman, Dr. James M. *Aesculapius on the Colorado, The Story of Medical Practice in Travis County to 1899.* Austin: Encino Press, 1971.

Coleman, W. L. *A History of Yellow Fever.* Houston. Chicago: The Clinic Publishing Company, 1898.

Cooke, Catherine Nixon, Linda Seeligson, Thomas Baker Slick, eds. *JWN: A Surgeon's Reflections.* La Jolla: Nixon/Slick/Pater/Taliaferro/Seeligson, Incorporated, 1978.

Cox, Mary L. *History of Hale County Texas.* Plainview: 1937.

Cranfill, Dr. J. B. *Dr. J. B. Cranfill's Chronicle.* New York: Fleming H. Revell Company, 1916.

Cremony, John C. *Life Among the Apaches.* San Francisco: A. Roman and Company, Publishers, 1868.

Crosthwait, William L., M.D. and Ernest G. Fischer. *The Last Stitch.* Philadelphia: J. B. Lippincott Company, 1956.

Crouch, Carrier J. *A History of Young County Texas.* Austin: The State Historical Association, 1956.

Crowder, Eleanor McElheny. *Nursing in Texas: A Pictorial History.* Waco, Texas: Texian Press, 1980.

Cupples, George, M.D. *Register of Cases, No. 2.* Location: UTHSCSA, San Antonio.

DeShields, James T. *Border Wars of Texas.* Tioga, Texas: The Herald Company, 1912.

Dixon, Charles D. *The Menace: An Exposition of Quackery Nostrum Exploitation and Reminescences of a Country Doctor.* Lodovic Printing Company, 1914.

Dobie, J. Frank. *The Guide to Life and Literature of the Southwest.* Dallas: Southern Methodist University Press, 1952.

Dowell, Greensville. *Yellow Fever and Malarial Diseases.* Philadelphia: Medical Publications office, 1876.

Duffy, John. *The Healers: The Rise of the Medical Establishment.* New York: McGraw-Hill, 1976.

Dunlop, Richard. *Doctors of the American Frontier.* Garden City, New York: Doubleday and Company, 1962–1965.

Eddy, Gay Marsh, ed. et.al. *The University of Texas Medical Branch at Galveston.* Austin: University of Texas Press, 1967.

Emmett, Chris. *Texas Camel Tales.* [Reprint.] Austin: Steck-Vaughn Company, 1969.

Faulk, Odie B. *The Last Years of Spanish Texas, 1778–1821.* London: Mouton and Company, 1964.

Feeter, Harvey Wickes. *History of the Eclectic Medical Institute, Cincinnati, Ohio, 1845–1902.* Cincinnati: Cincinnati Publishing House, 1902.

Flexner, James Thomas. *Doctors on Horseback.* New York: The Viking Press, 1937.

Foote, Henry Stuart. *Texas and the Texans,* Vol. I. Philadelphia: Thomas, Cowperthwait and Company, 1841.

Fornell, Earl Wesley. *The Galveston Era*. Austin: University of Texas Press, 1961.

Fulmore, Z. T. *History and Geography of Texas as Told in County Names*. Austin: Press of E. L. Steck, 1915.

Gallaway, B. P. *The Dark Corner of the Confederacy*. Dubuque, Iowa: Kendall/Hunt Publishing Company, 1968.

Gambrell, Herbert. *Anson Jones: The Last President of Texas*. Garden City, N.Y.: Doubleday and Company, Incorporated, 1948.

Gambrell, Herbert and Virginia. *A Pictorial History of Texas*. New York: E. P. Dutton and Company, 1960.

Gatschet, Albert S. *The Karankawa Indians, The Coast People of Texas*. Vol. I, No. 2. Cambridge, Massachusetts: Peabody Museum of American Archaeology and Ethnology, 1891. (Millwood, NY: Kraus Reprint Company, 1974).

Geiser, Samuel Wood. *Horticulture and Horticulturists in Early Texas*. Dallas: Southern Methodist University Press, 1945.

———. *Naturalists of the Frontier*. Dallas: Southern Methodist University Press, 1948.

Ghormley, Pearl. *Eastland County, Texas: A Historical and Biographical Survey*. Rupegy Publishing Company, 1969.

Gilpin, Laura. *The Enduring Navaho*. Austin: University of Texas Press, 1968.

Haggard, Howard W. *Devils, Drugs, and Doctors*. New York: Harper and Brothers, 1929.

Haley, J. Evetts. *Fort Concho and the Texas Frontier*. San Angelo: San Angelo Standard Times, 1952.

Herff, Ferdinand Peter. *The Doctors Herff: A Three-Generational Memoir*. Vol. I. San Antonio: Trinity University Press, 1973.

Hertzler, Arthur E., M.D. *The Horse and Buggy Doctor*. New York: Harper and Brothers, 1938.

Hill, Jim Dan. *The Texas Navy*. New York: A. S. Barnes & Company, 1937.

Hogan, William Ransom. *The Texas Republic: A Social and Economic History*. Austin: The University of Texas Press, 1969.

Hoyt, Henry F. *A Frontier Doctor*. Boston: Houghton Mifflin Company, 1929.

Huson, Hobart, ed. *Dr. J. H. Barnard's Journal*. Goliad Bicentennial Edition, 1950.

Jones, Billy M. *Health-Seekers in the Southwest, 1817–1900*. Norman: University of Oklahoma Press, 1967.

Karolevitz, Robert F. *Doctors of the Old West: A Pictorial History of Medicine on the Frontier*. Seattle: Superior Publishing Company, 1967.

Kaufman, Martin. *Homeopathy in America*. Baltimore: Johns Hopkins Press, 1971.

Leger, Theodore. "Essay on the Particular Influence of Prejudices in Medicine over the Treatment of the Disease most common in Texas, Intermittent Fever." Brazoria: People Press, 1838.

Linn, John J. *Reminiscences of Fifty Years in Texas.* Austin: The Steck Company, 1935.

Littlejohn, E. G. *Texas History Stories.* Richmond: B. F. Johnson Publishing Company, 1901.

Looscan, Adele B. *Heroes of Texas: Micajah Autry, A Soldier of the Alamo.* Houston Union National Bank.

Lukes, Edward A. *DeWitt Colony of Texas.* Austin: Jenkins Publishing Company, The Pemberton Press, 1976.

Lyons, Albert S. and R. Joseph Petrucelli, II, *Medicine, An Illustrated History.* New York: Harry N. Abrams, Incorporated, 1978.

Marti-Ibanez, Felix, ed. *History of American Medicine: A Symposium.* New York: MD Publications, Incorporated, 1958.

Massengill, Samuel Evans. *A Sketch of Medicine and Pharmacy.* Bristol, Tennessee: S. E. Massengill Company, 1943.

McCarty, F. M. ed. *Texas Guidebook,* 5th Edition. Grand Prairie, Texas: Lo-Ray Company, 1970.

McCullough, William Wallace, Jr. *Dr. William Dennis Kelley: Texas Physician and Surgeon 1825–1888.* Galveston: Private Printing, 1961. (Microfilm at The Southwest Collection, Texas Tech)

McIlvain, Myra Hargrave. *Texas Auto Trails, The Southeast.* Austin, University of Texas Press, 1982.

———. Memorial and Biographical History of Dallas County, Texas. Chicago: The Lewis Publishing Company, 1892.

Neville, A. W. *The Red River Valley Then and Now.* Paris, Texas, 1948.

Newcomb, W. W., Jr. *The Indians of Texas.* Austin, The University of Texas Press, 1961.

Newell, R. C. *History of the Revolution in Texas.* Austin: The Steck Company, 1935. (A facsimile reproduction of the original published by Wiley and Putnam, 1838.)

Nixon, Pat Ireland, M.D. *A Century of Medicine in San Antonio.* Lancaster, Pennsylvania: Lancaster Press, Incorporated, 1936.

———. *A History of the Texas Medical Association: 1853–1953.* Austin: University of Texas; Press, 1953.

———. *The Medical Story of Early Texas: 1528–1853.* Lancaster, Pennsylvania: Lancaster Press, Incorporated, 1946.

Notson, William M. *Fort Concho Medical History: January 1869–July 1872.* San Angelo: Fort Concho Press and Museum, 1974.

Novotny, Ann and Carter Smith, eds. *Images of Healing.* New York: Macmillan Publishing Company, Incorporated, 1980.

O'Connor, Kathryn Stoner. *Presidio La Bahia.* Austin: Von Boeckmann-Jones Company, 1966.

Osgood, Charles. *The Causes, Treatment, and Cure of Fever and Ague and Diseases of Bilious Climates.* New York: 1867.

Packard, Francis R. *History of Medicine in the United States.* 2 vols. New York: Paul B. Hoeber, 1931.

Philips, Shine. *Big Spring, The Casual Biography of a Prairie Town.* New York: Prentice-Hall, 1942.

Pickard, Madge E. and R. Carlyle Buley. *The Midwest Pioneer: His Ills, Cures, and Doctors.* New York: Henry Schuman, 1946.

Reagan, Rocky. *G. P. Reagan: Country Doctor.* San Antonio: The Naylor Company, 1963.

Red, George Plunkett. *The Medicine Man in Texas.* Houston: Standard Printing and Lithographing Company, 1930.

Reeves, L. H. *Medical History of Fort Worth and Tarrant County: One Hundred Years. 1853–1953.* Fort Worth: Tarrant County Medical Society, 1954.

Rice, Lawrence D. *The Negro in Texas.* Baton Rouge: Louisiana State University Press, 1971.

Richardson, Rupert Norval. *The Frontier of Northwest Texas: 1846–1876.* Glendale, California: The Arthur H. Clark Company, 1963.

Risse, Guester B., Ronald L. Numbers, and Judith Walzer Leavitt, eds. *Medicine Without Doctors: Home Health Care in American History.* New York: Science History Publications/USA, 1977.

Rister, Carl Coke. *Fort Griffin on the Texas Frontier.* Norman: University of Oklahoma Press, 1956.

Rothstein, William G. *American Physicians in the 19th Century.* Baltimore: The Johns Hopkins University Press, 1972.

Schmidt, Charles F. *History of Washington County.* San Antonio: The Naylor Company, 1949.

Shelton, Hooper and Homer Hutto, Sr. *Jones County, Texas — The First 100 Years.* Stamford: Shelton Press, 1978.

Shyrock, Richard Harrison. *Medicine in America — Historical Essays.* Baltimore: Johns Hopkins Press, 1966.

Silverthorne, Elizabeth. *Ashbel Smith of Texas.* College Station: Texas A&M University Press, 1982.

Smart, Charles, *The Medical and Surgical History of the War of the Rebellion, Part III,* Vol. I, Medical History. Washington: Government Printing Office, 1888.

Smith, Ashbel. *Reminiscences of the Texas Republic.* Austin: The Pemberton Press, 1967. (Brasada Reprint Series)

Spiller, Wayne. *Handbook of McCullock County History,* Vol. I. Seagraves, Texas: Pioneer Book Publishers, 1976.

Steen, Ralph W. *The Texas Story.* Austin: The Steck Company, 1948.

Steiner, Paul E. *Physician-Generals in the Civil War: A Study in Nineteenth Mid-Century American Medicine.* Springfield, Illinois: Charles C. Thomas, 1966.

Stephens, I. K. *The Hermit Philosopher of Liendo.* Dallas: Southern Methodist University Press, 1951.

Stone, Eric. *Medicine Among the American Indians.* New York: Hafner Publishing Company, 1962.

Tarpley, Fred. *1001 Texas Place Names.* Austin: University of Texas Press, 1980.

Thompson, Samuel. *New Guide to Health*, Ninth Edition. Columbus, Ohio: Jarvis Pike & Company, 1833.

Vernon, Walter N., Robert W. Sledge, Robert C. Monk, Norman W. Spellmann. *The Methodist Excitement in Texas: A History.* Dallas: The Texas United Methodist Historical Society, 1984.

Wallace, Ernest and E. Adamson Hoebel. *The Comanches: Lords of the South Plains.* Norman: University of Oklahoma Press, 1952.

Webb, Walter Prescott. *The Texas Rangers: A Century of Frontier Defense.* Austin: University of Texas Press, 1935.

Webb, Walter Prescott, ed. *The Handbook of Texas*, I and II. Austin: The Texas State Historical Association, 1976.

Weems, John Edward. *Weekend in September.* New York: Henry Holt and Company, 1957.

Wharton, Clarence R. *History of Texas.* Dallas: Turner Company, 1935.

Whisenhunt, Donald W. *Chronology of Texas History.* Burnet: Eakin Press, 1982.

White, Gifford. *1830 Citizens of Texas.* Austin: Eakin Press, 1983.

Wilkes, William O. *History of the Waco Medical Association.* Waco: 1931.

Yoakum, H. *History of Texas: 1685–1846.* Vol. II. Austin: Steck Company, 1855.

Zachry, Juanita Daniel. *History of Rural Taylor County.* Burnet: Nortex Press, 1980.

Periodicals, Journals, and Annuals

Almonte, Juan. Trans. Carlos Castaneda. "Statistical Report on Texas, 1835." *Southwestern Historical Quarterly,* 28 (January 1925), p. 183.

Anderson, H. Allen. "Mountain Pass: A Texas Frontier Landmark." *West Texas Historical Association Year Book,* 53 (1977), p. 69.

Andrassy, Richard J. and Clyde O. Hagood, Jr. "Chief Surgeon of the Alamo." *Surgery, Gynecology and Obstetrics,* 145 (December 1977), pp. 913–915.

Baird, Violet M. "Nineteenth Century Medical Journalism in Texas: With A Journal Checklist." *Bulletin of the Medical Library Association,* 60 (July 1972), pp. 375–381.

Barker, Eugene C. "The San Jacinto Campaign." *Quarterly of the Texas State Historical Association.* 4, pp. 296–301.

Boatright, Mody C., editor. "The Healer of Los Olmos and other Mexican Lore." *Publication of the Texas Folklore Society,* 24. Dallas: Southern Methodist University Press, 1951.

Breeden, James O. "Health of Early Texas: The Military Frontier." *Southwest Historical Quarterly,* 80 (1977), pp. 357–364.

Cary, E. H. "Eye, Ear, Nose, and Throat as a Specialty in Texas in the Past Century." *Texas State Journal of Medicine,* (May 1953), pp. 298–300.

Cash, Philip. "The Medical Community of the Last Century." *Nineteenth Century,* 7 (Autumn 1981), pp. 35–37.

Clarke, T. Wood. "Anson Jones: Doctor and Diplomat." *New York State Journal of Medicine.* 50,1 (1 January 1950), pp. 65–68.

Cooper, Texas Jim. "True Texas Tales." *Suburban News.* Carrollton, Texas, 17 December 1964.

Farmer, Jo Ann. "Sandstone Sentinels." *West Texas Historical Association Year Book,* 34 (October 1958), pp. 122–130.

Geiser, Samuel W. "The first Texas Academy of Science, (1880–1887)." *Field and Lab,* 13, (1945), pp. 34–39.

Goar, Everett L. "Ophthalmology." *Texas Medicine,* 63, (March 1967), p. 82.

Green, William Elton. "Dr. William Notson: The First Historican of The Concho Country." *West Texas Historical Association Year Book,* 49, (1973), pp. 78–89.

Haggard, J. Villasana. "Epidemic of Cholera in Texas, 1833–1834." *Southwestern Historical Quarterly,* 40, (January 1937), pp. 216–230.

Harrison, R. H. "The Great Storm at Galveston — From a Medical Standpoint." *Texas Medical Journal,* 16 (1900–1901), pp. 164–169.

Harper, Cecil O., Jr. "Before They Were Populists: Politics and Politicians in Jack County, 1884–1892." *West Texas Historical Association Year Book,* 53 (1977), pp. 106–120

Hatcher, Mattie Austin. "Letters of Antonio Martinez, the last Spanish Governor of Texas, 1817–1822." *Southwestern Historical Quarterly,* 39 (January 1936), p. 229.

Hearde, T. J. "The Diseases of Washington, Texas, for 1851, including its Topography." *Transactions American Medical Association,* 5 (1852), pp. 678–685.

Hildreth, Peggy. "The Howard Association of Galveston: The 1850s, Their Peak Years." *East Texas Historical Journal,* 17, No. 2 (Fall 1979), pp. 35–41.

Hood, Maurice. "Medicine In the Civil War." *Texas Medicine,* 63 (March 1967), pp. 53–55.

Jacobs, Kenneth R. and Ernest Wallace, eds. "History in West Texas." *West Texas Historical Association Year Book,* 54 (1978), p. 102.

Jochims, Larry. "Medicine in Kansas, 1850–1900." *The Emporia State Research Studies,* 28 (Fall 1979), Number 2.

Kemp, Hardy A. "One Hundred Years of Health Guardianship and Health Progress in Texas." *Texas State Journal of Medicine,* 49 (May 1953), pp. 308–311.

Kyle, J. Allen, J. Edward Hodges, Lyman C. Blair. "A History of Organized Medicine in Harris County, Texas." *Historical Committee of Harris County Medical Society,* October 28, 1948.

Labadie, N. D. "San Jacinto Campaign." *The Texas Almanac for 1859*, pp. 46, 47.

Marriott, Alice L. "Indian Medicine." *Southwest Review*, (Autumn 1944), pp. 61–66.

McCraven, William. "Houston, Texas: Its Topography, and the Diseases of 1851." *Transactions American Medical Association*, 5 (1852), pp. 669–678.

———. "Letter to Dr. E. D. Fenner, New Orleans." *New Orleans Medical and Surgical Journal*, (1849/1850), pp. 60–64.

Medical Record and Annals, Vol. 57 (1964), Vol. 58 (1965), Vol. 59 (1966), Vol. 60 (1967).

"Medicine in the Lone Star State," *MD, Medical Newsmagazine*, 20, 6 (June 1976), 57–60.

"Memoranda." *The British Medical Journal*. June 17, 1891. [In Papers of James Edwin Thompson, Rosenberg Library, Galveston].

Nixon, Pat Ireland. "Surgery: A Cultural Factor in Early Texas." *Texas State Medical Journal*, 53 (March 1957), pp. 159–164.

Padgitt, James T. "The Padgitts and Saddle Leather." *West Texas Historical Association Year Book*. 29 (October 1953), pp. 36–37.

Paine, J. F. "History of Medical Teaching in Texas." *Texas Medical Journal*, 22 (November 1906), pp. 173–183.

Parker, H. C. "Some Account of the Yellow Fever as it appeared in Galveston and Houston, Texas, in 1867, together with its symptoms, Treatment." Bound with "Yellow Fever and its Treatment Homeopathically," 1868. Moody Medical Library, Galveston, Texas.

Rodin, Alvin E. and Albert O. Singleton, Jr. "Two Early Leaders: Medical Branch." *Texas Medicine*, 63 (March 1967), pp. 113–116.

Rouse, M. O. "Medical Education in Texas." *Texas State Journal of Medicine*. (May 1953), pp. 320–22.

Rutherford, Robert. "History of Quarantine in the State of Texas from 1878 to 1888." *Public Health Reports and Papers*, 14 (1888), pp. 125–133.

Singleton, Albert. "Address of the President: The Surgeon in the Romantic Story of Texas," *Annals of Surgery*, 3 (May 1940), pp. 673–87.

Swearingen, R. M. "The Quarantine System of Texas." *Public Health Papers and Reports*, 19 (1894), pp. 111–115.

Smith, Ralph A. "The West Texas Underground Frontier, 1870 to 1890; Settling the Land Six Feet Down." *West Texas Historical Association Year Book*, 53 (1977), pp. 18–41.

Tandy, Charles C., Robert B. Krause, and Russell F. Bonham. "Anesthesiology." *Texas Medicine*, 63 (March 1967), pp. 61–63.

Taylor, Lonn. "The McGregor–Grimm house at Winedale, Texas." *The Magazine Antiques*, (September 1975), pp. 515–521.

Thames, W. D. "An East Texas Pioneer." *Texas State Journal of Medicine*, 60 (August 1964), pp. 665–667.

———. "Transactions of the Texas State Medical Association Sixth Annual Session, 1874." 6 (1874). University of Texas Health Science Center at Dallas.

———. "Transactions of the Texas State Medical Association." 9 (1877). University of Texas Health Science Center at Dallas.

Thompson, Jesse E. "Sagittectomy — First Recorded Surgical Procedure in the American Southwest, 1535." *New England Journal of Medicine.* 289, No. 26 (December 27, 1973), pp. 1403–07.

Travis, J. M. "Progress in the General Practice of Medicine in Texas During the Last Century." *Texas State Journal of Medicine.* 49 (May 1953), pp. 279–81.

Viener, Saul. "Surgeon Moses Albert Levy: Letters of a Texas Patriot." *The Publication of the American Jewish Historical Society,* 46 (December 1956), pp. 101–113.

Williams, Al. "Early Concern for Public Health Hinged Upon Devastating Epidemics." *Texas Health Bulletin,* 32 (January 1979), pp. 3A–5A.

Williams, Clayton W. "A Threatened Mutiny of Soldiers at Fort Stockton in 1873 Resulted in Penitentiary Sentences of Five to Fifteen Years." *West Texas Historical Association Year Book,* 52 (1976), pp. 78–83.

Winkler, E. W., ed. "The Bexar and Dawson Prisoners." *Quarterly of the Texas State Historical Association,* 13 (April 1910), pp. 292–94.

Wooster, Ralph. "Wealthy Texans, 1860." *Southwestern Historical Quarterly,* 71, No. 2 (October 1967), p. 171.

Papers

Cupples, George. "Register of Cases, No. 2." Nixon Library of the UTHSC at San Antonio.

Ghent, H. C. "President's Address Before the Texas State Medical Association." Houston, Texas, April 21, 22, and 23, 1885.

The Handbook of Texas. Ann Arbor, Michigan: Edwards Brothers, Incorporated 1 and 2, 1952.

Shaw, Lucy. Letters of Lucy Shaw. Rosenberg Library, Galveston, Texas.

Long, James. James Long Papers. Barker Collection of University of Texas at Austin.

Medical History of Post: Fort Concho, Texas. Records of Adjutant General's Office in Fort Concho Library, copied from the National Archives. 401, 403, 404, 407.

Papers of Dr. Menger. Nixon Library of the UTHSC at San Antonio.

Smith, S.L.S. S.L.S. Smith Medical Records. San Angelo: Fort Concho Museum Library.

"Texas National Dispatch." Austin, Vols. 1–4.

Thompson, James Edwin. Papers of James Edwin Thompson. Rosenberg Library, Galveston, Texas.

INDEX

D

E

F

N

O

P

R

S

Editor: Shirley Denise Ratisseau